MEMOIRS OF AN ANZAC

Born in 1883, John Charles Barrie grew up in Victoria. He joined Australia's militia in 1909, and remained an army man his entire life, retiring with the rank of colonel. An officer in the AIF from the start of World War I, Barrie was involved in the landing at Gallipoli, and later served at the Western Front. He was wounded twice during the war. Barrie died in 1957, survived by his wife and daughter. His memoirs have been made available by his granddaughter, Judy Osborne.

Ross McMullin is a historian and biographer who has written extensively about the impact on Australia of its involvement in World War I. Dr McMullin's books include his biographies, the award-winning *Pompey Elliott* and *Will Dyson: Australia's radical genius*. His most recent book, *Farewell, Dear People: biographies of Australia's lost generation*, was awarded the Prime Minister's Prize for Australian History.

MEMOIRS OF AN ANZAC

A FIRST-HAND ACCOUNT BY AN AIF OFFICER IN THE FIRST WORLD WAR

JOHN CHARLES BARRIE

INTRODUCED & ANNOTATED BY ROSS MCMULLIN

SCRIBE
Melbourne • London

*In loving memory of my mother, Isabel Ruff,
the daughter of John Charles Barrie*
Judy Osborne

Scribe Publications
18–20 Edward St, Brunswick, Victoria 3056, Australia
2 John St, Clerkenwell, London, WC1N 2ES, United Kingdom

First published by Scribe 2015

Text copyright © Judy Osborne 2015
Introduction and notes copyright © Ross McMullin 2015

All rights reserved. Without limiting the rights under copyright reserved above, no part of this publication may be reproduced, stored in or introduced into a retrieval system, or transmitted, in any form or by any means (electronic, mechanical, photocopying, recording or otherwise) without the prior written permission of the publishers of this book.

Indexed by Richard McGregor
Typeset in Minion Pro 11.5/15.25 pt by the publishers
Cover photograph © Australian War Memorial, RELAWM01070, Silver-plated 'Class A, Victor' bugle engraved by subscribers: C Company, 13 Battalion AIF.

Printed and bound in Australia by Griffin Press

The paper this book is printed on is certified against the Forest Stewardship Council® Standards. Griffin Press holds FSC chain of custody certification SGS-COC-005088. FSC promotes environmentally responsible, socially beneficial and economically viable management of the world's forests.

National Library of Australia
Cataloguing-in-Publication data

Barrie, John Charles, author.

Memoirs of an Anzac: a first-hand account by an AIF officer in the First World War / John Charles Barrie; introduction by Ross McMullin.

ISBN: 9781925106497 (paperback)
ISBN: 9781925113686 (e-book)

1. Barrie, John Charles. 2. Australia. Army. 3. Australian and New Zealand Army Corps–Biography. 4. Soldiers–Australia–Biography. 5. World War, 1914-1918–participation, Australian–Biography. 6. Australia–Biography.

Other Authors/Contributors: McMullin, Ross, writer of added text.

940.3092

This project has been assisted by the Australian government through the Australia Council for the Arts, its arts funding and advisory body.

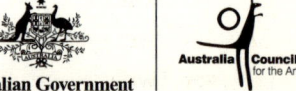

scribepublications.com.au
scribepublications.co.uk

Contents

Abbreviations in the text *ix*
Formations in the military hierarchy *xi*
Preface by Judy Osborne *xiii*
Introduction by Ross McMullin *1*

Chapter One *3*
Chapter Two *10*
Chapter Three *19*
Chapter Four *28*
Chapter Five *32*
Chapter Six *40*
Chapter Seven *53*
Chapter Eight *64*
Chapter Nine *75*
Chapter Ten *91*
Chapter Eleven *107*
Chapter Twelve *123*
Chapter Thirteen *142*
Chapter Fourteen *160*
Chapter Fifteen *175*
Chapter Sixteen *187*
Chapter Seventeen *204*
Chapter Eighteen *221*
Chapter Nineteen *234*
Chapter Twenty *242*
Chapter Twenty-one *255*

Afterword by Judy Osborne *273*
Index *279*

Abbreviations in the text

A.I.F. Australian Imperial Force
A.M.C. Army Medical Corps
A.P.M. Assistant Provost Marshal
C.C.S. Casualty Clearing Station
C.M.G. Commander of the Order of St Michael and St George
C.O. Commanding Officer (sometimes reversed as O.C.)
C.S.M. Company Sergeant Major
D.C.M. Distinguished Conduct Medal
D.S.O. Distinguished Service Order
G.O.C. General Officer Commanding
H.E. High Explosives
M.C. Military Cross
M.L.O. Military Landing Officer
M.M. Military Medal
M.O. Medical Officer
M.S.M. Meritorious Service Medal
N.C.O. Non-commissioned Officer
Q.M.S. Quartermaster Sergeant (sometimes Q.M.)
R.M.O. Regimental Medical Officer (sometimes M.O.)
R.S.M. Regimental Sergeant Major
R.T.O. Railway Transport Officer
T.M. Trench Mortar
V.C. Victoria Cross
V.F.L. Victorian Football League

Formations in the military hierarchy

Formations, in descending order, are as follows:

Army
Corps
Division
Brigade
Battalion
Company
Platoon
Section

Preface

By Judy Osborne

I never met my grandfather Colonel John Charles Barrie, as he died a year before I was born, but I heard many tales of his adventures and achievements as a husband and father, a horseman, and an officer of the Australian Army in the First World War. He wrote this book in the 1930s, and I remember the much-cherished original manuscript being in my grandmother's care, and then my mother's, until she gave it to me some 25 years ago.

I read and enjoyed the book then, and, finally, I decided that 80 years was long enough for it to have been kept in the cupboard. Grandpa's story is worth telling, and I want to share it.

Against his mother's wishes, my grandfather joined Australia's militia in 1909, and had attained the rank of lieutenant when the First World War broke out in 1914 and he was appointed to the Australian Imperial Force. He was ready, willing, and able to embark on the HMS *Benalla* in October that year, which took him and the 8th Battalion from Port Melbourne to the shores of Gallipoli on that fateful first Anzac Day. His spirit saw him through this famous battle, and beyond.

Grandpa was not known as John, or even Charles. He was Charlie to most of his friends and family — but, to my grandmother, he was Peter, because she said he was like Peter Pan, the little boy who never grew up (and, in fact, he was, and I am, related to Peter Pan's author, J.M. Barrie). To his digger mates in the AIF, he was known as Dan, and this is his story.

Introduction

By Ross McMullin

'I like soldiering, and duty was always a pleasure to me', J.C. Barrie writes in these illuminating recollections of his years in the AIF. Such attitudes can sound like platitudes, but Barrie's memoirs confirm that, in his case, these sentiments were genuine. An officer from the start of the war, Barrie was wounded at Gallipoli, and yearned to return to the front. But he found himself repeatedly frustrated, because during his recuperation he made himself indispensable in various training roles that he performed with characteristic diligence and effectiveness. It was 'harder to get to the war than away from it', he lamented. Eventually, though, he managed — via distinctly unorthodox means — to get back to his unit. He relished his association with comrades of like-minded conscientiousness, and was full of admiration and compassion for the men he led.

Barrie describes his experiences with verve and flair. Frank and forthright in his assessments of individuals and events, he chronicles unhackneyed anecdotes, is good at dialogue, and enjoys humour. But this is no frivolous exercise in avoidance of the ghastliness of the war. The reality of the conflict is depicted with vivid authenticity. Admired comrades die, or endure dreadful wounds; Barrie is severely wounded himself at both Gallipoli and France, and almost drowns in a quagmire of mud one dark night near Delville Wood.

Moreover, there is plenty here to interest specialists and aficionados who have read widely about the AIF in World War I. Accounts of the landing at Gallipoli routinely highlight the brave and selfless contributions made by British Navy personnel, so it is startling to read in these pages about a punch-up between an AIF officer and a British ship captain that stemmed from the Australian's determination to prevent the apprehensive skipper from taking his ship away from the danger zone before its quota of the landing force had disembarked. Also, the story of four battalion commanders conspiring with an obliging doctor to use a dodgy diagnosis to remove an incompetent and obnoxious brigadier is superb. Other splendid vignettes include Barrie's description of Pompey Elliott playing football behind the lines in France. Barrie was something of a Pompey protégé. He had been trained by Elliott in the pre-war militia, wanted to serve under him again in the AIF, and eventually did.

Barrie is scathing about someone else he served under, but does not name this commander. However, the officer concerned is identified in the footnotes I have compiled to accompany Barrie's recollections. The aim of these notes is to identify notable persons Barrie has mentioned but not named, to provide additional information about individuals who are significant in Barrie's memoirs, and to contribute elaborative context for some of the events he has described. Unless otherwise stated, place names in these notes are Australian, and the ages attributed to individuals in the notes relate to the time when they appear in Barrie's narrative (although military records often reflect what soldiers said their ages were, and are therefore not necessarily always accurate).

Chapter One

In the year 1832, just 100 years ago, my grandfather, then living in Perth, Scotland, decided to emigrate and seek his fortune in a new land. The reason which prompted him to make this decision was the sorry state of his wife's health, she being stricken with grief at the loss of four children which had been born to them and all of whom had died in infancy.

They decided to come to Australia, and landed in Tasmania at the latter end of that year. There they lived for four years, and in February 1836 my father was born. A few months later, while he was still a baby, the family came to Victoria, then known as the Port Phillip Bay District, where Batman and Fawkner, having crossed from Tasmania a few months previously, had founded a settlement on the banks of the River Yarra, which has since grown into the City of Melbourne. In the course of time, two more sons and three daughters were born and lived.

At the first land sales in Melbourne, my grandfather purchased a block of land in Collins Street, running from Swanston Street, half way up the hill to Russell Street, and back to Little Collins Street. On this site, where the Melbourne Town Hall now stands, he erected a building and for several years carried on business there.

We could wish today that he had been possessed of greater foresight and retained his original purchase, for that block of land today is worth many times more per foot than he paid for the whole area. However, he sold it, and purchased another piece nearer the centre of the township, in Queen Street, and there his building still stands behind the Titles Office.

My father and my aunts have often told me stories of their childhood days when they lived in Queen Street and there was no building to the east of them, and how they used to run home terrified when they saw blacks coming up the hill from where the G.P.O. now stands in Elizabeth Street.

My people were originally of the Du Barri family of France, who, like so many French Protestant families, left their native land after the massacre of the Huguenots and sought sanctuary in Scotland. They later dropped the 'Du' and added an 'e' to their name to distinguish them from the Barrys. I remember asking my father why they changed their name, and he assured me quite solemnly that they had to drop the 'Du' as a 'Jew' could not live in Scotland. I could not quite see the point at first, but, when it finally dawned upon me, I realised it was the origin of the famous joke.

My father and his brother, as young men, like all others of the time, developed 'gold fever', and spent a good part of their early days seeking gold at Bendigo, Ballarat, and Castlemaine, and afterwards for a time in New Zealand. They were fairly successful, and when their father died in 1870 were well-established and successful businessmen in Melbourne.

The new country had been good to the family and they had become firmly established in it. But in 1892 came the crisis of the land boom, the closing of the banks, and the general financial crash which brought about the ruin of so many people and more or less hurt everybody.

My father was fortunately not involved in land transactions, and therefore escaped lightly by comparison. He was not ruined, but his investments suffered severely. The banks repaid only a fraction of deposits, companies and business firms failed, values of securities dropped to almost nothing, and a considerable part of his fortune was swept away. I remember one company in which he had invested 2,500 pounds — shares which were considered gilt-edged security at the time he purchased them — repaid only 150 pounds.

However, he survived the disaster, and carried on his business until his death in 1900, at the age of sixty-four.

At the time, I was just over sixteen years of age, and my elder brother just a few years older, and as neither of us were old enough or sufficiently experienced to undertake the responsibilities of business, the business was sold and my mother was left with a modest income, which, though not as big as she had been used to, or had expected to have, was still sufficient to keep her and the family in comparative comfort. Then came the problem of 'what to do with us'. I had my own ideas — first I wanted to be a soldier, and, failing that, to go on the land. Like so many mothers who live in the city, she did not like the country, and no amount of pleading would persuade her to consider the land idea, and she was equally adamant on the idea of soldiering.

I have often thought since how foolish it is of mothers to endeavour to shape the destinies of their children, and how many men's lives are spoilt by being pushed by their parents into a channel to which they are utterly and entirely unsuited. My mother was a very fine woman, and we owe a tremendous lot to her. I know she thought she was doing the very best for me, and did not realise that my nature was entirely unsuited to the path she chose for me.

It so happened, fortunately or unfortunately for me, that at this time an uncle was general manager of one of the biggest banking institutions in Australia, and my mother wrote to him, asking if he could find a place for me in the bank. He replied requesting her to send me in to see him. I went. He asked me a lot of questions, and then handed me over to a clerk who was instructed to give me an examination paper, and I sat down to another school examination. This was no trouble. I was told I had passed, and was duly appointed to the service. My adventures as a banker are of no particular interest, except perhaps as a study in psychology and the methods by which some of those who are in high places today have crawled to their respective positions, not by any display of outstanding ability, but by methods which disgusted most decent youngsters, and prompted many of them, including myself, to get out as soon as possible.

I made an effort soon after joining to follow my natural bent and become a soldier, by endeavouring to enlist for the South African War, but I was under age and could not quite reach the physical standard, which was a very high one, so for the present I resigned myself to my job.

After serving for some time in a branch office, I was transferred to the head office of the bank in Melbourne, and it was there that the full extent of the hypocrisy and wire-pulling tactics of those who were determined to get on was brought home to me, and I no longer wondered why men of proved ability were kept on unimportant jobs and small salaries, and why so many of them left and accepted posts in commercial houses outside. As soon as it became apparent that a young man was possessed of outstanding ability, he became a menace to those senior to him, and at all costs he must be prevented from obtaining too quick promotion. If the name of such a man should be mentioned for promotion, it would be — 'Yes! Quite good at his work, sir, but I am afraid he drinks a little,' or 'A bit too fond of racing, sir. I am afraid he is not quite trustworthy.' And so his character would be slowly but surely undermined, so that his ability availed him nothing, and the promotion went to one who would not be a worry to his seniors.

In one post which I held while at head office, my duties took me into the general manager's room frequently to refer certain documents for his authority or signature. He had the reputation of being a bully (my uncle had by this time retired), and I used to be first astonished and then amused at the antics of very senior officers preparing for their daily interview with him. Each morning at about 9.30 a.m. the manager would approach the door of the sanctum with nervous steps and affix his eye to the crack, and there he would remain, almost motionless, often as long as twenty minutes, until such time as the 'old man' laid down his pen (I believe he often kept on writing on purpose). Then the manager would knock gently and cough, advance on tip-toe across the linoleum to the edge of the carpet, and say 'Good morning, sir,' getting a grunt in reply. He would then advance to the table, and the interview would proceed. On completion, the manager bowed again and retired backwards, mopping his brow as soon as he was clear of the door.

It appeared to me to be so absurd that one in his position, which carried with it a certain dignity, should be so overcome with moral funk at the prospect of a mere business discussion. I had been warned what to expect when I took over this job, but was far too busy to stand for twenty minutes on the doorstep, so adopted the normal practice of knocking and entering, and that, coupled with the fact that I failed to tip-toe across the linoleum, threw the secretary, who was in the room, into a state of nervous prostration. He put his finger on his lips and emitted a very subdued 'Sh'. But it did not appear to upset the old man. I placed the documents before him, he attended to them immediately, and I retired in the normal fashion.

It was not long before the secretary interviewed me, and scolded me severely for my intrepidity in daring to enter the general manager's room in that manner. He was horribly scandalised when I told him that I did not have time to humbug, waiting on the doormat, and anyway if the old man had anything to say, from what I had heard of him he probably would not hesitate to say it. After a few days of this sort of thing, and being further admonished by the secretary, I entered one morning in my usual way, met by a frown from the secretary and his finger to his lips, and in a spirit of devilment I crossed the room on the linoleum instead of the carpet. I thought the poor chap would have a fit when I stood alongside the old man and smiled across at him, and I verily believe the old man smiled, too. I think he held their 'Uriah Heep' methods in secret contempt, for he was always courteous to me and never passed me outside without a smile and a nod and sometimes a cheery word.

I was afterwards transferred to a country branch and remained in the country, though not in the same branch, until the war broke out.

While at school, I had joined the School Cadet Corps, and after leaving had joined a volunteer corps, in which I served for some years.

In 1909, I applied for and received a provisional appointment to commissioned rank in a militia unit, the 5th Australian Infantry

Regiment. In those days, the process was somewhat different to the present method of appointment. One had to be personally recommended by an officer of the forces as of good character and education, and in possession of the necessary qualifications to fit one to become an officer. The brigade major was my sponsor. An interview was arranged with the adjutant, I was duly introduced, and he sized me up. I apparently met with his approval, for he then arranged for an interview with the commanding officer. Again I was successful, and finally had to face the state commandant. During all these interviews it was impressed on me that there were no vacancies in the Regiment at present. Nevertheless, one occurred shortly after my interview with the state commandant, and I was duly gazetted to a provisional appointment with the rank of 2nd lieutenant (prov.). I qualified at the first examination, and my appointment was confirmed six months later, and dated the 9th August 1909.

In those days, our training was a good deal more thorough than it is today, and our officers and N.C.O.s were very efficient. Each company paraded every Tuesday night, and the battalion allotted one Saturday afternoon per month for field work, and throughout the summer and autumn months spent about three Saturdays a month on the rifle range. Any exhibition of slackness on the part of officers resulted in an interview with the commanding officer and a warning. The warning was not repeated. If the offence was, the individual was quietly told that an application for transfer to The Reserve would be favourably considered.

In addition to our weekly parade, classes of instruction were held, which all junior officers were expected to attend as follows: Monday night — drill; Tuesday night — company parade; Thursday night (once a month) — lecture; Friday night — musketry; and very often on Sunday, junior officers would go out into the country under a staff officer for instruction in map reading, tactics, or engineering.

Most of my spare time was thus taken up in the study of military affairs, but it was interesting. I met a very fine lot of fellows, and became proficient at the job.

Our staff officers told us then that with very little doubt we would be at war within five years. They were very efficient and very keen, and did not mind giving up their Sundays or any other time that suited us for instruction. They did a lot to inspire us with the same enthusiasm, and their work was amply demonstrated when the 1st Australian Division was formed in 1914, and was almost entirely composed of those militia officers. They made that division the very efficient organisation that it was, and laid the foundations of the wonderful traditions achieved by the Australian Imperial Force in the Great War.

Chapter Two

As I have said, I was in the country, in a little town in the north of Victoria, when the news of the European crisis reached us in July 1914. I was still on the active list of the Defence Force and had just passed my examination for captain's rank, but had not yet been promoted. How eagerly everybody watched the news in those days, until the fatal 4th of August, and how little they knew that war was a foregone conclusion, that all the efforts of our diplomats were so much waste of time, no matter how sincere they were. The Kiel Canal had been completed in June, and Germany was at last ready. The assassination of an archduke in Sarajevo had no bearing on the question, but was simply used as a ready excuse to break off diplomatic relations. Germany was ready to enforce her policy on the nations of Europe, and the declaration of war was the culmination of forty years' effort.

The Commonwealth government immediately offered to raise and equip a division for service overseas, and the offer was accepted by the British government, and for the next fortnight I was consumed with anxiety in case I should be left out of it. How eagerly I scanned the papers each day for the announcement of the appointment of brigade and unit commanders. I had already sent an application for appointment to district headquarters. Then followed letters and telegrams to everyone I knew who was likely in any way to have any influence in the appointment of officers to the force.

My first reply was something of a disappointment from General (then Lieut. Col.) H.E. Elliott, telling me that units were to be raised territorially, and he regretted that I was not in his area. He had, however, sent my application, with a recommendation, to the officer appointed to command the battalion to be raised in my area.[1]

Dear old 'Pompey'. He had been adjutant of the old 5th in the days when I was a brand-new subaltern. How those of us who knew him loved him. Hard as nails on duty, ruthless on an officer who railed, but always just, always ready to fight the troubles of anyone under his command, and always ready to go anywhere he ordered his troops to go. Brave as a lion, and more concerned about his men than himself. And he kept a job up his sleeve for me until he definitely knew that I was appointed to the 8th Battalion. So after all I was lucky, for I was chosen in two places, though I did not know at the time. He told me when I met him in camp, and after congratulating me he said, 'I reserved a job for you with me in case you did not get into the 8th, but now you are alright I can fill it.'

I thanked him and told him that I almost regretted having been appointed to the 8th as I would like to have served with him, and moreover I knew his officers almost to a man, while I knew very few in the 8th.

About 10.00 a.m. on Monday the 17th of August, I received a telegram informing me that I was appointed to the 8th Battalion and instructing me to take charge of the quota from that area and report by first available train to Drill Hall, Surrey Hills, Melbourne.[2] There was no train until ten minutes to six the next morning, so I packed

---

1 Harold 'Pompey' Elliott's renowned leadership in World War I was to make him a household name. Barrie had known him well since 1909, when they were in the 5th Australian Infantry Regiment together. After the outbreak of war in August 1914 a new expeditionary force was created, the Australian Imperial Force (AIF), and Pompey Elliott was appointed to command the 7th AIF Battalion.
2 John Charles Barrie had just turned 31 when he joined the AIF. He was an unmarried bank clerk, 5 feet 8½ inches tall (174 cms) and weighing 10½ stone (66 kgs). His next-of-kin was his mother, Jessie Barrie, of Holyrood Street, Sandringham.

up, handed over my job, and assisted the doctor in examining recruits until 10.00 p.m. The news did not take long to spread, a send-off was arranged at the leading hotel, and about ten o'clock I duly presented myself. What a night! Nobody went to bed, the send-off lasted until the train went, and I was driven to the station in good style. A lorry was drawn up in front of the hotel, minus horses, my bags were put on it, and I was then shouldered and carried out to the 'carriage' and ordered to stay there. I had no hope of getting off. My friends surrounded the lorry, some took the pole, while others pushed on the sides and rear, and away we went to the cheers of the populace, with the local constable heading the procession with his bagpipes.

It was late in the evening when we reached Surrey Hills, and I reported myself at the Drill Hall and spent the remainder of the night, until about 4.00 a.m., swearing in recruits and making out attestation papers. Next morning, there was a general muster at Victoria Barracks, and we marched through the city and out to Broadmeadows, twelve miles away, to camp. The work of organising and training the company fell on me, as my company commander did not arrive in camp until some weeks later, and when he did I found that though he had served in the South African War he had not done any service since, so that I practically had to train him as well as the company. But he was a very fine chap, and it did not take him long to pick up drill and infantry tactics. He left me to complete the organisation, and we turned out a very smart and very happy company.[3]

We had an extremely fine lot of men, many of them with militia service, and enlisted mainly from Stawell, Horsham, Ararat, and surrounding districts.[4] After being in camp a few weeks, the brigade was asked to send a representative company from each battalion to a military tattoo at the Exhibition Oval. Each of the other battalions sent

---

3 Barrie was in E Company of the 8th Battalion. In charge of the company was Lieutenant Gerald Cowper, a 34-year-old estate agent from Pascoe Vale.
4 The 8th Battalion had a strong connection with Ballarat, and many of its originals resided in that city. Other early enlisters in the unit came from Melbourne, Geelong, Gippsland, and Mildura.

a composite company made up of chosen men from each company, under chosen officers, but our commanding officer announced that he would send a complete company, and it would be the one that he considered the smartest and best trained in the battalion.[5] He chose my company, and I could not help feeling very proud. I had worked very hard with them, but that was sufficient reward. We were fully clothed and equipped by this time, and I will never forget the way those fellows marched through the streets that night. No regulars could have done better.

Of our training in Broadmeadows, there is little to tell. We were there nine weeks; it seemed a long time with everybody itching to get away. After two or three disappointments, when we packed up and fell in ready to move only to be ordered back to our lines again, we finally embarked on the 19th October on H.M.S. *Benalla*.[6] She was a very comfortable ship of 11,000 tons, and we were not overcrowded, having only our own battalion and two Army Service Corps companies on board. I had a very comfortable two-berth cabin to myself all the way. We had an uneventful voyage as far as Albany, which was the rendezvous for the convoy, and there we remained about a week, waiting for the New Zealand convoy to join us.

The day after our arrival, the commanding officer gave us leave to go ashore in batches of half a dozen at a time. I was named in the first batch. A very heavy storm had come up during the night, and as we were lying in open roadstead we got the full force of it. Our only means of going ashore was on the customs launch which visited us each day, and we had to watch for our chance to jump aboard. One minute she was level with the deck, and the next she was thirty or forty feet below. Four of us got on board; the other two decided they

---

5 The commander of the 8th AIF Battalion was Lieutenant-Colonel William Bolton, an experienced soldier with a distinctive moustache, who was aged 53 in August 1914. He had two of his sons with him at the unit's headquarters: one, like Barrie, was a lieutenant from the start, while the other was initially a private but became an officer after the early Gallipoli casualties.
6 The AIF's departure was delayed because Prime Minister Andrew Fisher was concerned about the threat to the troopships posed by marauding German warships.

would wait until the gale was over and go another day. We had to call at two or three other ships, and it was about three hours before we got into the harbour, and we lost our 'crew' overboard on the way. The crew consisted of a bright lad of about seventeen years of age, a nephew of the skipper. As we were pushing off from another vessel, the launch gave a sudden lurch, and he lost his balance and went over the side. Everybody yelled, but the skipper seized a boat hook, and when the lad appeared on the surface he deftly fixed the hook in the seat of his pants and we hauled him aboard. I could not quite determine whether he was grateful for the rescue or not — he just stood on the deck with the water running off him and swore solidly for five minutes, and as near as I can remember he did not repeat himself once. It was a very creditable performance in one so young. Then he went below to the engine room and dried his clothes.

When we reached the landing stage, we were met by the district naval officer, who informed us that the flagship had arrived and signalled — 'No Leave'. He therefore regretted that we must return to our ships, at which we all looked very glum. However, we were soon cheered again when he told us that as the storm was increasing he could not allow any boats to go out of the harbour, and we would be quite safe until eight o'clock that night when we must report to his office for instructions. The gale was still blowing, and we had to stay ashore and report again at 8.00 a.m.

At 8.00 a.m. he told us there would be no hope of getting out that day, and we could go and amuse ourselves for twenty-four hours. We spent a very enjoyable day and a half in Albany, to the great indignation of those who had waited for finer weather.

A few days later, the New Zealand convoy, consisting of twelve ships, joined us, and our convoy being now complete (with the exception of the Western Australians, who joined us off Fremantle), we shortly afterwards put to sea. It was a wonderful sight to see those forty-eight ships, each leaving her anchorage at the appointed time, steam out of the Sound and take up her allotted position in the convoy, which was formed some miles out at sea in three long lines, with ships at 800-yard intervals and 800-yard distance.[7] Our escort consisted of four warships — H.M.S. *Minotaur* from the China Squadron (our flagship), in front; H.M.A.S. *Sydney* in rear; H.M.A.S. *Melbourne* on the left flank; and the Japanese cruiser *Ibuki* on the right. We steamed without lights, except that each ship showed a light astern for the guidance of the ship in rear, and this was carefully encased in a box to prevent it being seen from any other angle.

On the morning of the 8th November, H.M.S. *Minotaur* left the convoy, and H.M.A.S. *Sydney* took over command, steaming through the convoy at about 10.00 a.m. to take her place ahead, leaving our rear unprotected.

That night, at about 8.00 p.m., H.M.A.S. *Sydney* signalled a special warning to be careful of lights, as she had observed the masthead light of a vessel crossing her course. This must obviously have been the German cruiser *Emden*. What a chance she missed. Had she been a couple of hours later and crossed in rear, which was then unprotected, what havoc she might have caused. She would certainly have met with a very sure fate, but she would have done a lot of damage first.

Next morning, to everybody's astonishment, we saw H.M.A.S. *Sydney* suddenly shoot off from her post at the head of the convoy and disappear over the horizon in a cloud of smoke. *Ibuki* followed, but soon turned back and took *Sydney*'s place. They were in wireless communication, and H.M.A.S. *Sydney* ordered her to return, while we in the convoy were still wondering what it was all about. Later, a wireless message, transmitted through the headquarter ship *Orvieto*, informed us that *Sydney* had overhauled a strange cruiser flying the German flag and was engaging her, and we could occasionally hear the boom of gunfire in the distance. The next message read — 'Enemy cruiser beached. Am chasing collier', and then a later one — 'Have captured collier. Enemy cruiser Emden total wreck'.

Imagine the excitement and the cheers throughout the fleet, with

---

7 There were, in fact, 38 troopships: 28 conveyed the AIF in three parallel columns ahead of the New Zealand contingent in its 10 transports. Barrie's ship, the *Benalla*, was the fifth ship in the starboard column.

more to follow when a half-holiday was announced to celebrate the victory. A few nights later, H.M.A.S. *Sydney* passed through the convoy on her way to Colombo with prisoners and wounded from the *Emden*, and we all turned out at about 4.00 a.m. to see her. She passed quite close to us, but her captain had requested that the troops should not make any demonstration out of consideration for the wounded on board, so we watched her go by in silence.

We were kept fairly busy on the voyage, and carried on a regular programme of training for the troops, with extra classes of instruction for officers and N.C.O.s, culminating in a lecture after dinner each evening at 7.30 p.m. This was held on the promenade deck, the weather being beautifully fine, and it was more pleasant outside on the deck than inside. These evening lectures were not very popular, but the colonel insisted, and we had to submit.

One evening it started to blow a bit and turned cold, and we were all full of hope that the lecture would be postponed. The adjutant[8] made the suggestion, but the only result was permission to use the guardroom. The guardroom was situated in what was the ship's second-class dining saloon, from which tables and chairs had been removed except one row along one wall, and over these the guard had swung their hammocks. We trooped into the room, I am afraid with rather a bad grace, and everybody squatted on the floor, prepared to be more or less bored for half an hour. A chair was brought for the colonel; the lecturer hung up his blackboard, and proceeded with his lecture. Finding the floor a trifle uncomfortable, I discovered that, by crouching under a hammock, I could get into one of the seats at a table, which two of us duly did.

About halfway through the lecture, I was fiddling with my penknife when I happened to glance up at the hammock above, in which a member of the guard, off duty, was resting. I noticed that his blanket had gone awry, and his bare skin covering that portion of his anatomy which he used for sitting on was protruding through the meshes of the hammock. Well! I ask you! What would you do?

---

8 The 8th Battalion's adjutant was 30-year-old Captain Alf Possingham. He was killed during the charge towards Krithia on 8 May 1915.

The temptation was too great for me. I jabbed it with the penknife. The victim emitted the most blood-curdling yell and literally hit the roof. Everybody jumped, the lecturer dropped his chalk and broke it in pieces, the dear old colonel fell off his chair, and for a minute or so pandemonium and consternation reigned. The colonel picked himself up and wanted to know what the hell the matter was. I thought, 'Now I'm in for it,' but the victim, appreciating the joke like a good sport, apologised for the disturbance and explained that he had been dreaming. Good lad! What wonderful chaps they were: quick on the uptake, full of resource, and absolutely dependable in a crisis.

We stayed a day at Colombo and a day at Aden, but were not allowed shore leave at either place. At Aden, the convoy split into two parts to save congestion at Suez while passing through the Canal, and while on our way between Aden and Suez we received the news that we were to disembark at Alexandria and complete our training in Egypt. The news was received with mixed feelings, as many thought it meant that we would be used merely to garrison Egypt and would not see any active service, though I think we all realised we were lucky to escape that winter on Salisbury Plain.

The only other excitement of the trip occurred in the Red Sea, when one night H.M.T. *Ascanius*, immediately in front of us, struck the stern of the ship in front of her, and in the commotion that followed a cry of 'man overboard' went up from the *Ascanius*. Our ship swung out to port to avoid collision with the *Ascanius* and lowered a boat to look for the missing man, then stopped to render assistance if necessary and to wait for her boat. Within a few minutes, H.M.S. *Hampshire* (which was afterwards sunk with Lord Kitchener on board) and which had taken over command of our portion of the convoy at Colombo, steamed up and her captain enquired through a megaphone, 'What the devil are you stopping for?'

Captain Symons was on the bridge of the *Benalla*, and replied that there was a man overboard from the *Ascanius* and he had lowered a boat. *Hampshire* retorted that that was nothing to do with him, that he was in charge of this convoy, and when he wanted anyone to stop he would issue orders about it. Would we please get under way at once and proceed on the voyage? Captain Symons replied he would proceed as soon as his boat returned. *Hampshire* said, 'To hell with your boat. You can pick it up at Suez if they can row that far. Get under way at once.'

After that, Captain Symons said no more, but the *Hampshire* made a complete circle of the *Benalla* with her captain talking all the time in true navy style, to the huge delight of the troops. He never missed a beat, and did not repeat himself once. It was a wonderfully sustained effort, and substantially increased my already great respect for the Royal Navy. Our sympathy, however, went out to Captain Symons, whom everyone liked. He was a very fine, quiet old gentleman, and we felt he did not deserve such treatment. We were glad when his boat returned, the alarm having proved a false one, as we knew he would have been very worried at leaving his boat behind, though doubtless some other ship would have picked it up.

The remainder of the voyage passed without incident, and we arrived at Alexandria on the 4th of December, forty-nine days after leaving Melbourne. It was a long trip, but our speed was regulated by the speed of the slowest ship, the old *Southern*, which could only do nine knots.

Chapter Three

We disembarked next morning and entrained for Cairo, and on arrival there the battalion marched to Mena, about ten miles out, where our camp was situated. I was detailed for duty in charge of baggage, which was conveyed by tram to the pyramids and thence by native donkey carts to the camp lines. It was a beautiful moonlight night. I will never forget the sight and the feeling of awe which inspired me when I got my first glimpse of the Great Pyramid, with the moon behind it, through the trees on the side of the road. It seemed to be towering over us while we were still miles away from it.

We arrived in camp about midnight with the baggage all complete, and found the battalion asleep in the sand. Tents had not been erected — we were to draw and erect them next day — and that night it rained, the only night during our four months' stay at Mena. When we awoke at daylight we found the camp site was located in a valley with an almost perpendicular wall on one side and the pyramid towering over us.

We started off at once on a scheme of progressive training to fit us to take our place with the British Army. We were all a bit soft after being seven weeks at sea, but we soon hardened up again, and training started in earnest. Our brigade commander had his own ideas (some of them very original) for making us fit. He forbade smoking during training hours — nobody would have minded this if he had set the example himself, but he was an inveterate cigarette-smoker and puffed them all day long in view of the troops, and of course they resented it.[1]

After church parade on Sunday, when there was general leave for the division, the 2nd Brigade was ordered to do a route march of not less than five miles, sticking to the sand. This became the joke of the division, and they all turned out and cheered as we marched through the camp. 'The 2nd Brigade *will* be fit' became a well-known slogan. Unfortunately, it had the opposite effect, and towards the end of our training the troops began to show signs of strain. They were weary and over-trained, and Division ordered the Sunday route march to be discontinued, and instituted an additional weekly half-day holiday.

The third notable effort to ensure our fitness was contained in an order to the effect that 'When on active service every soldier is required to carry 150 rounds of ball ammunition in the pouches of his web equipment. In order to accustom the troops to this extra weight, pebbles will be issued in lieu of ammunition. Platoon commanders will be responsible that every man is issued with 150 pebbles every morning before parade, pebbles to be returned to, and checked by them each night before dismissing.'

This was marked 'Urgent' and delivered by a brigade runner one evening while we were at mess. When it was handed to the commanding officer, I saw him go red in the face as he read it and then throw it at the adjutant, saying, 'Read that!' The adjutant read it and grinned. We all wondered what was up. It quite spoilt the colonel's dinner, and he could hardly contain himself until the loyal toast was drunk, after which he left immediately for brigade headquarters to lodge his protest in person. We never knew the outcome of that interview, except that he was not alone, the other three C.O.s following on his heels. After the C.O. had gone, the adjutant read us the order, which was greeted with roars of delight, especially from the subalterns, who began to calculate how many pebbles would be required to issue forty-eight men with 150 pebbles each. The result

---

1 Brigadier-General James McCay, commander of the 2nd AIF Brigade, was talented and industrious — his wide-ranging achievements had included a stint as Australia's Defence minister — but he was also pedantic and irascible, with a notorious tendency to alienate others unnecessarily.

is 7,200, so that each platoon commander was required to find that number and issue them before eight o'clock the next morning, check them in again in the evening, and repeat the performance daily. Some of the bright lads proceeded immediately to organise a pebble hunt, but most of us decided on Cairo instead. I am afraid we did not take that particular order as seriously as perhaps we might have done, and though the C.O. did not confide in us the result of his interview, the order was never carried out.

As marching was an important part of our training, we had to march about five miles out into the desert every day, where each unit was allotted a certain area for training. One day, each platoon was given a definite area in which to work, and platoon commanders instructed to site and dig a trench and then to practise a bayonet charge from the trench, choosing an objective not less than 100 yards away, the work to be inspected and criticised by battalion staff and reasons to be given for the site chosen. My area was at the junction of two valleys. I duly sited the trench and got it dug, the staff inspected it, and were apparently satisfied. They rode off, leaving instructions to carry on practising the charge. I chose my objective straight down the valley, so that we had level ground to charge over.

Half-right from us on the top of the high bank, a family of orange sellers were squatting, waiting for the midday rest to sell their wares. I gave the necessary instructions to the platoon, pointed out the objective, gave the order to fix bayonet, and, on my whistle blast, all were to leap from the trench, cheer, and charge. I drew my sword, blew my whistle, scrambled out of the trench, and ran for the objective. The platoon followed, but as soon as they were clear of the trench, to a man they turned half-right; with the bayonets down and yelling like maniacs, they made straight for the orange sellers. I had almost reached my objective before I realised what was happening and had no hope of stopping it, so followed my platoon, not knowing whether to swear or laugh, and wanting to do both. Needless to say, the natives did not wait; they got the fright of their young lives, and streaked for the skyline, leaving their oranges behind. I did not actually see anyone take any oranges, and sincerely hoped that they would not do so. I commenced to abuse all and sundry, but the humour of the situation got the better of me and I was forced to join in a general laugh. I marched them back to the job, and half an hour later observed a black head appear very cautiously over the bank, then beckon to his mates. They appeared quite relieved to find oranges still in their baskets, but there were nevertheless a few suspicious bulges in the trouser pockets of my platoon.

In February 1915, a little excitement was caused by the news of the Turkish attack on the Suez Canal, and the Australian Division was required to send one infantry battalion to Ismailia to strengthen the garrison there, the 2nd Brigade being ordered to supply it. The brigade commander decided, in order to distribute the honour, to send two companies from the 7th Battalion and two from the 8th Battalion, and to our huge delight my company was one of the chosen.

We marched to Cairo and entrained for Ismailia, where we bivouacked on the desert just outside the town, which is the headquarters of the Suez Canal Company and situated on the shores of Lake Timsah. That night it rained again. The town itself is, I think, one of the prettiest little places I have seen, the streets being all asphalted and lined with trees, and the houses well built, each standing in its own ground, with the most beautiful tropical gardens. It was originally one of the worst mosquito-infested fever spots in the world, but today there are no mosquitoes, and it is a health resort of Cairo where many people have their summer homes.

I could never understand the system of defence employed on the Canal, the garrison being in trenches practically on the Canal bank, so that the Turks were able to bring their artillery close enough to fire into and over it, and every ship, before entering the Canal, had to build up sandbag protection on the bridge. Several ships were hit, and one ship's captain killed on his bridge. The destruction of the Canal, or even the sinking of a ship in it, would have had a very serious effect on our communications, but it was not until the visit of Lord Kitchener to Gallipoli in November, after which he inspected the Canal defences, that the garrison was moved, under his instructions, ten miles out into the desert.

We did not get an opportunity of getting into action, though our other company did a tour of trench duty during an attack at Kantara, but it did not develop on their front.

About the fourth or fifth day, orders came to us that we were to form part of a column to go out into the desert after a Turkish force estimated to be about 4,000 strong, was reported by the Air Force in a certain position, and considered easy of capture. Some British troops and the Bengal Lancers, who were bivouacked close to us, making a total strength of about 4,000, were detailed for this job. Camel transport was allotted to us, three days' rations drawn, and each man was issued with 200 rounds of ammunition. Reveille was arranged for 2.00 a.m., the column to move at 3.00 a.m. and cross the Canal before daylight. Everybody was keyed up to a great pitch of excitement, and we were forbidden to leave the bivouac lines and were ordered to get as much sleep as possible. The bivouac was quiet at 8.00 p.m., the troops lying on the sand with their equipment alongside them, blankets having been handed in. I think most of us only half-slept that night, anxiously waiting for 2.00 a.m. and reveille. It seemed a long time coming, and eventually, to our astonishment, the sky began to lighten and the first streaks of dawn appeared. I jumped up in a fright, my first waking impression being that I had been left behind, and was very relieved to find the regiment still there.

It was not long before they were all awake and wondering, like me, what had gone wrong. All the colonel could, or would, tell us was that the show had been postponed. About 8.00 a.m., after his return from headquarters, where he had been ordered to report, the colonel told us that the show was definitely off. What had happened was that the G.O.C.–Canal Defences was under direct instructions from the War Office in London and could not move without permission. The War Office had cabled instructing him not to go out, but to remain where he was and allow the Turks to come in. The Turks, unfortunately, were not quite so simple and had no intention of coming in, and after a few days they withdrew. It was only a raid, made with the object of forcing our people to keep a big garrison in Egypt and so weaken the Western Front, and it succeeded. It was another bright example of the stupid interference by politicians with the plans of an army commander.

It has been the same all through British history. The politicians, after making a mess of diplomacy, run the country into war, and call upon the army to get them out of it. Then, having committed the army, they cannot leave them to do the job, but literally tie the commander's hands and rob the army of its victory or the fruits thereof. The outcome of what came to be called World War I turned out to be one of the worst examples on record. Instead of it being 'a war to end war', the fruits of the victory won by the British Army and their allies at such tremendous cost were snatched from their grasp by the Armistice and the 'Peace' of Versailles, arranged by politicians headed by a pedantic old schoolmaster, so that now it will have to be fought all over again. The indications are that the time is not far off.[2]

I cannot help thinking that there were many times in the last war, and in nearly every other war we have fought, when we did not deserve to win, and probably would not have won, if we had not had a Divine Providence watching over us.

The next night, the Turks made a definite attempt to cross the Canal by building a pontoon bridge across it at a spot where there was a break in defences. Unfortunately for them, a battery of Egyptian field artillery had been moved to this spot that day, and though the Turks were unaware of the fact, they built their bridge right under the muzzles of the guns. The battery lay quiet until the bridge was completed and the troops commenced to march across, then they opened fire at point-blank range, killing 136 and wounding many more, a great number of whom escaped. Only four reached our bank unhurt, and they were captured next day. The pontoons were riddled with shrapnel and sank, but were raised and brought into Ismailia dock the next day, where I saw them. After that failure, the Turks withdrew, and a few days later we returned to Mena.

Shortly after our return, I was detailed for picquet duty in Cairo, the picquet consisting of four officers and N.C.O.s and 100

---

2 As these comments indicate, Barrie compiled his recollections in the 1930s.

men, made up of one officer and twenty-five other ranks from each battalion in the brigade. The four officers detailed were all friends, and we had a very happy time on that job. Captain McKenna of the 7th Battalion was in command, and the three subalterns were Balfe (6th), Caughey (5th), and myself (8th).[3] The picquet was accommodated in tents in Kasr-el-Nil barracks, and the officers had the option of living in tents and using the barracks mess, or living in a hotel. We elected to stay at a hotel, and put up at the National close by, thinking we would be more free to do some sight-seeing as we had no duty in the daytime, except ordinary routine. Only small picquets under N.C.O.s were required during training hours when the troops were on duty, officers being required for duty with larger picquets during the evening when the troops were on leave. We had very little trouble, and the behaviour of the troops was remarkably good, considering there were 30,000 young, fit men from Australia and New Zealand, mostly between the ages of eighteen and thirty-five years, set down in a strange and fascinating country, and released from the restraining influence of home life. Our duties took us into the lowest quarters of Cairo, where every door had to be opened on our demand, but where no man dared enter unaccompanied, and I saw some sights there which astonished and disgusted me and which, while they themselves were to me a practical object lesson, I cannot set down here.

After a payday the troops would become quite festive, and a few would overstay their leave, so that the picquet would have to remain on duty perhaps until 4.00 a.m. to clear the last of them out, and sometimes we would find it necessary to arrest one or two for their own safety. After midnight one night, I discovered a man, whom I had previously warned, still trying to evade us in one of the lowest haunts

---

3 Neither Balfe nor McKenna were to survive the Gallipoli landing. Edward McKenna, a 37-year-old soft-goods manager, was married and admired. Rupert Balfe, a 25-year-old medical student, was gifted and revered — a VFL footballer, a champion athlete, and so admired that his friend Robert Menzies was moved to eulogise him in verse after his death. Ross Caughey, a 25-year-old clerk, survived the war.

of the city. I took an N.C.O. and a file of men, and went through the house and eventually ran him to earth. He was somewhat inebriated and had ninety pounds in notes in his pocket. He had just arrived from Australia with the 4th Brigade and was determined to see the sights, but did not realise the risk he was taking. Men have had their throats cut for less than that in that quarter, so we locked him up for his own safety. That night I visited the police station at Bab-el-Hadid on our way back to barracks, having instructed two men, whom I had sent off as escort to a prisoner, to wait and rejoin us there. I found the sergeant on duty (an Englishman) in the guard room, and went in and spoke to him. I remarked on the noise the prisoners were making, and he replied, 'Oh yes, but we'll stop that directly, sir. We are just going to turn in now. Would you like to have a look at them?'

I replied that I would, and he opened a slot in the door for me to see through. There were about twenty there, all singing and some dancing. I said, 'You'll never stop that, Sergeant.'

'Oh, yes, we will, sir,' he replied. 'Come, and I will show you how we do it.'

With that he led me onto the verandah, where he had a hose attached to a tap, and seizing the nozzle of the hose he threw up the window, poked the nozzle through the bars, and demanded silence. Nobody took any notice and the revelry continued, so he turned to a man at the tap and said, 'Alright, Corporal, turn it on.'

The hose spurted, and he gave it one quick swish around the room. The effect was wonderful; there was instant silence and then a final warning.

'You can all go to sleep now,' he said. 'The guard is going to turn in. Any more noise and I will give you a proper sousing.' Then, turning to me with a confident smile, he said, 'That will be all tonight, sir. We'll turn in now.'

I thanked him for the exhibition, returned his salute, and wished him goodnight. It's a great life in the army.

Soon after our return to Mena, at the termination of our tour of picquet duty, a stir was caused throughout the division by the sudden departure of the 3rd Brigade for an unknown destination. In

February the navy had begun their attack on the Dardenelles ports, and all sorts of rumours were flying around as to the fate of the 3rd Brigade. However, we had become so used to rumours by that time that no-one took them seriously, though it bucked the troops up considerably to think that perhaps after all we were going to be used for something more than garrison duty. As a matter of fact, they had been sent to Lemnos with the idea of co-operating with the navy in the attack on the forts, though we did not know of this until we joined them there ourselves, early in April. They were, of course, not used until we joined them, as the Turks had by then sent a strong garrison to the Peninsula, which rendered any effort by one brigade entirely out of the question. Therefore they were landed at Lemnos and waited there until the arrival of the remainder of the force.

Chapter Four

Ever since our arrival at Mena, I had wanted to inspect the Great Pyramid, or Cheops, as it is called, but we had been kept so busy in the daytime that we had little opportunity for sight-seeing. I had, of course, been to see it and the Sphinx just below, and had even climbed it, but had not been inside until we were granted our weekly half-holiday, when I took the first opportunity of achieving my desire.

Nobody who has not seen the Great Pyramid can have any conception of the magnitude of the building. It is built on a rocky plateau, close to the edge of the inundated area of the Nile. It is 470 feet high, the base covering thirteen acres of ground, and it is built of tiers of stones, each stone being about fifteen feet long and three feet square. About 400 yards away is the second pyramid, almost as big, with its top covered with alabaster, and very difficult and dangerous to climb, it being possible only on one side, where there is a crack in the alabaster affording little better than a toehold. A divisional order was issued a few days after our arrival warning the troops against climbing this pyramid, and pointing out that only very few of the cleverest native guides were able to reach the top, and any attempt on the part of the troops would probably result in a fatal accident. Next morning, a Western Australian flag was floating from the summit. It was never discovered who put it there, but it was a very eloquent expression of 'Never let it be said that an Australian soldier cannot do what an Egyptian native can!'

One day, in company with two other officers of my battalion,

I climbed the Great Pyramid. We each engaged a guide, as even though we were all fit and in good, hard condition, it is a fairly hard task to reach the summit without assistance, for as I have previously explained, each step is three feet high. An extra guide attached himself to our party, and though we tried to 'shoo' him off and told him we would not pay him, he refused to leave us and accompanied us right to the summit, rendering assistance to each of us wherever he thought it necessary on the way.

It took us, with the help of our guides, about forty minutes to reach the top, which is uncompleted and has a flat surface about forty feet square. There was a native on top selling coffee. We each had a cup, and sat down to enjoy the view, which stretches for miles and miles across the desert on every side. It was wonderful. Then our spare guide approached us and offered to bet us ten shillings that he could descend the pyramid and climb to the top of the other one in nine minutes. We laughed at him and told him we wouldn't take his money. It had taken us forty minutes to climb this one, and he undertook to descend it, run 400 yards across the sand and climb the other in nine minutes. However, he was very persistent, so we told him we would not bet him, but would give him two shillings each if he succeeded. He promptly threw off his cloak, while we produced our watches and gave him the word 'go'. He trotted to the edge and right down the face of the pyramid, taking each step in his stride. We watched him across the sand and up the side of the other pyramid until he reached the summit, where he turned and waved to us. His time was eight minutes. After resting there a minute or so, he descended, climbed to the top of our pyramid again, collected his cloak and his money, and helped us to the bottom. We returned to camp in a disconsolate mood, feeling that we were not fit at all.

We decided on our next half-holiday to 'do' the inside of the pyramid. It was impossible, of course, amongst the native guides to find one who knew the story of the true significance of this wonderful edifice. The popular theory is that it was built as a tomb by one of the ancient kings of Egypt, and in the centre are the king's and queen's chambers with sarcophagus complete, but there is no record of any body having been found in either of them, and they were probably placed there merely as a blind to mislead anyone who broke into it before the time was ripe for its real secrets to be revealed.

I regret that I was not sufficiently well versed at the time in the true story of the pyramid to enable me to take full advantage of the opportunity for a close inspection, but in the light of knowledge which I have since acquired on the subject, there appears to be little room for doubt that it is an inspired edifice, and is very aptly termed 'The Bible in Stone'.

Another interesting trip which I was anxious to do was to the Tombs of the Sacred Bulls at Sakhara. This meant a ride of about eight miles across the desert, which I was able to accomplish with the connivance of our transport officer, Lieut. John Bolton (son of our commanding officer), who wangled two horses and accompanied me.[1] At Sakhara is also what is reputed to be the oldest pyramid in Egypt, known as the 'Step Pyramid'. Its construction is somewhat different from the others; it is small in comparison and crumbling with age. We passed it on the way, but did not have time to spend more than a few minutes there, and pushed on to the tombs. Leaving our horses in the charge of our guides, we located the caretaker, who conducted us through them.

The tombs are underground and are carved out of solid rock, with a ramp at the entrance, which is protected by an iron grille. They consist of a long, narrow corridor, with compartments each about fifteen feet square opening off the corridor on either side, the floor of each compartment being about three feet lower than the floor of the corridor, and each containing a granite sarcophagus large enough to contain the body of a bull standing up. These sarcophagi are beautifully carved and polished, and each is cut from a solid block of granite with a sliding lid, which is pushed back so that the inside may be seen. Each sarcophagus weighs several tons and, apart from the weight, the dimension of each is greater than that of the doorway.

---

[1] John Gillies Bolton, a blue-eyed, fair-haired 32-year-old engineer, survived Gallipoli, was wounded and decorated in France, and returned to Australia in 1918.

The question that immediately arises in one's mind is 'How were they got there?' But I have not met anyone who was able to supply the answer. These bulls were held to be sacred, and were worshipped by the ancient Egyptians, and on death their bodies were embalmed and buried there. They have all now been removed, but I have seen some of them in the museum in Cairo, wonderfully preserved, where are also the mummified bodies of several kings and queens of Egypt, including that of the Great Rameses III. Egypt is certainly a land of mysteries and a most fascinating place. We had tea in the desert, and enjoyed a most wonderful ride home in the moonlight.

Chapter Five

Our training was now sufficiently far advanced to enable us to undertake divisional manoeuvres, and during this stage we often spent a night in bivouac on the desert. The days were getting hot, and the troops went out lightly clothed in the morning, and in consequence they suffered rather severely from the cold at night, as a result of which we had a good many cases of pneumonia, especially amongst the 2nd Brigade, where the men were still suffering from the effects of strain and over-work from the extra work imposed on them at the outset. I have often thought that the gentleman who composed that well-known song 'Till the Sands of the Desert Grow Cold' had very little experience of his subject, for I don't think I have ever tried to sleep on anything colder. Though perhaps, after all, there was method in it, for it was certainly not a very binding promise. They grew very cold every night.

General Birdwood arrived from India to take over the command of the Australian and New Zealand Army Corps, and rumours began to develop into something more definite.

Towards the end of March, General Sir Ian Hamilton also arrived from England. He inspected the division and declared them fit for active service.[1] But before this event I also had succumbed to sickness

---

[1] Birdwood, then 49, arrived in Egypt shortly before Christmas 1914. Hamilton, who was 62, arrived four months later, having been appointed as commander-in-chief of the allied Mediterannean Expeditionary Force. Both were highly experienced British commanders.

and was a patient in Mena House, which had been taken over as an Australian Hospital.[2] I had been in bed about a fortnight and was then allowed to get up for two hours in the afternoon, when one day Colonel Springthorpe, Medical Officer in Command, came to my room and asked me how I felt, felt my pulse, had a look at my chart, and after some discussion with the sister, informed me that he had a note from my C.O. stating that the battalion was marching out from Mena the next day to entrain for Alexandria for embarkation, and enquiring if I was fit enough to re-join.[3]

He asked me what I thought about it. I replied, 'I am alright, sir. I would hate to be left behind.'

He then told me that I could go and see my C.O. that afternoon and tell him that, though not fit for duty, I could go by train to Cairo and join the battalion there, and if allowed to rest on the voyage, the sea trip would probably fit me up.

I did this, and returned to hospital, but unfortunately on my visit to camp I must have picked up another germ of some sort, for I woke up in the morning with a violent headache and feeling very sick. However, I said nothing until the nursing sister came and told me my bath was ready. I jumped out of bed, and fell flat on the floor. The sister picked me up and helped me back to bed, felt my pulse, took my temperature, which showed over 103 degrees, and sent for the doctor.[4] Needless to say, I did not get to Cairo that day, and my battalion went without me after all. The colonel, however, sent his report to my C.O., and my baggage was sent to the hospital.

---

2 Barrie was diagnosed with bronchial catarrh, and admitted to hospital on 23 March.
3 Doctor J.W. Springthorpe was an energetic and prominent physician and lecturer in Melbourne, where he involved himself in the organisation of dentists, nurses, ambulances, masseurs, and child welfare, as well as recreational pursuits such as art and cycling. When he reviewed Barrie's recovery in Egypt, 'Springy' was a 59-year-old physician at No 2 Australian General Hospital with the rank of lieutenant-colonel.
4 According to official records, Barrie had been in hospital at Mena House for 10 days when his temperature, hitherto normal, suddenly climbed to 101 degrees (38.3 Celsius) on the morning of 3 April. It remained high for three days, peaking at over 102 degrees (39 Celsius) on 5 April, before subsiding.

A few days later, when I imagined they would be well at sea, a wire came from Alexandria saying that the troopship would be at the wharf coaling until six o'clock that evening, and enquiring if I was yet fit to re-join. I begged permission to go, and armed with a chit to say I was not fit for duty, the colonel sent me into Cairo in an ambulance to catch the midday train. Unfortunately, the ambulance was late starting and missed the train, and I had to wait until four o'clock for the next one, which did not arrive at Alexandria until 10.00 p.m., and my ship had gone. However, the M.L.O. procured a cabin for me on another ship that night, and next morning arranged a passage for me on the *Ittria*, a British India ship, carrying the 6th Battery A.F.A. There were two other infantry officers on board, Scanlan (6th) and Layh (7th), both of whom had been sent ashore on duty at Alexandria and their ships had pulled out before they returned.[5]

Major Mills, in command of the 6th Battery, turned a cold eye upon us all.[6] He was of that peculiar type that looks down on all infantrymen, and was quite certain that we had all been ashore pleasure-seeking and had missed our ships on purpose. It was obvious to us that he was not acquainted with Colonel Elliott or Colonel Bolton. Explanations were unavailing; he would not listen, but took pains to assure us that he would make us work. We resented his attitude so much that I did not even bother to show him my certificate, and did my tour of orderly duty with the others, and whatever other duties were required. Evasion of duty had never been a hobby of mine. I like soldiering, and duty was always a pleasure to me.

However, I had an opportunity before leaving the *Ittria* of getting

---

5 Lieutenant Jack Scanlan was, in fact, with Captain Bert Layh in Pompey Elliott's 7th Battalion. Both were soon to be wounded at Gallipoli, but became proficient and decorated battalion commanders in Elliott's 15th Brigade at the Western Front. Scanlan was to become a prisoner of the Japanese for three-and-a-half years in World War II.
6 Major J.B. Mills, commander of the 6th Battery, was a 44-year-old barrister and former journalist from Western Australia. He had served in South Africa, and had been an artillery officer ever since. Mills was wounded in the abdomen at Gallipoli and died on 30 May 1915.

even with him. In fact, I think I was one up. At dinner on the last evening, when we were approaching Lemnos, the battery officers, several of whom I knew and who enjoyed the joke tremendously, toasted the 'derelicts', as they had christened us. Captain (now Colonel) Geo Stevenson proposed the toast, and in a humorous speech he made some facetious remarks about the infantry and particularly the 'derelicts' whom they had on board — all, of course, in a good and friendly spirit, which we took in good part and enjoyed.[7] The 'derelicts' nominated me to reply on their behalf, which I duly did in the same vein, and in conclusion I asked the ship's officers to join us in drinking the health and good fortune of our 'auxiliary arm, the artillery'. This evoked shrieks of delight from the 'derelicts' and ship's officers, and even some of the artillery people joined in, but I am afraid the dear old major did not appreciate the joke. He went red, and got really angry about it, refusing to speak to me again. The artillery is, of course, auxiliary to the infantry, but it is not safe to mention the fact to some of them.

I think one of the best jokes I have heard occurred that night at the commencement of dinner. The ship was manned by a Goanese crew, and the chief officer had a personal servant named Jesus (which is quite a common name amongst them) who, in addition to his other duties, waited at table in the saloon. As we took our seats, the captain said, 'Well, gentlemen, this is probably our last meal together. God knows what is going to happen tomorrow. And, by Jove, there are just twelve of us. It reminds me of the Passover Feast.' At that moment, the door opened and the chief officer remarked, 'Yes, sir, and here's Jesus with the soup.' And it was so.

We entered Lemnos Harbour the next morning. It is quite a large harbour, and was crowded with shipping. There was a boom across the entrance, which was closed at night as a protection against

---

7 George Stevenson, a 32-year-old Scottish-born accountant, was also an experienced artillery officer. He was more fortunate than Mills, ending the war after durable service at Gallipoli and the Western Front as Lieutenant-Colonel Stevenson CMG, DSO (mentioned in dispatches on four occasions) without having been wounded, sick, or gassed.

attack. Transports arriving had to judge their time accordingly so as to arrive in daylight. I have never seen so many ships congregated in one place before, and do not suppose I shall again. The navy used it as their base of operations against the forts, and there was a great number of battleships, cruisers, destroyers, and submarines, both British and French, in addition to the huge number of transports necessary to accommodate the Australian and New Zealand Army Corps, the 29th British Division, and a French division, all of which were congregating there in readiness for the now-famous landing at Gallipoli. As soon as the *Ittria* dropped anchor in her allotted position, we said goodbye to our friends on the ship, and they sent us off in a boat to re-join our respective troopships. I received a warm welcome aboard the *Clan Macgillivray*, and as I was already feeling fairly fit after the few days at sea, I resumed duty at once. Duties on this ship were confined to routine; there were no lectures now, our training having been completed. The troops enjoyed a well-earned rest, and it was of wonderful benefit to all ranks.

We lay there three weeks, during which time several practice landings were made on the beach, using the ship's boats, and we were allowed ashore once or twice on leave. There were only two small villages on the island, and nothing much to see. On a fine day, we could see the hills of Gallipoli, where the Turks were busy preparing for our reception, for they must by then have been fully aware of the reason for our presence at Lemnos. One day, two hospital ships steamed into the harbour, and one of them, the *Gascon*, took up position opposite us. The next day, the battalion went ashore to practise a landing and then to do a route march to exercise the troops, returning at about 6.00 p.m. I was on guard duty, and, with two other officers, had to remain aboard.

During the day, we saw some of the nurses on the *Gascon* practising semaphore signalling; so, procuring a set of flags, we called them up. Sending our names, we asked who they had aboard, and found there were two nurses whom I knew. They invited us to tea at 4.00 p.m. We were not expecting relief until 4.00 p.m., but they replied that they would wait tea for us, and we gladly accepted the invitation. The difficulty was to get across, as all the ship's boats were ashore. But we could not allow a little thing like that to daunt us, and when our relief returned, we persuaded the sergeant in charge of the boat to wait for us, and row us over on his way back to the beach, picking us up again after his last trip.

I was surprised to find Colonel F.D. Bird, a well-known Melbourne surgeon whom I knew, and his son Captain Dougan Bird, on board.[8] We received a very warm welcome from them and the sisters, one of whom had nursed me in Mena, and spent a very pleasant couple of hours until at about 6.00 p.m. we saw our last boat return to the *Clan Macgillivray*. We watched him unload and then push off to come across for us, then he stopped and there appeared to be some altercation, and the boat pulled into the side of the ship and, to our dismay, was hauled on board. We were absent from the ship without leave. The chief officer semaphored our captain and explained the position, but he replied that it was nothing to do with him, he would not lower a boat again, and we could make our own arrangements. Colonel Bird, who had already invited us to dinner, turned to us with a smile and said, 'Splendid! You'll have to stay to dinner now.' Then to his son he went on, 'Dougan, tell the steward to put some champagne on the ice.'

That put the lid on it. We accepted the situation and stayed. There was nothing we could do anyhow, and when the colonel suggested that there were plenty of comfortable beds in the hospital ward, in addition to the prospect of a good dinner, we put our worries aside, got a message to the C.O. explaining our predicament, and set out to enjoy the present. We certainly enjoyed a beautiful dinner, vastly different from the fare we were getting on the *Clan Macgillivray*, which, without doubt, was the worst ship I had ever sailed in, and after dinner we danced on the deck to the music of a gramophone until ten o'clock, to the envy of our friends on the 'Clan'.

---

8 Fred Bird was a prominent, eminent, and well-connected 56-year-old surgeon. He had accompanied the AIF to Egypt with his own self-funded team of nurses and equipment, and in February 1915 was appointed consulting surgeon to the British forces in Egypt with the rank of lieutenant-colonel.

During the evening, after again refusing to send for us, the captain ordered a light to be hung at the foot of the companionway, right at the water's edge, to guide us home. We saw it going down the side of the ship and hang there, then at our suggestion the chief officer signalled again, thanking the captain, but regretting that it was a bit too far to swim. At ten o'clock, we returned to the saloon for supper, and as we had still not been called for, went to bed in the hospital ward, enjoying a good sleep in a comfortable bed. We had only our valises on an iron deck on the troopship. At seven o'clock next morning, the hospital ship lowered a boat, manned by a crew of medical officers who rowed us back to our ship. The whole battalion turned out to welcome us home and gave us a rousing reception, mingled with the admonition,

'Wait 'til you see the C.O.!'[9] That was what we were thinking, too, and went to report ourselves, but finding the colonel was in his bath, we went to breakfast hoping to delay the ordeal until he had his breakfast and might be expected to be in a mild mood. I was still at the table, though the others had finished and fled, when the colonel came in. He looked at me with a frown and said, 'Hello, Barrie! So you're back?'

I stood up, prepared for all that was coming to me, and replied, 'Yes, sir.'

'You seem to have had a good night.'

'Yes, sir.'

Then, still frowning, but with a twinkle appearing in his eye, he said, 'Well, if you ever arrange a show like that again without letting me into your party, you and I will have a row.'

I promised faithfully to let him know next time, and that was the end of it. The dear old colonel, he was very soft hearted in spite of his bluster; and though he kept us up to the mark, I think he was really fond of us all.

Later that day he, in company with other C.O.s and formation staff, went on board H.M.S. *Queen* and made a reconnaissance of the

---

9 The 'C.O.' refers to the commanding officer of the unit — that is (in this instance), Lieutenant-Colonel Bolton.

coast of Gallipoli from Bulair to Helles, and the plan of attack was made known to them. That evening after dinner, we were issued with maps, and the C.O. gave us all the information possible. We were allotted a very definite task and were responsible for the security of the right flank of the map, and our instructions were that we had to get to it and hold it at any cost. The 25th of April was fast approaching, though we did not even then know when the great event would take place. About the 23rd we were told that the attack would be made on Sunday. Iron rations were issued, and we checked all kits to see that every man's issue was complete, including his field dressing. A company of the 7th Battalion under Captain Mason was transferred to our ship for convenience in landing.[10]

Saturday the 24th was a wet day, everything was ready, and the troops were allowed to rest. In the afternoon, sixteen of us foregathered in one cabin, of which there were only three besides those occupied by the ship's staff, and, in a spirit of fun, Lieut. Jack Paul forecasted our fate. He was a big, fine-looking chap, the son of a soldier and one of the best himself, liked by all of us. Taking each in turn, he told us what would happen to us on the morrow, and that he himself would be killed. He was killed that first day, and, strangely enough, his entire forecast almost came true.[11]

Early that evening, we left the harbour and steamed to a harbour at the north end of the island, which was our starting point for the run across to Gallipoli.

After receiving final instructions from Colonel Bolton regarding our job on the morrow, everybody turned in early to get as much sleep as possible, wondering when we would get the next.

---

10 Both the 6th and 7th Battalions were aboard the *Galeka*. To ease congestion, A Company of the 7th under Charles Mason was transferred to the *Clan Macgillivray*. Mason was a 36-year-old lawyer who had served in the South African War.
11 Jack Paul had attended Geelong College, and worked in the wool industry for Dalgetys. He had just turned 22. His body was not found and identified (from his identity disc) until two months after his death.

Chapter Six

We were roused next morning at three o'clock to find the ship under way. The weather was beautifully fine, with a clear sky and a late moon reflected in a perfectly calm sea. We dressed hurriedly and in silence, then went below where the troops were falling in, and checked the roll. Everything was done in a whisper, as we were ordered to maintain strict silence; smoking was forbidden, as noises and lights carry a long way at sea on a still night. After roll call, we dismissed for breakfast. It was a strange sight to see all those ships steaming along in the moonlight with not a light showing anywhere and in dead silence.

The 3rd Brigade was to land first, and half of the brigade had been transferred to some of the warships the evening before, two companies of each battalion to the *Queen*, *Prince of Wales*, and *London*, and the remainder distributed between seven destroyers. These warships were steaming ahead of the convoy, and would go in as close to the shore as they could with safety, and then land the troops in their boats. They were timed to reach the beach at 4.30 a.m. At about four o'clock we saw the dim outline of the hills in the moonlight, and as we slowly approached them everyone was watching and listening, and wondering what sort of reception the 3rd Brigade would get. Would they succeed in getting ashore?

It was just about 4.30 a.m., when the first streaks of dawn were appearing in the sky, that a light was seen on the cliffs (apparently a signal light) followed by a few scattered rifle shots and then a machine gun. We knew then that they had been seen, and wondered what was happening, but our own duties left us little further time for wondering. The ship had stopped, and we had to get breakfast and prepare to disembark.

I have said that the *Clan Macgillivray* was a rotten ship, but we did not realise what an extremely rotten ship she was until that morning. Several of our officers had tried some days before to purchase some whisky or brandy, thinking it would be very useful to have in the event of casualties. But the chief steward regretted that there was not a bottle on the ship, and no amount of persuasion could succeed in making him produce any. Now, at the last minute, we found he had an unlimited supply at one pound per bottle. We were so disgusted to think that a man would stoop to exploit the troops under those circumstances, many of whom we knew were looking upon their last sunrise, that everyone refused to trade with him, and he did not sell a bottle.

We were to go ashore in two parties — headquarters and three companies in two destroyers, and one to return for the remainder. My company, with that of the 7th, was to be the last to go. We waited for breakfast until the others had finished, as accommodation was limited, and when the saloon was clear we went down for ours. All the dirty dishes from the last sitting were still on the table, and there was not a steward in sight. We called, searched the galley, where we could only find dirty pots and pans, and then proceeded on a search of the ship, but failed to find anyone, nor did we ever find them, and we finally went ashore with empty stomachs. A few shells had by this time begun to fall in the vicinity of the ship, and the whole crew from the captain downwards had gone to earth in a panic.

The ship was carrying a large quantity of ammunition and military stores, and our first reinforcements, who had joined us in Mena, were left on board as a working party to unload them, with Lieut. J.E.T. Catron of my company in charge.

The two destroyers, *Chelmer* and *Ribble*, came alongside about 7.00 a.m., one on each side of the ship, and the three companies got quickly aboard and left for the beach. We cheered them off and sat down to wait our turn. Shrapnel was falling pretty thickly around the ship, and the troops were kept under cover. The forecastle deck was empty, and I walked out to the forecastle head to see what was happening. Hearing an altercation on the bridge, I was astonished to see Catron and the captain in a heated argument. The captain was rushing backwards and forwards on the bridge, literally tearing his hair and waving his clenched fists in the air, invoking divine wrath on all and sundry, and shouting, 'My ship will be sunk, my ship will be sunk.'

Catron was standing guard over the engine-room telegraph, and by physical force preventing the captain from using it. The captain then signalled the *Queen Elizabeth*, who was lying near to us, firing broadsides into the hills, 'I am under fire, am standing out to sea.'

The *Queen Elizabeth* immediately trained a gun on the ship and replied, 'If you move I will sink you.'

At this, the captain went madder than ever, and Catron finally struck him, then seized him by the shoulders and ran him off the bridge, and, to his everlasting shame, the captain stayed off. He sought sanctuary below somewhere, and remained there.

Seeing the scuffle, I proceeded at the run to Catron's assistance, but he was quite equal to the job, and had literally kicked the captain down the steps before I arrived. Catron told me that the captain had actually signalled the engine room to move the ship. I said, 'What is going to happen now, Joe? It's a pretty serious thing to kick a captain off his bridge.'

'That will be alright. I'm captain now,' he replied, 'and if there is any trouble, I have got a hundred good men behind me.'[1]

---

[1] Joe Catron, a 23-year-old lieutenant, had been appointed the ship transport officer with the specific task of ensuring that the 1,200 men (the 8th Battalion plus Mason's company of the 7th), with their accompanying equipment, were disembarked efficiently from the *Clan Macgillivray*. He felt a profound sense of responsibility about this task, which no doubt contributed to the way he dealt with the ship captain. Also instrumental was his boxing and wrestling prowess — he had been Geelong's champion in both types of combat before the war. Joe Catron's older brother, Bill, was also an 8th Battalion original. Initially a private in Joe's company, Bill was made an officer on the day after the landing, but was evacuated from Gallipoli with appendicitis. He had

The ship was in good hands, temporarily at any rate. She wouldn't desert her post under that skipper.[2]

Three weeks prior to the landing, the *Clan Macgillivray* had been warned that, in the event of heavy casualties, she would be used as a hospital ship. As we only had two hospital ships, with accommodation for 400 cases each, there seemed little doubt that she would be required, but not even a bale of straw was provided for the comfort of the patients. When, later in the day, 850 badly wounded men, of whom I had the misfortune to be one, were sent aboard her, they were simply laid out in rows in the holds and on the iron decks, with nothing under them, and no blankets to cover them. Many a poor chap died on that ship, who might have pulled through with reasonable care and a little comfort. She was a blot on the escutcheon of the British Merchant Service, one of the finest services in the world.[3]

It was not long before the *Chelmer* returned for us. We got on board quickly, and she started in at once. She had seven or eight ships' boats in tow, which were drawn alongside, and we clambered into them while she was still underway. She took us in as far as it was safe for her to go, then slowed down and cast us off. A naval pinnace then picked us up, and towed us in as close as she could, then each boat threw off its ropes and rowed the rest of the way. As we reached the beach, there was a hail of shrapnel tearing up the sand and the water's edge, but we were fortunate enough to get ashore without casualties. My platoon sergeant, Taylor, was in the

---

two operations, endured constant pain, and was sent home to Australia, but left Melbourne to return to the war in October 1916. Joe was wounded, decorated, and survived the war, but Bill was killed in France in March 1917.
2 Typically, AIF soldiers were highly complimentary of the selfless assistance they received from British Navy personnel during the landing, which makes Barrie's account of the missed final meal and the punch-up with the captain all the more arresting.
3 Barrie was understandably aggrieved about his experiences aboard the *Clan Macgillivray* on 25 April 1915, but the neglect concerned not only his troopship. The British medical arrangements for the whole operation were scandalously and culpably negligent.

bow of the boat, and I was in the stern.[4] I had instructed Taylor to get ashore first and form the platoon up under cover of the cliffs, while I saw to the disembarkation and made sure that nothing was left behind. The water was deep at the stern of the boat, and we had to disembark from the bow, which made the operation comparatively slow. It took only a few minutes, actually, but I seemed a long time standing there under fire. When the boat was at last clear, I was just preparing to jump into the water myself when Sergeant Taylor waded in and shouted, 'Hold on, sir.'

'What's the matter?' I said. 'Have you forgotten something?'

'Yes, sir,' he replied as he laid his hand on the gunwale. 'We forgot you. Get on my shoulders. There is no need for you to get wet.'

I told him to go to the devil. Everybody else was wet up to the waist, and if it was good enough for them, I was not going to shirk it. However, he looked so disappointed and hurt at my refusal after wading in for me, that I gave in and he carried me ashore with dry feet. He was one of the best, a young commissioned officer of the Citizen Forces at home, who had resigned his commission and enlisted, and was one of the first to gain his commission in the field.

My platoon had just formed up when a shell from the fort at Gaba Tepe burst right over our heads, causing several casualties amongst another boatload who were just disembarking a few yards away along the beach. I shifted my men as close in under the cliffs as we could get, and reported to Major Field, my company commander, for instructions.[5] He was with Major Blamey of Divisional Staff, who

---

4 Robert George Leslie Taylor was a 22-year-old draper from Stawell. He became a lieutenant three days later, but a significant Gallipoli wound in his left wrist, compounded by ill-health, ended his active war service.

5 John Field had become Barrie's company commander after the internal structure of AIF battalions was altered to conform to arrangements in the British Army. This switch from eight companies to four resulted in the merger of the 8th Battalion's former A and E Companies, with Field in command of the new A Company, and Captain Cowper as his deputy. Field, a 50-year-old brewery employee from Castlemaine, had been an officer in the militia since 1893. He was severely wounded at Gallipoli, but survived the war.

directed us to battalion headquarters, where we would get detailed instructions.[6]

I got my platoon under way immediately, and crossing the first low hill, where the engineers had cut a path through the scrub, we dropped down into Shrapnel Gully in single file at the double, under fairly heavy fire. We reformed under an almost perpendicular cliff at the other side of the gully, and here my first casualty occurred. Private Baensch was standing alongside me when he was wounded by a sniper from the head of the gully.[7] We moved on at once and found the battalion headquarters, where Colonel Bolton directed us to our objective and gave us very definite instructions that we were to hold it at all costs and we were not to move from it. We had to climb two or three ridges to get to it. These ridges were so steep that we had to pull ourselves up on the scrub with which they were covered. We finally reached our objective, where we found some of the battalion spread out on the top of the ridge, and, finding a gap in the line, we dropped into it. It was a steep ridge, dropping almost straight down onto the beach and looking across a fairly wide valley, afterwards known as 'Death Valley'. There was a wheat field just in front of my position, but the rest of the country was thickly covered with scrub. We were under fairly heavy shrapnel fire, and shells directed at the beach and the ships were whizzing over our heads.[8]

When we first arrived we could not see anything to fire at; moreover we knew that some of our own men were out in front, and we had to hold our fire until they returned. I heard an N.C.O. giving

---

6 Major Blamey became commander-in-chief of Australia's military forces in World War II.
7 Herbert Ernest Baensch, a 26-year-old labourer, was a prominent target for a sniper when standing in the open — he was tall and well built. It was a severe chest wound, and he did not rejoin the unit for six months. He later transferred to the 58th Battalion, and rose through the ranks to become a lieutenant in France before being killed by a shell in June 1918.
8 After reaching the shore, the 8th Battalion was engaged on the right — or southern portion — of the area the Anzacs occupied. The most prominent feature in this sector became known as Bolton's Ridge, and Bolton's unit was positioned along and near it. Barrie and his men were directed to a position in this area, and had to proceed over hills to reach it.

fire directions to his men some little distance along the line, and ran along to see what he was aiming at. Using my field glasses, I was able to distinguish his target as a party of our own troops, and was just in time to stop him. The fire on our left had by this time increased to tremendous volume, and seemed to be working closer to us. What was happening was that Kemal Pasha, with a force of 36,000 men, had arrived at the scene to oppose us, and his men were coming into action as fast as they could deploy, and soon we were busy, too.

Colonel Bolton, accompanied by the adjutant, Captain Possingham, inspected the position, and further impressed on us the necessity for holding it. As he was leaving, he said to me, 'Don't leave this place, whatever happens. Get dug in if you can.'

There was little chance of digging in under rifle fire, but many of the men had scraped out small rifle pits for themselves with their entrenching tools. As the Turks began to appear on the opposite ridge, the parties in front began to come back at the run through the scrub, and the fire began to increase. We had all been wondering how our men would shape under fire, and now the test had come — a severe one, too. We were all a bit anxious because we knew that if we could not hold what we had got, there was no retreat for us. We could never get off again. I was very proud of my platoon, and I know every officer felt the same about his own command, but there was just the feeling that we were not regulars, and this was our baptism. We need not have worried. I made my way along my line to see how my men were taking it, and to encourage them if necessary, but they were all as cool as cucumbers, doing their job with not much more concern than they displayed at a field day on the desert. They were wonderful.

A message came along the line for me to report to the major on my right in command of that sector.[9] I went and found him. He

---

9 The officer in command of the sector was Lieutenant-Colonel Robert Gartside, who was second-in-command of the 8th Battalion. Gartside, an orchardist of Harcourt, was about to turn 53; he had been severely wounded in South Africa. After Pompey Elliott was wounded at the landing, Gartside was transferred to command Elliott's 7th Battalion, and he was killed leading it into action in the charge towards Krithia on 8 May 1915. (The 8th Battalion had three lieutenant-colonels — Bolton, Field, and Gartside — which was

instructed me to go back to battalion headquarters and tell the C.O. that he was going to advance his line on to the next ridge. I looked at him with astonishment and said, 'But, sir, we can't leave here. It will throw our flank right open.'

He ordered me to leave that problem to him and do as I was told. Remembering the C.O.'s injunctions, I took the risk of reminding him of them, saying, 'I'm afraid, sir, the colonel would shoot me if I took him that message.'

He replied, 'I will if you don't, so you had better go at once.'

It left me in a nasty quandary. It was a serious job for me, a subaltern, to disobey a direct order from a senior, but I knew at the same time that by doing as he instructed, he was acting in direct contravention of the orders of his superior, and the move would leave us with an open flank. I also knew Colonel Bolton's manner towards those who blundered or disobeyed, and I did not relish my reception with the message.

I replied, 'Very good, sir,' and turned on my heel. But I never delivered the message. Fate intervened. I made my way back to my platoon sector to let my sergeant know where I was going. I threw myself down alongside him and told him, but even then I did not leave at once. I preferred the enemy's fire to the colonel's wrath, though I can't say I was enamoured with either. A few minutes later, I saw a rush of a big body of our troops coming up the slope towards us. It looked like a panic. Knowing how quickly panic can spread, and thinking they might go through our line and perhaps cause it to break, too, and go with them, I drew my revolver and ran to the point where they were coming in. As I reached one end, I saw Captain Sergeant, one of the company commanders, running towards the other. He shouted to me, 'Shoot anyone who goes past.'

I waved in acknowledgment and shouted at the men to stop. But it was no panic. As they reached the line, each man turned and dropped into it. They had been driven off the ridge in front. The Turks were coming up so thickly that they had to run for their lives to get back. It

---

unusual, so it was understandable that Barrie, writing in the 1930s, would presume that Field and Gartside had been majors in April 1915.)

was not long before we realised the presence of the Turks there, and the question of an advance was definitely settled. It would have been fatal for us had we attempted it.

After we had stopped the rush, Captain Sergeant came across to my position to find out the situation and get in touch with our end.[10]

H.M.S. *Bacchante* was steaming along, close inshore, firing into the fort at Gaba Tepe, the guns from which were enfilading the beach and causing a good deal of damage. A Turkish field battery commenced firing at the *Bacchante*, which they could just reach by skimming the hill on which we were lying. Their shells were clipping the leaves off the bushes under which Captain Sergeant and I were sitting. Captain Sergeant was discussing the situation with me, and what would be best to do in the event of the Turks attacking, when a shower of leaves fell on us, and he remarked that we were in an uncomfortable position and had better move. We both turned round to look at the *Bacchante,* and were just about to get up and move to another position when a shell burst a few feet from us, and I felt a blow like a sledge hammer on my left shoulder and another on my right leg, and I toppled over. I tried to pick myself up, but my left arm was broken and crumpled up under me, and I flopped again. I managed to sit up, and found Captain Sergeant sitting up also. I asked him if he were hit. He smiled and said, 'Yes, but it's nothing,' and fell back dead.

The nose cap had hit him in the back. I got three pellets that came past him. Poor old Sergeant, I shall never forget him. He and I had been friends all through. He was one of the finest of our officers, a quiet, courteous gentleman, who had also served in South Africa, and one who would probably have achieved high rank and distinction, had he lived. He died smiling, so typical of all those fellows. Of all the wounded, both officers and men, whom I met later, and several of whom died, I never heard one breathe a word of complaint, no matter what his sufferings were.

---

10 Major John Sergeant was a 45-year-old grazier and vigneron from East Goorambat. Married with children, he had extensive experience in the militia, and had served in the South African War.

One of my N.C.O.s ran to my assistance and carried me down the hill, out of fire, and bound up my wounds. He got me down to the beach a little later. The beach was literally covered with wounded men from the cliff to the water's edge. It was still being shelled, though not so severely as earlier in the morning, and the wounded were being wounded again, and some killed, as they lay there. I was laid out amongst them. I was in terrific pain by this time, as although I did not know it then, the bullet which broke my arm had gone through my chest, fractured one of the vertebrae of my spine, and lodged in my liver.[11] I could not breathe except in gasps. After a time, an A.M.C. sergeant came and had a look at me. Looking very hard at me, he said, 'Is your name Barrie?'

I replied that it was. He was a lad whom I had known as a baby but had not seen for about fifteen years, when he was a kid in knickerbockers. It was an act of providence that sent him to me. He procured a rough splint and bound up my arm, gave me a draught of something to drink, then got a stretcher for me to lie on, and told me he would get me off to a ship as soon as he could. I had been wounded about half past three in the afternoon. He got me onto a boat about six o'clock, and I was rowed back to the old *Clan Macgillivray*.[12] As the boat drew alongside the companionway, the naval petty officer in charge said, 'All those who can walk, go up the companionway. The remainder will be taken over the side in slings.'

As the last of the walking cases stepped from the boat, I said to the petty officer, 'I think I can walk up.'

He looked at me doubtfully and said, 'Do you think you can manage it, sir?'

'I will have a shot anyway, if you will help me out,' I replied.

He assisted me out of the boat, and waited a minute or two to see how I got on. My right arm and left leg were still good, but my

---

11 He had a compound fracture of the humerus bone connecting his left shoulder to his elbow.
12 Barrie was relatively fortunate, in that the appalling medical arrangements resulted in many wounded Australians remaining on the beach for much longer.

right leg was bent at the knee as a result of injury, and I could not straighten it. However, I was able to reach each step with my toes, and hop onto it with my left foot, gripping the rail with my right hand, and so I got right to the top unassisted. At the top was a short flight of steps dropping onto the well deck, but I could not go down unassisted. However, Catron had seen me coming up, and came to my aid. He helped me up to the bridge deck, where I was instructed to go, unrolled my valise for me, and helped me into it. From that moment, for a period of six weeks, I was unable to raise my head from my pillow, and for most of the time could not even turn right or left. I have often wondered since how I managed that climb up the companionway, from the water's edge to the deck, but men did things that day which in no other circumstances would have been remotely possible.

Two medical officers, Captain Benjafield and Captain Campbell, with two A.M.C. orderlies, had been sent aboard the ship, and a naval surgeon had been lent by one of the warships to assist. As I have previously stated, there were 850 cases sent on board, and the ship provided nothing in the way of comfort and had no medical stores. The M.O.s had a very limited supply of bandages, and could not even attempt a change of dressings on very bad cases. They reserved them for those they thought they could save, and even then they had to wash the old bandages and use them again. We were five days on the ship, and during that time, in company with many others, my bandages were never removed. It was not the fault of the doctors, God knows they worked, but they had no material to work with.

The naval surgeon came and had a look at me, and gave me an injection of morphine. Some time later, he came again and gave me an opium draught. The pain was so great that the morphine had not taken any effect, and between then and midnight he gave me another dose of morphine and another of opium. None of them had the slightest effect on my pain.

About midnight, a destroyer came alongside and hailed us. I heard her skipper give instructions to send every available boat to the beach to bring the troops off. It had been decided to evacuate.

Imagine our feelings when we heard that, knowing of the thousands that had been killed and wounded, and all for nothing, and knowing also what was in store for those who were left if they attempted to get off. However, that order was countermanded later, when the troops themselves declined to leave. They had dug trenches under cover of darkness, and declared that they could hold on; so, instead of bringing them off, the balance of the force was disembarked.[13]

In the morning, Captain Benjafield visited me again, and when in reply to his query I replied that I was feeling splendid, he grinned and said, 'Well, I'll see if I can fit you up a bit better.'[14]

I think he was surprised to see me alive. He got me into one of the few available bunks, which had been occupied by a man with only a broken arm, and made me as comfortable as possible. I heard some time later that he told that man he could probably have his bunk back again in the morning, as he did not think I would live through the night.

The ship did not move from her position until Tuesday night,[15] and during the whole of that time we could hear the incessant roar of rifle fire, which did not cease even for the space of a minute. It died down at about six o'clock on Tuesday night, and, except for occasional outbursts, ceased about dark. We had won, up to the point that the Turks had failed to drive us off. Our position was established, and even the wounded on the ships felt a glow of pride in the victory. But at what a cost! Our total casualties up to that time were 10,000, of

---

13 Re-embarkation was indeed under consideration. Birdwood, the most senior shore-based commander, referred this momentous decision to the commander-in-chief, Hamilton, who was aboard the *Queen Elizabeth*. Meanwhile, a provisional order was sent to every ship to lower all their boats and be ready to send them to the beach. This was no doubt what Barrie heard from the *Clan Macgillivray*, but it was contingent upon a decision being made to re-embark. Hamilton, having been advised that there was insufficient darkness left for re-embarkation to be feasible, accepted this advice and sent a message urging that the only possible approach was to 'dig yourselves right in and stick it out'.

14 Vivian Benjafield was a 35-year-old surgeon who had graduated from the University of Sydney.

15 That is, 27 April. The landing had started before dawn on Sunday 25 April.

which 6,000 occurred the first day, when we had had to fight without cover. About 50 per cent were killed and wounded. I think, according to all recognised standards of military ethics, we were licked, but, unfortunately for the Turks, we did not know about it. There was no-one there to tell us so, and I verily believe the spirit of the troops was such that if the other 50 per cent had become casualties also, they would still not have acknowledged defeat, and the last man would have died fighting.[16]

I cannot refrain at this juncture from paying a tribute to the gallantry of the 29th (British) Division, which carried out the landing at Cape Helles. I think our people in Australia were so engrossed with the doings of their own men that they were perhaps inclined to overlook the fact that there were other people engaged as well as us. This is of course natural, but I think the 29th Division had even a worse time than we had. They encountered barbed-wire entanglements in the water, and a long open beach with very little cover. They were shot down as they floundered in the wire, and scores of them were drowned by the weight of their equipment. The landing from the *River Clyde* was so costly it had to be stopped until dark, and the few who succeeded in getting ashore hung on by the skin of their teeth, taking cover under a blade of grass, and remained there all day, fighting desperately, waiting for the help which could not come to them until darkness fell. One of their brigades had four brigadiers in two hours. No-one on earth but the British soldier could have done what those fellows did that day, and the men of the 1st Australian Division looked on them with admiration and affection which lasted throughout the war, and still holds good amongst the individuals of that division who are still alive.

---

16 According to Charles Bean's *Official History*, the Australian and New Zealand casualties from 25 April to 3 May amounted to about 8,100.

Chapter Seven

On Tuesday evening, the ship weighed anchor and proceeded on her way to Alexandria. The weather was still fine, and we had a smooth passage all the way. On Wednesday morning, Captain Benjafield visited me again. I was suffering severe pain as he came into the cabin and asked me how I was. I told him to go to the devil, and that he did not appear to be worried how I was. I had not had even a wash, let alone a change of dressings, and I thought he had only come to see if I was ready to be put over the side so he could have my bunk for someone else. I refused to die, despite him.

Dear old Benjafield. I did not realise the extreme difficulties under which he was working. I apologised for my outburst when I met him again some months later, and we laughed about it, though he told me then that my determination not to die was probably the only thing that saved me, as I was beyond all medical aid.

However, a medical orderly came soon after and washed me, for which I was duly grateful. In addition to my other wounds, I had a slight wound on my head. It had bled a good deal, and my face was covered in blood.

We reached Alexandria early on Friday evening. I was carried ashore immediately after the ship tied up, and was placed in an ambulance in company with Captain Mason of the 7th Battalion, who was also aboard *Clan Macgillivray*, suffering from a severe stomach wound.[1] We were taken at once to the Deaconess's Hospital, a beautifully equipped hospital run by the German community of Alexandria, and staffed entirely by German nurses, with an Austrian doctor in charge. It had been taken over by the government, and an English R.A.M.C. colonel appointed to command with a staff of British medical officers, but the services of the Austrian doctor and the German nurses were retained. The nurses were members of a religious order, and unconcerned with worldly affairs. They were very good to us, and we liked them. One of them told me that her brother was serving with the German Army, but she was only concerned with the good of humanity, and had no concern for the rights and wrongs of the war.

We drove through a huge crowd of natives all the way to the hospital, and the city was seething with excitement. A rumour had been circulated that we had failed at Gallipoli, and the enormous crowd of casualties arriving, British as well as our own, gave credence to the rumour. The authorities were very worried for some time, for fear of a native revolt. Although the Turks were not popular in Egypt, there was a good deal of sympathy for them amongst the natives, on religious grounds. We got through without incident, but some of the ambulances were stoned, and the situation, for a time, was very nasty. We arrived at the hospital about 8.00 p.m. I was taken straight to the operating theatre, and there my field dressings were removed, and my wounds dressed and bandaged. This was the first time they had been touched since they were adjusted in the field the previous Sunday, five days before.

It was a wonderful relief to get my clothes off, for I was still dressed as I had landed on the beach, even to my boots. Except that I had lost my tunic, which had been cut off me on the field, none of my clothes had been removed. I was washed, dressed in clean pyjamas, and put into a comfortable bed. I think I slept that night for the first time without an opiate.

---

1 Mason was classified as permanently unfit and sent home to Australia, but he ended up commanding a battalion in Pompey Elliott's brigade at the Western Front. He was awarded the DSO for his fine leadership at Polygon Wood.

We were lucky to get into such a good hospital, as there was not sufficient hospital accommodation in Alexandria to accommodate everybody, and thousands of cases were dumped into buildings such as schools, which had been hastily taken over with no preparation for their reception. Carpenters and workmen were called in to make the necessary alterations suitable to a hospital, and the noise of sawing and hammering went on all day, to the intense discomfort of the patients.

On the Saturday morning, the colonel and his staff made a tour of the hospital and inspected each patient. He spent some time with me, and ordered an X-ray of my chest and leg, where a nasty lump had formed below the knee. The Austrian doctor was in charge of the X-ray, and he was instructed to produce the plates next morning. Though the German nurses were good, the Austrian doctor was not so good. He overlooked me. Next morning the colonel asked for the plates, and was very annoyed when he found I had not been done. He gave instructions that I was to be done that day without fail. Again I was overlooked. Next morning he was furious, and threatened to have the doctor interned if the plates were not ready on the morrow. That day, I was taken to the X-ray room. My leg was photographed first, then my shoulder, and I was lifted back onto my perambulator. I asked him if he was not going to do my chest. He replied, 'There is nothing in your chest. The bullet has broken your arm, and then it bounced out.'

I would have laughed if I could, but I could not with a hole in my chest, so I said nothing. I had known my arm was broken a week before; it did not need an X-ray to disclose that.

Several English ladies living in Alexandria volunteered their services, and used to attend the hospital daily. They were very good to us. One, especially, I remember, who looked after me and did everything she could for me. I was pretty helpless and had to be fed on broth through a spout out of a receptacle like a teapot. I was very grateful when she refused to allow the orderlies, who were mostly Greeks or Arabs, to attend to me. She also wrote letters for me, and sent a cable to my mother.

There were two other patients in the room with me. An electric bell push was fitted in the wall at the foot of one of the beds, which the occupant could just reach with his toe. None of us could get up, and he was appointed official bell-pusher for the ward. He became quite adept at pushing bells with his big toe, and got plenty of practice, but never succeeded in waking an orderly. One of the nurses would come eventually, and I do not think even they discovered the orderlies' hiding place. The situation had its humorous side, and one day it got the better of me and I had to join in the general laugh. I will never forget it. My breathing was still painful and I could not take a full breath, so that when I laughed it distended the wound in my chest, and the agony was almost unendurable. The laughter ended in weeping, and that joke nearly cost me my life. My pals were very upset, and I am afraid I cramped their style a bit after that, but they were very considerate in their efforts not to make me laugh again.

On Sunday morning, a barber visited the hospital. He was a Greek, too. I had not had a shave for a week, and asked that my name be put on the list of those desiring his services. I looked forward with pleasure to the prospect of being clean again, and submitted gladly to his ministrations, not even complaining when I got some of his lather in my eye — partly because I was glad to get shaved, and partly because I was afraid to open my mouth in case his brush slipped in. Shaving soap is cheap in Egypt. He lathered all over my mouth, and both my ears were full of it. Then he produced his razor and commenced to shave.

It went along very smoothly at first. I did not feel it at all, and was prepared to forgive him the lather. I did not realise however, that his razor was of the stump-jump variety, and had not touched my beard. He lathered again and applied more force, with a little more success to him, and a deal more pain to me. He removed a portion of the beard that time — by the roots! Again he lathered and repeated the process, while I repeated my complaints. After about ten minutes of this, I could endure no more, and ordered him to desist. He handed me a mirror, and I was shocked at the result. My face had almost completely disappeared, but the whiskers still remained. His razor must have been made of hoop-iron. He offered to come each day and shave me for a shilling. He appeared quite hurt when I offered to pay him two shillings each day to stay away.

It soon became apparent that the casualties from Gallipoli could not be accommodated in Egypt, and instructions were issued that all cases who were likely to be any length of time in hospital were to be sent to England to relieve the strain. I was too ill to be moved with the first shipload, but left on the second ship on the 8th of May. The doctor wanted to operate on my leg where the lump was growing daily, but thought I was too ill to stand it, and told me he thought I would be alright until I reached England. He sent a special report to the hospital ship, requesting that my leg be watched on the voyage, and I went on board the *Letitia*, a very comfortable ship of the Indian Medical Service. There was an English colonel in charge, and English nurses, the other doctors being Indians. One of the Indian doctors did most of the dressings in our ward, where there were twelve officers, but the colonel himself attended to me and one or two other bad cases. He was very good to us, and went out of his way to do everything possible for our comfort. The Indian doctors were also very fine men, and we liked them immensely.

After we had been at sea two or three days, the colonel told me he was a bit worried about my leg, as the abscess was still increasing in size, and he thought he would have to operate; but he did not want to do it if it could be avoided, as his theatre was below decks, and he had some nasty septic cases and was afraid of infection. He looked at it again next day and said that he thought it had better be done. He decided to arrange it for the next morning. Early next morning he came and told me he would operate about eleven o'clock, and I was not to have breakfast. I liked him very much, but I did not realise how good and thoughtful he really was. He had decided it was too risky to take me downstairs, so he cleared out a small ward next to ours which had contained three warrant officers, fumigated it, and brought all his theatre equipment up there, especially for my operation. I was taken in about eleven o'clock and duly done. When I woke up he presented me with a brass detonator cap of a Turkish shell, which he had removed from my leg and which I still retain as a souvenir. The cause of the abscess was easily explained with that inside me.

At eight o'clock each evening, an orderly came on duty, and remained in the ward all night to attend to patients. He was not a bad lad up until 10.00 p.m. Then the lights went out, and he retired to a corner of the ward where he kept his own light burning, pulled a curtain across, from below which we could see his white shoes peeping, and was ostensibly at the service of patients. He was often wanted during the night, but no-one ever succeeded in waking him. He was one of the best sleepers I have ever met. Patients made a practice of collecting missiles to throw at him, but all to no effect. It took a shipwreck to wake him.

Two nights after my operation, we ran into a very thick fog when approaching Gibraltar. The ship slowed down to a crawl, and every few minutes sounded ear-splitting blasts from her siren. We heard another ship reply in the distance, very faintly at first, but gradually getting louder as the ships approached each other, until finally she appeared to be right alongside us, and both sirens were going at intervals of about a minute. I do not know what time it was then, but it was after 'lights out', and the orderly pitched forward on his face, with a table full of bottles on top of him. The poor chap got an awful fright, and I think at first he thought some of the patients were wreaking vengeance on him. Then he picked himself up, and the last we saw of him was his white shoes going up the staircase, three steps at a time.

Those patients who could, sat up in bed and said, 'What the devil's up?'

Those who could not, said the same thing.

Then one of the wags said, 'Well, I don't know what it is, but it seems to have awakened the orderly, so it must be damned serious. I'm going up to see.'

That broke the tension, and everybody laughed; then all who were able to, got out of bed and trooped up on the deck, leaving three of us who could not move — Lieut. Tarrant, 2nd Battalion A.I.F., Lieut.

Mostyn, Worcester Regiment, and myself. Someone came down and told us there had been a collision, and disappeared again. Tarrant, who was always a cheery cuss, asked me if I could swim and if I had any idea of the distance to Gibraltar. Mostyn piped up at this and declared that we would not get a chance to swim; we would be drowned where we were, in our beds. I offered to bet him ten shillings the ship would not sink. He took me up. It was one of the best bets I ever made, and I wished it was bigger. The ship did not sink, and I got my money. If it had sunk we probably would have drowned, and I would not have had to pay.

We learned afterwards that there had been a collision alright. The other ship, an Italian cargo vessel, though passing very close to us, would probably have cleared us if she had stuck to her course but, unfortunately, through the fog she saw the glare of the red cross on the side of our ship, and, mistaking it for the ship's navigating light, she swung around and came right across our bows, so that we struck her amidships. She sank in a few minutes, with the loss of several lives. The *Letitia*'s bows were split open from the deck to below the water line, but fortunately the bulkheads were closed and held, and we remained afloat. We hove to until daylight, then proceeded slowly to Gibraltar. We stayed there two days, and they filled the forward compartment with cement. Then we continued the journey to England. There were five shipwrecks in the vicinity of Gibraltar that night. Three other ships went ashore on the coast of Spain, and one on the Moroccan coast. We reached Southampton on the 22nd of May, without further incident.

A hospital train was waiting at the quayside at Southampton, and we disembarked at once. The colonel was waiting at the gangway to say goodbye to each of us as we went ashore. He had been awfully kind to me, dressing my wounds himself throughout the voyage, and had gone out of his way to do everything possible to relieve my pain and make me comfortable. I thanked him as well as I could for all that he had done, but he did not appear to think any thanks were due to him. It was his job. Perhaps it was, but there are different methods of doing a job, and he certainly did his in the nicest possible way. He was one of those gentlemen whom one feels better for having met.

As soon as the train was loaded, we started off, travelling via Reading and Oxford to Manchester, arriving there at about 5.00 p.m. I was in a lower bunk, and enjoyed seeing the country all the way up. I think England is the most beautiful country in the world, and coming straight from Egypt, where for months we had seen nothing but sand, it looked wonderful. There was a big crowd of people at the station at Manchester, and they all seemed to have their pockets full of cigarettes. We were soon unloaded and driven to the 3rd Western General Hospital, quite close to the London Road Station. It had been a technical school, now transformed into a hospital, and here we met our friends who had preceded us in the first shipload.[2] Everybody was very good to us, and I made a lot of friends during the weeks that I was there. Many of the businessmen of Manchester had formed themselves into an association, and gave one afternoon a week each, with their cars, and took the patients out for a drive every afternoon. It was a good while before I was fit enough to go, but in the meantime several of them spared a little time now and then to come and see me, and sent their friends, so I got to know quite a lot of very fine people.

I was in bed there for several weeks. My chest healed up, so I was able to breathe again, and I was finally out of danger. It had been a very close call. I was X-rayed again several times, and the bullet finally located in my liver. I was rather thankful when the doctors decided to leave it there. They said that as it had been there so long without raising complications, it would probably not cause further trouble, and as it would be a very dangerous operation, I would be well advised to leave it alone. I very gladly took their advice, and it is still there. My leg was straightened out under massage, and I began to take an interest in life again. Then, one day, the doctor told me I could go for a drive in the afternoon.

---

2 According to military records, Barrie was admitted to the 2nd Western General Hospital at Manchester on 12 May 1915. Private Baensch, who had been the first casualty in Barrie's company, was also conveyed to England on the *Letitia*, and admitted to the same hospital in Manchester.

CHAPTER SEVEN

Mr H.M. Gibson, secretary of the Manchester Ship Canal Company, who was the first man I met in Manchester, and who drove me to the hospital, came for me. My arm was still in a sling, and I could not use my right leg, but they carried me into the car and he drove me across to Warrington near Liverpool, where he had to attend to some business, then he took me to his home for dinner. It was a wonderful day to get out into the world again. After that I went nearly every afternoon, always with Mr Gibson if he was free, and, if not, with some of his friends whom I had met. There was generally a telephone message in the morning to say that someone would call for me, and asking me to wait for him, so that I had the added pleasure of driving with someone I knew. We went to a different place each day — sometimes to someone's home for tea, and sometimes to some place of historic interest.

One of the first places I went to was the home of the Earl of Sheffield at Alderley Edge. The earl's son Sir Arthur (now Lord) Stanley was then governor of Victoria. We had tea, and spent a very pleasant afternoon. On one of my early trips, our host had been delayed on business and was a little late arriving, and apologised for the necessity of stopping at a garage to get petrol. We did not mind. Lieut. Mackenzie of the Black Watch was with me. There were no bowsers in those days, and our host drove into the garage. It was a very big building with a very large parking space inside. We stopped alongside another car in which three ladies were sitting, also waiting for petrol. Mackenzie and I were sitting in the back seat talking, when suddenly at the other end of the garage someone started up a motor bike, and we both dived on the floor. It sounded exactly like a machine gun, and scared the wits out of us. Then we sat up and laughed at each other. The ladies were at first inclined to be sympathetic, then they saw the funny side of it and joined in the laugh.

We went to Chester that afternoon, a beautiful place and one of the oldest and most historic places in England. It was the scene of many a battle in early English history, and the walls are still intact. It has, of course, far outgrown its original size, but the old gates are still there as you enter the old town. One of its peculiar features is a double tier of shops. Flights of steps run up from the footpath above with rows of shops, the same as those below.

One of the most interesting trips that I did was to Haddon Hall in Derbyshire, the scene of the romance of Dorothy Vernon.[3] It is a beautiful place, built on rising ground, with a stream running at the foot of it and an oak wood behind, not far from the village of Bakewell. A great gateway in the wall opens into a cobbled courtyard, at one end of which is the family chapel, which is quite as big as many little country churches, and where the family retainers attend divine service. At the other end of the courtyard, a door opens into the banqueting hall. The hall is panelled in oak, and contains a solid oak table reputed to be 600 years old. There is a musicians' gallery at one end, and iron rings attached to the wall, into which the wrists of refractory guests were clamped and their drinks poured down their sleeves until they were prepared to return to the table and take their drink with company. Leaving the banquet chamber, a winding staircase ascends to the ballroom. The staircase consists of solid blocks of oak cut from a tree in the wood, and shows hardly any signs of wear.

When, eventually, my arm healed and I was able to dispense with a sling, I was presented with a crutch, and was able to get about myself. Even that was a wonderful change to being lifted into a wheeled chair and pushed about by an orderly. Soon after this, Lieut. Evans of the 11th Battalion[4] and I were invited to lunch at the Union Club by Mr Midwood, one of the gentlemen we had met, and who

---

3 *Dorothy Vernon of Haddon Hall*, a popular historical novel by Charles Major, was published in 1902.

4 Military records do not appear to confirm that a Lieutenant Evans was among the 11th Battalion's officers at the landing. There was, however, a Lieutenant J.A. Evans of the 12th Battalion, who was wounded in the early fighting at Gallipoli and conveyed to England to recuperate. He was a 34-year-old Western Australian, who was married and had been employed at the Royal Mint in Perth. It is conceivable that Barrie, compiling these recollections later and remembering Evans as a Western Australian, may have presumed that he was in the 11th, which was the initial battalion from Western Australia.

had been very kind to us. Mr Midwood had invited us both to spend our convalescence at his home in Cheshire as soon as we were able to leave hospital, and now he arranged this lunch to celebrate our recovery so far. Evans had a rifle bullet in his spine, and though he could not straighten his back, he could get around with the aid of a stick.

It was a wonderful lunch. There were about a dozen of the leading businessmen of Manchester present, and we met many more in the club. It seemed they could not do enough for us. The lunch did not finish until about three o'clock. Our health was toasted, and they appeared to think it wonderful that we Australians had come so far to fight for England. We tried to point out to them the intense pride we felt in belonging to the British Empire, and how in fighting for it, we were fighting for ourselves. I have often thought since that the war did a great deal of good in that way, that it brought the people of Great Britain and the dominions into closer touch, and led to a better understanding between them.

After lunch, Mr Midwood took Evans and me to his works, and showed us the process of manufacture of cotton goods from the raw material to the finished article. It was a very interesting and instructive afternoon. We returned to the hospital feeling we had had a most enjoyable day.

Chapter Eight

About the end of July, Mr Midwood interviewed the C.O. of the hospital and offered to take Evans and me to his home for our convalescence, if we were fit to leave hospital. There was some hesitation about letting us go at first, as we were still under treatment, but to overcome that he offered to provide whatever medical treatment was necessary, and even to arrange for a masseur to visit me daily, pointing out that the hospital would then have two more beds available.

The C.O. eventually agreed to let us go, and Mr Midwood took us out to his home next day. He lived in Cheshire, about twenty miles from Manchester, in a beautiful old home, and we spent several happy weeks there. I protested against the expense of a masseur, as my leg was getting quite strong again, and it was only a matter of use and exercise now to make it right once more. I considered it was good enough of him to take us into his home, without going to all that extra expense on our behalf. He argued that it was little enough for him to do; it was his way of helping in the war, as his son was too young to go. However, he gave way 'for the present,' he said, when I threatened to return to hospital. He did not tell us then, though he did later, that they had lost their eldest son and only daughter, aged nineteen and seventeen respectively, in an epidemic a couple of years before. It was a tremendous grief to him and his wife. His younger and only remaining son was at school at Harrow and would ordinarily have stayed there another year; but, having reached his eighteenth birthday while we were there, he left at the end of that term and joined the army. Who could have blamed them if they had kept him at home? But the thought did not seem to strike them. Their only thought was that England needed him, and he went. He served in Mesopotamia, and I am glad to say he returned safely home at the end of the war.

I think they were the most wonderful people I have ever met, and our own fathers and mothers could not have done more for us than Mr and Mrs Midwood. Mr Midwood gave instructions that the car was at our disposal every afternoon, and told us to tell the chauffeur when we wanted it, and where to go. When they noticed that we felt a bit diffident about giving instructions to the chauffeur, they arranged things for us, and Mr Midwood often came with us.

One of the days that I enjoyed immensely was the meeting of a quoiting club at the little village of Mobberley. All the members of this club were members of the Union Club of Manchester, and it was their practice to meet once a month, though they had not met since the outbreak of the war until this day. We went by car, meeting Mr Midwood there, and he drove home with us afterwards. The meeting was held at the village inn, but they brought their lunch in hampers from the club, under the care of two club stewards, and it was laid in a large room upstairs. This club was over 100 years old, and the minutes of every meeting since its foundation were preserved. They not only recorded the names of the members and visitors present and the business of the meeting, but were a full record of all the happenings of the day, written in a very witty style, and were well worth perusing. After an excellent and lengthy luncheon, at which our health was again toasted, and we were called upon to speak, the party adjourned to the quoiting green and proceeded to play.

The game is played on a green, at one end of which is a small circular heap of sand with a feather stuck in the top of it. The quoits are flat iron rings with a sharp edge. They are thrown overarm with the sand as the target and the feather as the bullseye.

As I could not play, during the afternoon I wandered across to the village church opposite, and was interested to read the inscriptions on the gravestones, some of which date back hundreds of years. It was a beautiful old church with an ivy-covered porch, and inside on the wall was a tablet containing the names of the vicars of the parish for seven or eight hundred years back, and the dates of their ministry. I was interested to note the same name appearing amongst them time after time, and on one or two occasions with the title of baronet. I was so interested there that I forgot the passage of time, and it was growing late when the chauffeur came looking for me. Nobody knew where I had gone, and my disappearance had created a small stir.

We went upstairs again, where another meal was laid out. It was taken standing this time, and after a half hour's enjoyment of good company, the party dispersed for home. It was a very enjoyable day. Every member present was over military age, and their sons and relatives were serving, and in some cases had already been killed, but they decided it was no use being downhearted. They were doing all they could to help in the prosecution of the war, and they resolved to continue their meetings. They were wonderful men, full of that spirit which has been the foundation of Britain's success throughout the ages. It was the spirit that won the war, that never knew the meaning of the word 'defeat'. We attended their next meeting a month later, and when the minutes of the last meeting were read, I was tickled to death at hearing a vivid and witty description of my experiences amongst the tombstones.

I attended an auction sale one day of gifts to the Red Cross Society, of which Lady Sheffield was president of the local branch. Mr Midwood was the auctioneer, and I do not think I have ever heard a better one. I never knew a man more universally liked and respected. He had a wonderful sense of humour, and when he mounted the rostrum, his first thought, as he put it, was to put the crowd in a buying mood. He made a very sound speech in a very witty manner, and soon had them laughing. The way he sold his articles was marvellous. About halfway through, a man standing next to me turned to go when a friend addressed him, saying, 'Are you going, George?'

'Ay,' said George, still smiling. 'There baint nothing left in my pockets but the linings, and th' old man'll have *them* next.'

The Red Cross certainly showed discretion in the choice of an auctioneer, and though a very busy man, Mr Midwood was always ready to lend his services in a good cause.

One day, Evans was ordered to present himself before a medical board at Shrewsbury. I do not know why, as it was a very long way to go, and we were still on the books of the hospital in Manchester. Mr Midwood insisted on him going by car, and I went with him. Shrewsbury is a garrison town and a very old place. One of the main items of interest is the famous Round Church, which I went to see. It is quite a big church, and round in shape. Inside, the walls and rafters were hung with regimental colours of many famous British regiments, some of them very old and tattered from hard wear in the days when the colours used to be carried in battle. Nowadays, of course, the colours are not carried on service, though they are still regarded as a sacred emblem and are only unfurled on ceremonial occasions under an armed escort, and are generally deposited in the church for safekeeping until the regiment returns.

Shortly after this, I was boarded again in Manchester, declared 'permanently unfit', and given fourteen days' leave, at the termination of which I was to report to the Australian Depot in Weymouth. My departure from 'The Grange' was like leaving home, and the Midwoods made me promise to come back for a weekend before my leave was up. I promised willingly and kept it. I went to London and spent a week there, staying at a quiet hotel in Bloomsbury. I had discarded my crutch by this time, but was still very lame and had to use a stick. It was on my first night there at dinner that I saw Captain Benjafield again. He was dining with friends, and I waited for him in the lounge afterwards. I caught his eye and smiled, but he did not know me. After his friends left, he came across and spoke to me. When I told him who I was, he said, 'Oh no, you are not Barrie. I know he died.'

He was very astonished when I finally convinced him that I was still alive.

That night, I went to see 'Potash and Perlmutter' at the Globe Theatre with Colonel Craig A.A.M.C. of Sydney, who was also staying at the hotel.

As we emerged from the doorway at the end of the show, a gun went off close by, followed by another and another, until in a minute or so there was a regular barrage. We got out on to the roadway. Scores of searchlight beams pierced the darkness from every direction, all focussed on one point, and there, thousands of feet up in the sky, were two zeppelins, looking like two little yellow cigars, with shells bursting all around them. It was a very pretty sight, but not altogether a popular one. All traffic was stopped, and as we were standing in the middle of the road gazing skyward, a sweet young thing came running towards me, and taking a flying leap at me, threw her arms around my neck and cried, 'Save me! Save me!'

Disentangling myself with great difficulty, I endeavoured to reassure her, but all to no purpose. She insisted on being saved. I waved my strong right arm and said 'shoo' to the zeppelins, but they did not take the slightest notice, and the lady retained a firm grip of my left arm. After twenty minutes or so, the zeppelins got away out of range of the searchlights, and the guns ceased fire, but the lady still retained her hold of my arm, and refused to be comforted. I finally lured her on to a bus, which was just starting again, gave the conductor a fare, and transferred her into his care, and as the bus started to move I stepped off and bolted while my luck was in. I hope it was the right bus. I found Colonel Craig again, who was enjoying the joke at my expense, and we started home.

On the way, we noticed an ominous red glare in the direction of the city. A policeman told us that the zeppelins had been dropping incendiary bombs and had caused a fire in the city, so we made our way there to see what was happening. There was a strong cordon of police guarding all the entrances to the affected area, but being in uniform they allowed us through. Practically the whole of the warehouse quarter of the city was blazing, particularly Silver Street and Wood Street. It was the biggest fire I had ever seen. The zeppelins certainly did some damage that night. They had splattered the whole area with incendiary bombs, one of which dropped within 200 yards of the Bank of England, and the fire burnt to within a couple of hundred yards of the G.P.O. It was pretty good shooting on the

Germans' part, for the city was practically in darkness, all electric arc lights having been painted black except for a small circle at the bottom, which threw a circle of light straight down on the ground. We were rather amused at seeing two girls, members of some women's organisation, wearing a neat blue uniform and carrying a stretcher big and strong enough to accommodate a large-sized doll, come down the street looking for casualties. One of them tripped over a fire hose and sat down, plop, into a pool of water. This rather damped their ardour. In fact, I think it wet it through completely, for they turned back and went home. As there was nothing we could do to help, we also went home at about 3.00 a.m.

The next morning, I searched the papers for an account of the fire and the damage, but there was not one word in any paper concerning it, and no-one in England except the eye witnesses knew of the damage done. I went that day to see the damage in daylight, and though the fire brigade had done wonderful work in confining the fire within certain limits, the damage was enormous. One bomb had dropped very close to St Bartholomew's Hospital, and every window on one side of the building was broken.

As I only intended staying a week in London, I determined to see as many places of interest as possible. I went to the Empire Theatre, and saw Tom Walls and George Grossmith. I had seen Tom Walls in Australia in his famous part of the Simplicitus in *The Arcadians* some years before. I saw Sir Henry Irving at the Savoy, Miss Vanbrugh at the Gaiety, and George Robey at the Coliseum. In the daytime, I got off the beaten track and sought places of historic interest. Walking down Fleet Street, I met Captain Jackson R.M.O. of the 8th Battalion, who had been invalided,[1] and we went to lunch at The Old Cheshire Cheese, an inn built in 1667 after the Great Fire, on the site of a Benedictine monastery. The entrance is on a narrow lane between two buildings facing Fleet Street. There is a small bar, and the dining

---

1   Harold Jackson, a 41-year-old Bendigo surgeon, was lofty and beefy. He had been the 8th Battalion's doctor from the start of the war until October 1915, when he was evacuated from Gallipoli with sore knees due to rheumatoid arthritis.

room opens off it. Nothing has been changed since the inn was built. In the dining room, there are wooden benches at the tables with oak partitions between, sawdust on the floor, and the waiters are William and Charles, irrespective of their own Christian names. If 'William' dies or leaves, 'Charles' becomes promoted to 'William'. This was a favourite haunt of Dr Johnson, and a brass plate is inserted in the wall at the place where he used to sit, and his chair is carefully preserved on a cupboard in the room. It is a celebrated place for lunch and dinner, and it is astonishing to see the names of visitors from all over the world in the visitors' book, which all visitors are asked to sign. They make a specialty of lark pie at a certain time of year when the birds are available, and this is put on three days a week. The pie season is opened with a 'dinner and smoke night' each year, to which all regular clients are invited and requested to wear the costume of the 17th Century. The host and the waiters wear these old world costumes, and the pie is borne in and opened with great ceremony. After dinner, each guest is provided with a church-warden's pipe, and the whole entertainment is carried out as nearly as possible in the atmosphere which prevailed at the date of the foundation of the building.

After lunch, we went down to the cellars (a special privilege) and had a glass of good port with the cellarman. The cellars are composed of part of the cloisters of the old monastery, and the cellarman turned off his lights now and then for us to get a sense of the proper atmosphere. He told us some of the history of the place, until we almost expected to see an old monk step around the corner.

The next day, I visited Madame Tussaud's, where, in accordance with custom, I said 'Good afternoon' to the policeman at the door. He was certainly lifelike.

I had often heard of the efficiency and courtesy of the London policemen, and their reputation is well deserved. They seem to know everything, and if they cannot answer a question, they can tell you where to find the answer. Coming out of a theatre one night, I found a real London fog had descended on the city. One who has not experienced a fog in London can have no conception of its density.

I made for the nearest island where I knew there was a policeman stationed, explained that I was a stranger in London, and asked him for directions to my hotel. He said, 'Well, it is no use directing you in this fog, sir. You'd soon be lost again.'

However, he told me where to find the next constable, and to tell him that he had sent me to him, and to send me on to the next. And so they did. I went from policeman to policeman, each one giving me proper directions to find the next one, until I found a landmark that I knew was quite close to the hotel. Here I bumped into a man in the fog. We both apologised, and he asked me where I was going. I told him, and he insisted that I was going in the wrong direction. He said that if I would turn about and go with him, he would see me home. I was sure I was right, and refused. He then said that he had been living at the Russell Hotel next door to mine for thirteen years and knew his way. I still refused, and he offered to go to the next corner with me and, when I found I was wrong, he would then conduct me home. At the next corner, to his great astonishment, we found my hotel — and I saw him home.

On entering the hotel, I was amazed to find it in darkness, and the lounge full of people in dressing gowns, each carrying a lighted candle. I asked the commissionaire what was up, and had I missed a fancy dress ball? He replied, 'No, sir. There's an air raid.'

I laughed, thinking he was pulling my leg, but he assured me seriously that it was a fact. Mr So-and-So had just come in and told them he had seen the lights of a zeppelin himself, flying very low. Mr So-and-So was a 'special constable' and could not be wrong, so they had roused the house. I knew the gentleman. I had heard him every meal time talking in a loud voice of his endeavours as a special constable. He appeared to me to be big and fit enough to be doing something better, and I did not like him. He was determined to achieve notoriety. I pointed out to the commissionaire that the fog was so thick, the lights in a second floor window were not visible from the street; that aircraft could not fly in a fog; and that, anyway, when they went on air raids they did not show their lights. In my opinion, Mr So-and-So was either a practical joker, or not quite right in the head. The latter appeared to be the general opinion, and everybody went back to bed. Mr So-and-So was not so popular the next day.

After a week in London, I went to Scotland. I had a pass to Nairn, my mother's birthplace. I also wanted to visit Perth, where my father's people came from, but did not have time to do either in the few days available. After a couple of days in Edinburgh, I went across to Glasgow, where I had promised to call on the father of one of my friends in Australia. In Edinburgh, my first visit was to the castle, where I spent a most interesting morning. Before leaving, in company with another officer with whom I had struck up an acquaintance during my tour of the morning, I visited the postcard shop, which is situated in a niche in the wall opposite the main gate. The girl in charge warned us that it was nearly one o'clock. Thinking she wanted to close up for lunch, we were hurrying through our selection, when suddenly from the battlements overhead a gun went off with a tremendous roar. It scared the wits out of us; we dropped the postcards and ran in different directions. Then we stopped and laughed at each other, and the girl laughed at both of us. It was the time-signal gun. The girl reminded us that she had warned us. That was all very well, but we did not know about the gun.

In the afternoon, I caught the train to Glasgow, arriving there at about 4.00 p.m. I left my bags at a hotel in Sauchiehall Street and set out to find the old man I had come to see. I located his office and found him in. I had, of course, never seen him before, but when I mentioned his son's name and said I knew him in Australia, he received me with open arms. He produced a box of cigars, and I had to sit down and tell him all about his son.

I finally dragged myself away, as I had promised to call on my friend's brother also, and I wanted to catch him before he left his office, so as I would have the next day free for sightseeing. The old man directed me to his other son's office, a shipping company not far away. He had gone home, but they insisted on me ringing him up. One of their ships had arrived in port that day, and he had taken the captain out to dinner. A boy got the number and I spoke to him on the phone. I told him who I was and that I would look him up in the morning. That was no good. I had to go at once to dinner. I got a taxi and went. He greeted me at the gate, and after greeting me like a long lost friend, enquired, 'Where are your bags?'

When I told him I had left them in Glasgow, he said, 'What the devil did you do that for?'

'Well, I intended staying there,' I said.

'Never mind. We'll get them afterwards. Come on in.'

His wife was waiting to receive me at the door, and greeted me just as cordially. I was a friend of Bob's, and that was enough. We had a very jolly dinner, and the captain invited us all to lunch on his ship the next day. His ship was at Greenock. The invitation was accepted, with the suggestion that Mrs Crombie and I should go down by boat so that I could see the Clyde on the way. It sounded quite interesting to me, but I felt quite sure that Mrs Crombie would not have gone if I had not been there. Any protestations on my part were howled down, and I let them have their heads. They were awfully good, and when the captain left at about 10.00 p.m., Mr Crombie drove me into Glasgow, retrieved my bags, and drove back to his home again. I was not allowed to stay anywhere else as long as I was in Glasgow. Next morning, Mrs Crombie and I left home early in time to catch the river steamer at about 10.00 a.m. The skipper met us at the gangway and took us up onto the bridge. Mr Crombie had been to see him and asked him to look after us on the trip and to point out anything of interest. He made it a wonderfully interesting trip for me. As we passed all the shipbuilding yards, he told me whose they were and what ships they were building. The river seemed at that time to be full of warships in all stages of construction, and the trip itself would have been very interesting to me as an ordinary passenger, but having the benefit of the view from the bridge with detailed information from the skipper made it doubly so. We landed at Greenock, found our ship, and had a very enjoyable luncheon on board. We returned to Glasgow by train.

Mrs Crombie gave up the next day to me also, and we went to Loch Lomond. We took the train to Balloch, had lunch there, and afterwards went on a motor launch up the loch. It was really beautiful. I do not wonder the Scots sing about it. The great expanse of blue water and the hills rising from it, wooded to the water's edge with their shading and colouring, are beyond my powers of description. I know I would like to have stayed longer and seen more of it, but in spite of very pressing invitations to do so, I had to leave next day on my return to 'The Grange' for the weekend. I spent a very happy weekend there. It was like going home. After promising to return for Christmas if in England, I left on Monday for the depot.

Chapter Nine

The Australian and New Zealand Depot was situated in Monte Video, about two miles from Weymouth, on the south coast. This was the collecting point for all ranks recovering from sickness or wounds, and where they were finally boarded and returned either to their units or to Australia. I was still very lame and could not walk without the aid of a stick. My great fear was that I would be sent home. I wanted to avoid that at any cost. All my pals were serving, or those that were left of them, and I was determined to get back to my regiment somehow or other. My leg would improve in time, if I could only wangle to stay there.

The depot was divided into three classes — 'fit', 'temporarily unfit', and 'permanently unfit'. I was allotted to the latter class, commonly known as the 'P.U.s'. We were a sorry looking crew at early morning parade, which even we had to attend for roll call, most of us on crutches or sticks. We were dismissed immediately afterwards, being all unfit for duty, and we were then faced with the problem of filling in a miserable and useless day. We would have been far better on leave. After a fortnight, I had to appear before a medical board again. We were 'boarded' once a month. As there was not a full board at the depot, I was examined by a board of English medical officers. Their decision was that I was 'permanently unfit and should be returned to Australia'. I lodged a protest at once. They were very nice about it. They listened to my argument and, after about twenty minutes of pleading, they finally altered their decision to 'home service', saying they would see how I was in a month's time — but did not hold out much hope of escape. Anyway, I had another month's grace, and had negotiated the first obstacle.

Life at the depot was pretty dull, especially for those of us who could not do duty. Having wangled 'home service', I interviewed the adjutant to see if there was any possibility of attending a school of instruction. I was in luck. General Birdwood had just written requesting that a machine-gun school be established at the depot, and as many officers and men as possible be instructed in the handling of machine guns while on convalescence. In those days, very few people knew anything about machine guns. A staff officer, Captain G.F.G. Wieck, was appointed to take charge of the school. He was very annoyed about it as he wanted to return to the front, but there was no-one else available. The depot had been allotted two vacancies for the next course commencing a week later at Hayling Island, a branch of the Hythe School of Musketry, and I was told that I could go. I threw my hat up for joy. A week later, in company with another officer, I left for Hayling Island for a three-week course of instruction of Vickers and Maxim guns.

Hayling Island is near Southampton, with the Isle of Wight showing in the distance across the water, and is connected with the mainland by a railway bridge. We changed trains at Southampton and boarded a local train for the island.

As I stepped from the train at our destination, I saw a very imposing looking figure on the platform, dressed in blue frock coat and brass buttons with gold lace on his cap, and whom at first sight I took to be at least an admiral. I gave him my best salute. He smiled and said, 'Good morning, sir,' as he returned my salute. I thought he was very polite for such an exalted person. When I pointed out to one of my companions that he had failed to pay him the respect due to an admiral, he replied, 'Admiral, be damned. He's the guard.'

And so he was. The joke was on me. When I looked again, he was blowing his whistle and waving a green flag.

The school was billeted in a hotel, which had been taken over for the purpose, close to the beach. There were no distractions on the island, and we had a very quiet time apart from the work of the school. But the work was interesting, and I enjoyed the school very much. Although the injury to my leg prevented me from qualifying in the time tests at the end of the school, I passed out with a qualifying certificate as an instructor in Vickers and Maxim guns.

Shortly after my return to the depot, the adjutant sent for me and asked me if I would like to do a course in Lewis guns at Chelsea Barracks, London. I jumped at the chance and answered in the affirmative. A few days later, I left for London to attend this school. I stayed at a hotel in London, and had to report at Chelsea Barracks every morning at nine o'clock. This school only lasted a week, and I qualified. In addition, it gave me the opportunity to see a little more of London, though mostly by night, as our class was not dismissed until 5.00 p.m.

The depot battalion, Grenadier Guards, were at Chelsea Barracks, and I used to arrive at about a quarter to nine every morning to see them fall in for parade. I had heard of the wonderful work of the Guards, and I never got tired of watching them. As I entered by the main gate and walked across the Barrack Square, there was not a soul in sight except the guard at the gate. At about ten minutes to nine, the R.S.M. appeared on the square and called for markers. Immediately, the markers appeared, marched across the square with sloped arms, fell in, and stood at ease. Following them came the drummers, who also fell in on a flank of the parade. The markers were called to attention, inspected by the R.S.M., and posted. All this time, there was still not another soul in sight. On a signal from the R.S.M., a bugler sounded the 'fall in', and immediately coming from every doorway of the buildings surrounding the square, a thousand men appeared. For a minute or so, it looked like hopeless confusion. But it was not. Every man marched out with his rifle at the slope, straight to his allotted place on parade, and fell in a pace and a half behind the marker, took up his dressing, and stood at ease. In an incredibly short space of time, every man was in his place, and what had looked like confusion had sorted itself out into perfect order. The sergeant major then called the parade to attention, and gave the command to 'fall in'. Every man jumped a pace forward, and with head and eyes to the right, shuffled up half a pace until the line was perfectly dressed, the drum meanwhile beating a roll. When the dressing was completed, the roll ceased, with sticks raised — then with one resounding thump on the drums, every head was turned to the front. One could almost hear the necks click as they came round. The perfect precision of their work was wonderful to watch, and I would like to have seen more of it, but it was nine o'clock and I had to go.

I was sorry when this school finished. It was very interesting, and I was the tenth to return to the depot. Shortly after my return, Colonel Elliott arrived at the depot. He had come to England on sick leave after the evacuation of Gallipoli.[1] He only stayed a few days, and left on the first available ship to return to Egypt. The A.I.F. was being re-organised — two new divisions were being formed in Egypt and one in Australia, making five divisions altogether, and Colonel Elliott had been appointed to the command of a brigade. I had a long talk with him, and he was interested to know that I had been to the two machine-gun schools. He offered me a job with his machine-gun company if I could get back to Egypt. I told him how I was situated, and asked if he could do anything to help get me away. He tried, interviewing the C.O. of the depot on my behalf, but failed to move him.[2] The C.O. produced my medical papers and pointed out that I was still unfit for service. It was impossible for him to let me go. I suppose it was, but I found it very disappointing, knowing there was a job with promotion awaiting me, if only I could get to it. However,

---

1 Pompey Elliott was evacuated from Gallipoli with illness in late August 1915. Diagnosed with pleurisy, he was sent to England to recuperate. Months later, having been passed fit, he left London on 14 November to return to Gallipoli, and it was evidently shortly before this that he caught up with Barrie (that is, before the evacuation rather than after it).

2 The Weymouth depot had several different commanders while Barrie was there. In charge from May to December 1915 was 45-year-old Lieutenant-Colonel Newton Moore, who had been premier of Western Australia for four years from 1906. He was succeeded at Weymouth by Lieutenant-Colonel Richard Courtney, who had been the 14th AIF Battalion's initial commander. It was just as well that this change of command had not occurred earlier: Pompey Elliott had fallen out with Courtney before the war, and retained a low opinion of him.

nothing could be done about it and it appeared that I would have to stay where I was until marked 'fit'. Colonel Elliott left a few days later, but promised me a job if I was ever able to return and come to him. For the present, I had to resign myself to the dull routine of the depot.

A couple of weeks later, I was sent for to report to Orderly Room, and was informed that I was appointed instructor in machine gunnery, to replace Captain Wieck, who was returning to Egypt as brigade major to (the newly promoted) General Elliott. Wieck had also interviewed General Elliott while he was at the depot, with greater success than I — but, of course, he was fit. General Elliott had cabled from Egypt on his arrival there, requesting that Captain Wieck be sent to him as brigade major.[3]

I received the news of my appointment with mixed feelings. I knew that, for the present, it would settle the question of my return to Australia, but I had no desire to be stuck on a depot job for the rest of the war. However, I decided I had better be satisfied for the present, and leave the other matter until the time came. I congratulated Captain Wieck on having wangled his release, and abused him for letting me in for his job. He grinned and told me what a nice job it was. It was quite a nice job, too, as far as it went, but it was not my ambition to serve through the war in the depot. I took over from him the next day, and he sailed a few days later for Egypt with the promise to find me a job if I came to the 15th Brigade.

I certainly enjoyed my work on the machine-gun school. I had a definite job to do at last, and my time was fully occupied on very interesting work. I applied for and got a Lewis gun, thus enlarging the scope of the school. Shortly after this, I also got an assistant instructor, whom I had trained myself, and I was able to take a much larger class. Each course lasted a fortnight. We trained quite a lot of men, finishing off each course with a course of musketry, including

---

3 George Wieck, aged 34 when Barrie succeeded him as the instructor, proved a highly capable staff officer at Pompey Elliott's headquarters, and also from mid-1917 at John Monash's divisional headquarters. He had served in South Africa, had an administrative role in World War II, and died in Perth soon after his 92nd birthday.

indirect firing.

While I was on the job, I did my best to make a success of it, as I realised the value of the instruction, and actually got quite a deal of kudos for my work. This was very nice as far as it went, but I felt between the devil and the deep blue sea. The harder I worked at the school, the more indispensable I became at the depot. Still, I was not yet fit, so there was no point worrying about it. I thought I would wangle something when the time came, and in the meantime I saw to it that each course included a proportion of officers, so that there would be someone available to take my place when the time came. I was still being 'boarded' periodically, but could get nothing better than 'home service'.[4] There were now three medical officers at the depot, constituting a full board. I knew two of them well. One night before a periodical examination, I interviewed one of them, and asked him as a special and personal favour, to mark me fit on the morrow. He laughed at first, and replied, 'Yes! Fit for Australia.'

I stuck at him and argued with him for two hours, until he admitted that he saw my point of view — but even so, there were others on the board, and I would have to get at least one other to agree. I knew that, of course, and told him that I intended to interview the other M.O. as soon as I had got his assurance.

'Alright,' he said, 'I'll come with you, and we will see what Mac has to say.'

We found him in his cubicle. I explained the situation and made my request. The result was an immediate and flat refusal. For half an hour, I had to argue against both of them, and it took me an hour to persuade him to agree. I went to bed happy that night. There was still the third and senior member of the board to be won over, and as I did not know him I could not approach him, but I had a two-thirds majority if they kept their word, and I did not doubt that once they had given it. The next morning, I reported myself at the appointed

---

4   For example, a medical board of three doctors assessed Barrie at Weymouth on 9 December 1915, and found that 'there is weakness in the right thigh which increases on exertion, and is accompanied by pain behind the knee'. They concluded that Barrie was fit for home service only.

time in a state of mild excitement. I discarded my stick and made a desperate effort to walk without a limp. It was hard to accomplish, but I knew there was not much space in the boardroom if they wanted to test me. It was only a few paces from one end to the other.

When I entered the room, the president was examining my papers. When he had finished, he bade me good morning and asked how I was. I replied that I was quite fit now. He only said 'Hmm,' and had another look at the papers. Then he made me show him my wounds, and after inspecting them and pummelling me for a few minutes, he sat me down and turned to the other two and said, 'Home service, I think. Don't you?'

I stared hard at them. They both looked at me and hesitated, and then the senior said, 'Oh, I think he might be alright now.'

Looking surprised, the president asked the junior for his opinion, and to my delight he agreed with the other member. But I was not over it yet. The president disagreed, and an argument ensued, but the two stuck to their word. The president was still not satisfied, and ordered me to walk across to the corner of the room and back. I did so, praying I would not limp. My knee was very weak, and I could not trust it. Another argument ensued. At the end, the president said, 'Oh well, if you both think so, we'll mark him fit, I suppose.'

But before he did so, he made me walk the room again. Then, after a few more remarks, I was dismissed. Hurrah! I was eligible to return to my unit, and though I knew this was only one step on the way, it was an essential one, and I now had solid grounds on which to base my case. I walked very carefully away from the medical quarters, as I had heard of doctors watching through windows before, and I knew the president was not entirely satisfied. I got safely away and returned to duty in a jubilant frame of mind.[5] Later in the day, I interviewed

---

5 The report of the Weymouth medical board that gave Barrie the all-clear on 18 February 1916 was signed by two officers from the Australian Army Medical Corps, Captains D.M. McWhae and J. Macdonald (so either could have been 'Mac'). Their report stated that 'there is now no disability present'. There is no third signature. Perhaps the president's scepticism prompted him to refrain from associating himself with it.

the C.O., told him that I had now been declared fit, and requested that he would allow me to return to my unit as soon as possible.[6] He told me to get the idea out of my head, as I could not be spared from the depot. It was useless to argue. He would not listen, and told me to get on with my job and forget about it. I obeyed the first instruction, but not the second. I had expected some such reply, and I could see I would have to use my wits to achieve my objective. It appeared harder to get to the war than away from it, but I determined to do it somehow.

I got a few days leave at Christmas, and spent a few happy days at 'The Grange' with Mr and Mrs Midwood. It was a real English Christmas. The whole countryside was white with snow, a proper atmosphere for a proper Christmas dinner. After the main course, the curtains were drawn and the room darkened, then the pudding was borne in, blazing. I enjoyed the few days immensely. The Midwoods were as kind as ever, though I knew it was not such a happy Christmas for them as it might have been. Their son had sailed for Mesopotamia and, though I knew their thoughts were with him and there must have been some anxiety underneath, they never showed it in any way. They spoke of him, of course, and were proud that he was doing his job, but that was all. I was sorry when it was time to leave again, and return to duty.

I walked into the mess one day and found a young staff officer howling with rage and cursing his luck. On enquiring the cause of his trouble, he told me he had just been ordered to report for duty at administrative headquarters in London, and being fit, he had hoped to get off with an early draft to re-join his unit. I sympathised with him and enquired what his job was to be. He told me it included compilation of draft rolls, and arrangements for transport of drafts

---

6 The CO at Weymouth was now Lieutenant-Colonel Courtney. A 45-year-old solicitor initially from Castlemaine, Dick Courtney had extensive militia experience, but his health was not robust. He was evacuated from Gallipoli with heart trouble within five weeks of the landing. His health continued to be troublesome at Weymouth, and in March 1916 he was sent back to Australia. He died in 1919.

for overseas. I knew it was the custom for that office to nominate to the depot the names of officers to go, so I extracted from him a promise that he would put my name on every draft list he sent down, until I went. He promised me faithfully that he would. He kept his word. It cost the depot quite a sum of telegrams asking for another name to be substituted for mine, as I was indispensable. Protests and applications from me were unavailing. They refused to let me go.

My pal, Lieut. Catron, turned up at the depot. He had been wounded in the knee at Helles on the 8th of May during the attack at Krithia by the 2nd Brigade. He was very lame and had to wear a steel plate over his knee to prevent it giving way when walking. Yates, another of our officers, also arrived. The three of us had been pals all through the war. Yates had hung out on the Peninsula for quite a long time and got the temporary rank of captain, which would be confirmed if held in the field for two months. He was suffering badly from dysentery and was invalided a fortnight before his time was up, thus having to revert to the rank of lieutenant. It was rotten luck for him after all he had been through. He did not stay with us long, but was sent home to Australia soon after.[7] Catron and I decided we would parade to the C.O. every time a draft list came out, and renew our request to be included. The list of names of officers to go was posted in the mess ante-room, and after inspecting the list, we duly presented ourselves at the orderly room and asked for our names to be included. We were treated politely at first, but our requests were refused. Nevertheless, every time a draft list came out we went again, and persisted in the practice, hoping the C.O. would get tired of us

---

7 Bill Yates, a 30-year-old farmer from Camperdown, had blue eyes, brown hair, and an eventful war. A wound to his right elbow in the early Gallipoli fighting resulted in his evacuation, and, after returning to the battalion in July, he contracted the severe illness that led to his return to Australia. In mid-1916, however, he accompanied an 8th Battalion reinforcements batch to England, and then rejoined his unit in France, only to be wounded by a shell near Bullecourt in April 1917. It was a severe head injury, and he again returned to Australia. But he still had not had enough of the conflict, and early in 1918 he headed to London once more. Bill Yates DSO survived the war.

in time and be glad to get rid of us. He did, but not in the way we had anticipated. He got angry with us and ordered us to desist. We still persisted — until, one day, he stood up at his table and ordered us out, saying,

'Catron, if you come here again with that request, I will send you to Australia on the first ship. As for you, Barrie, get back to your job and stay on it, and you will stay in this depot as long as I do.'

We saluted and went. It was no use arguing while he was in that mood.[8] When the next list appeared, I said to Catron, 'What about it, Joe? Are you going to chance it again?'

'Yes,' he replied. 'Are you coming?'

So off we went. We hardly got inside the door this time. The C.O. cut us short and said, 'Hullo. You two here again? Very well, you are for Australia, Catron,' and, turning to me, he went on, 'Barrie, any further requests of this nature from you will be treated as a breach of discipline. Now get out, both of you.'

We went, but did not think he would put his threat into execution. He did though. Catron's name appeared in a draft list a few days later, bound for Australia.[9] After that, I thought I had better keep quiet for a while, and try another scheme.

There were always a few in the depot who obviously did not want to return to the front, even if they were fit, and who would give anything to get a job that would keep them safe from the war. They were only a small proportion, but easily discernible. Those of us who were there against our will felt very self-conscious about it, in case those who did not know included us in the number of those who did not want to fight.

There was one in particular (I'll just call him Dash) who was fully determined not to leave if he could possibly avoid it. He always wore

---

8 The CO at Weymouth was still Courtney. The state of his own health would not have helped his mood.

9 Joe Catron returned to Australia early in 1916. Like his brother Bill, he left Melbourne later that same year to go back to the war, and rejoined the 8th Battalion. He left it in November 1917 to take up a commission in the Indian Army.

a mitten on one hand, and I could never discover what his injury really was, or whether he had any at all. It did not seem to cramp his style in any other way, and as far as I could see, the only thing it prevented him doing was getting back to the war. It is a true saying, 'birds of a feather flock together'. His friends were all more or less of the same type. He seized the job of mess secretary. There was no trouble about that, as no-one else wanted it.

Our sleeping quarters were in huts, each containing about ten cubicles opening on to a passage which ran the length of the hut, except for the two end rooms, which were larger than the others and included the width of the passage. The allotment of sleeping accommodation was part of the mess secretary's job. He established himself in one of the large end rooms. Unfortunately, it was next door to mine. That did not matter so much, except that he developed the habit of giving late parties in his room which disturbed my rest. The mess gramophone, which was out of order, was repaired under his instructions and paid for out of mess funds. On its return, the gramophone was established in Dash's room, for the entertainment of himself and his friends.

It was their usual practice to go to Weymouth every evening after mess, returning at about 11.00 p.m. before the mess steward closed down, have a few drinks in the mess, then retire to Dash's room with a few bottles, and continue the party there. I was invited to join them. I went once, but left early. I did not like the company, and though the invitation was repeated, I always found some excuse and did not attend again. Dash asked me one day why I did not join his parties. I told him they did not appeal to me, that I had a job to do and required my rest at night. Moreover, I was trying to get fit to return to the front, and could not stand the strain of sitting up at parties every night until 3.00 a.m., as I had to be out at reveille, and did not breakfast in bed. This rather hurt, because he did breakfast in bed, although it was forbidden, except on authority from the medical officer — but, being mess secretary, he controlled the kitchen staff and stewards, and some of them were rather anxious to keep their jobs, too. I think he was convinced by this time that his views and mine did not coincide, and he set out to annoy me.

He and his friends would troop into the hut every night around midnight, talking loudly and stamping the floor. As they filed into the room, they banged on my wall with their sticks. Then the gramophone started up, corks popped, and there were sounds of revelry by night. This went on until 2.00 a.m. or perhaps 3.00 a.m., and I certainly did get a bit annoyed, though I said nothing at the time, thinking they would probably get tired of it. Then one morning after a particularly bright party, Dash asked me how I enjoyed it. I told him candidly that I was getting a bit fed up with it, and suggested it would be a good idea if some of his friends entertained him in their huts for a change. He seemed quite pleased to know that they really had succeeded in annoying me, and assured me that they would continue where they were. I advised him in that case to make less noise, as, though I did not want to be a 'nark' altogether, if they continued to disturb me I would have to seriously consider stopping his parties. He laughed at that, and told me to do my worst. His parties would continue, and he would make as much noise as he liked in his own room.

That was a direct challenge. I replied, 'Very well. I will give you fair warning then. You can do as you like as long as you don't annoy me, but if I am disturbed tonight, that party will be your last.'

He got angry at that, and said, 'Hmm. Tell tales to the C.O., I suppose.'

I assured him that I had no such intention and would handle the affair myself, advising him again with a smile not to forget the warning. He replied that I could do as I liked but I would not stop him, and walked off.

I had already thought out a plan, and decided to put it into action. It would be worth it, if only for the joke.

I interviewed a man of my own battalion who, being unfit for service, was employed in the motor garage as mechanic and chauffeur to the C.O. After swearing him to secrecy, I propounded my scheme to him. He was full of glee when he grasped the idea, and cheerfully agreed to provide the necessary material, which consisted of one acetylene gas generator, one length of rubber tubing, and a brace and bit. He charged the generator at once, and accompanied me to my hut. We bored a hole in the wall at a spot opposite Dash's bed on the other side where it would not be seen, poked the tube through and attached it to the generator. We pulled my bed into position, so that all I had to do was to reach down and turn on the tap. There was nothing more to do now but wait for zero hour. This gang and their parties were annoying others besides me, and the joke was too good to keep, so a few of my pals whom I knew I could trust were let in on the secret. They chuckled with delight, inspected the works, and determined to watch the proceedings from a secluded position.

The British Army had not used gas up to that time, and I had the distinction therefore of being the first officer in the British Army to conduct a gas attack, which I did with great success, resulting in a complete rout of the enemy.

I retired at about 10.00 p.m., and lay reading until the party arrived. I heard them coming at about 11.30 p.m., all talk and laughter. They trooped up the steps; each one banged on my wall three times with his stick and stamped on the floor as he walked into the room. It was an extra-large party — the gang had been mobilised in full force to witness my discomfiture. So much the better. The gramophone was turned on, and the whole crowd seemed to be talking and laughing at once, each vying with the other to see who could make the most noise. Then a wrestling match started — chairs were knocked over, bodies banged against the wall, and rolled and kicked on the floor, while the onlookers barracked and cheered in good style. They were determined to assert their superiority and settle me for good and all. The wrestling match finished, and the combatants demanded a drink. Corks popped and they all had one, to the accompaniment of more jokes and much laughter.

I let them go for about half an hour, then when the party was at its height and the din as loud as ever, I let them have it. I leaned out of bed and turned on the tap. Nothing happened for a few minutes. Then, I think I have never heard anything so funny. As the gas began to generate and pour into the room, the din gradually decreased until finally for a few seconds there was dead silence. I would love to have been able to see them, but did not want to risk discovery and spoil the joke. Someone said, 'Who's playing jokes with carbide?'

Another voice declared it was a rotten joke, anyway. Someone looked at the water bucket, but there was nothing there. Presently, everyone was blaming everyone else, and there was very nearly a real fight amongst several members of the party. They pulled the furniture out, and turned the whole room upside down, and failed to find a clue. Then someone said, 'I know, there is someone underneath the hut blowing it through a hole in the floor.'

Immediately, there was a stampede for the door, and they all rushed out, determined to catch the miscreant and deal with him.

The hut was built on the side of a hill, and supported on brick pillars, which at one side were six feet high. I heard them underneath, chasing themselves around these pillars for ten minutes or so. Several captures were made, but in every case it turned out to be one of their own party. Then the hunt ceased, and a 'council of war' was held. In the meantime, the old generator was still working at top speed, and by this time was making so much gas that it began to whistle. I turned it off and the whistling ceased, but there was still a deal of gas to escape, and there was not the slightest smell in my room. Presently, the party returned and attempted to enter the room, but the fumes were thicker than ever, and they could not get in. Then there was a knock at my door. They had decided to inspect my room. Splendid! They were welcome to do so, but I did not want to appear too eager for it, so I ordered them off. The knocking persisted, and they asked me quietly to open the door. I finally did so and asked them what they wanted. Four of them came in, walked around my room, and sniffed in every corner, but smelt nothing. They all agreed there was nothing there, and prepared to depart. I suggested that they might tell me what it was all about before they went. One said, 'Oh, someone has been playing jokes with carbide, and we wondered if you knew anything about it.'

I asked them if they were satisfied.

'Yes,' said one of them, 'there is nothing here.'

I bade them goodnight and locked my door again.

The party was still pow-wowing on the doorstep. Dash put a handkerchief over his nose and made a gallant dash into the room, flinging open a window. A few minutes later, he repeated the process and opened the other window. It was a cold frosty night, and the party started to get fidgety. At length, someone said, 'It's no use standing here in the cold. I'm off to bed.'

Everybody agreed, and gradually the party drifted away, leaving the host sitting alone on the cold doorstep. He could not enter the room for an hour or more after that, and when he finally did get in, he was of the same opinion as I, that that was the last party he would give.

At breakfast next morning, the whole mess was laughing over the 'gas attack', except the victims, whose sense of humour did not stretch that far. They were obviously furious and threatening all sorts of dire punishment on the culprit if they found him. One of my pals beckoned me as I entered, and I sat down next to him. He whispered, 'Congratulations. It was a wonderful success. I watched it from my window.'

I whispered back, 'Do they know anything?'

'Not a thing. They are blaming me just now. I have already been threatened with a hiding.'

'Hope you get it.'

'It's not worrying me.' It certainly was not. He was a big chap and an excellent boxer.

For a week or more, the gas attack remained one of the leading topics of interest in the mess, and the victims had to endure a continuous fire of raillery, while the identity of the perpetrator remained a mystery. At the end of a fortnight, the interest was dying down and it was being gradually forgotten, when it suddenly blazed into prominence again. Entering the ante room one day before lunch, Dash approached me, looking furious, and said, 'I have discovered the secret of the gas attack. You are the —— who did it. My batman found the hole in the wall this morning when he was scrubbing the floor.'

I laughed, and said in a tone of surprise, 'But it hasn't taken you all this time to discover who did it, surely?'

'Yes, it has. But we know now.'

Still laughing, I said, 'My dear old chap, there was no secret about it. I told you the morning before the party that I would stop it. You challenged me to do it, you know, and I accepted your challenge.'

As he turned away in disgust, I stopped him and said, 'Dash, I suppose it is fair to let you know, in case you are thinking of having more parties, that I still have the outfit.'

There was a general laugh at his expense, and another round of chaff, which put him in a towering rage. He would have been wise to have kept his secret. He did not have any more parties.

Chapter Ten

Life proceeded smoothly at the depot after the rout of the 'leadswingers' — my rest was disturbed no more, and I slept in peace.

I regret that I did not receive any official recognition of my successful demonstration on the use of gas. I do not even think there is any record of it in the archives of the War Office. But that is always the way, a pioneer seldom reaps the fruits of his victories.

The machine-gun school was still going strong, turning out about eighteen men each course. The standard of training was good, and I still continued to put my best efforts into it, while never neglecting a chance to escape.

About ten o'clock one morning, I received a message to report to Orderly Room at once. Five other officers were there. We were marched in, wondering what it was all about. We saluted, and stood at ease. The C.O.[1] picked up a sheet of paper from his desk and said, 'Gentlemen, I have just received this telegram from London — "Six officers with machine-gun experience report to this office by first available train. After forty-eight-hours leave, proceed to France. Undermentioned officers will proceed on this duty."' The list of our names followed, with mine at the head. My pal was still true to his promise. Good lad. The C.O. continued, 'The train leaves Weymouth at twelve o'clock. You will pack your kits at once. Transport will be

---

1 The CO at Weymouth was now Lieutenant-Colonel J.L. Johnston, a 53-year-old stockbroker from Boulder in Western Australia. He had commanded that state's initial infantry unit, the 11th Battalion, for the first year of the war.

provided, leaving here at eleven o'clock. Report to the adjutant before leaving for, travelling warrants. I wish you good luck.'

Then the expected blow fell again. Turning to me, he said, 'Barrie, you will stand fast. Remainder — dismiss.'

Another hope dashed to the ground. When the others had left the orderly room, the C.O. said to me, 'I'm sorry, Barrie, but of course we can't spare you. You are quite indispensable. I have wired to London for another name to be substituted for yours. You will stand by until I get a reply.'

I did not even protest. I simply said, 'Very good, sir,' saluted, and marched out.

I was too downhearted to speak to anyone. I had trained every one of the other five, and was being left again myself. I wandered slowly across to my quarters, sat down on my bed, and made an appreciation of the situation.

What was I to do? My name was on the list, and the train left in less than two hours. A wire had been sent, asking for my name to be cancelled. Would the reply arrive in time, or would my pal be able to hold it up until the train had gone, counting on me to act? Until my name was cancelled, I was under instructions from a superior authority to catch that train, though the request would have to be dealt with by a senior officer, and would certainly be complied with. If I stood by and missed the train, my chance was gone. What would I do if positions were reversed? I would find some way of delaying that reply. Having put my name on a telegram with only two hours notice, would my friend expect me to take the chance? I thought he would.

I decided to take it. I sent for my batman and started to pack. I interviewed the man in the motor garage, and he promised to have a taxi waiting a few hundred yards down the road at 11.15 a.m., and help my batman to get my luggage out without being seen. Having completed packing, I wandered out through the back of the camp and across the fields. There, sure enough, was the taxi. I got in and waited. In a few minutes, my baggage arrived. Taking my batman with me, I said goodbye to the garage man, thanked him for the assistance he had given me on several occasions, and off we went. So far, so good. I was sorry to leave without saying goodbye to anyone, but did not dare do so. My troubles were not yet over, by any means. We would have half an hour to wait for the train. It was not safe for me to go to the station, so I got out and hid myself in a hotel opposite, instructing my batman to stay with my bags on the platform until I arrived. At two minutes to twelve, I went across. My batman was sitting on my baggage arguing with the guard, and refusing to load it until I came. I asked him if anyone had been enquiring for me. He had heard nothing. The other five officers were standing in a group close by. They knew nothing and had a warrant for six people, so I loaded my luggage, tipped my batman, and jumped on board as the train started to move. I was off at last, but I knew what a row there would be when my absence was discovered, and at every station I was expecting enquiries to be made for me. Nothing happened, and we reached London safely. Administrative headquarters was then at 72 Victoria Street. We drove straight there and reported ourselves. Leaving the others, I made straight for my pal's room. He laughed as I entered, and said, 'Hullo. You got here?'

'Yes. Didn't you expect me?'

'Well, I did actually,' he replied, 'but they sent a wire asking for your name to be struck off.'

'What did you do with it?' I asked.

'Oh, I kept it in my drawer until the train had left, to give you a chance, then I had to hand it on. The reply has since been sent, cancelling your name. Anyhow, I'm glad you made it, but now you had better clear out of here, and for goodness' sake don't come here again. Your disappearance has been reported, and the A.P.M. is after you. You will have to lose yourself in London for a couple of days and then make your own way to France.'

Thanking him for his co-operation, I shook his hand and left. My appreciation had been correct. He had done just as I had anticipated.

I put up at a quiet and little-known hotel in the West End, where I was not likely to meet anyone, and although I did not go to the extent of hiding myself, I kept away from popular haunts of the Australians.

Nothing happened during the two days, but I had that rotten feeling all the time that someone would tap me on the shoulder at any moment. I was 'absent without leave', and although I knew I would be posted as a deserter, seven days had to elapse before that could be done. Even so, I was deserting to the war, not from it, and did not expect any drastic punishment, even if I was caught.

I made the most of my short leave, deposited my surplus luggage at Cook's, and in the evening of the second day, I took a taxi to Waterloo in time to catch my train for Southampton. All terminal stations were under military control, with a railway transport officer in charge, and it was necessary to report to him to have my warrants checked and dated. At the ports, his office was on the quay and he was called the Military Landing Officer (M.L.O.). Here, the same procedure was followed. This presented the next difficulty, but it had to be overcome.

A porter was on the spot as the taxi stopped. I engaged him and told him to wait there with my baggage for a minute. Making a quick reconnaissance of the position, I found it was hopeless to try to get onto the platform in the ordinary way. There was a seven-foot picket fence across the entrance with only a narrow opening, on one side of which was a ticket collector, and on the other a military policeman. Of course, I had to evade the R.T.O., and no-one could get through that gate until he had seen him. The next platform, however, was open and vacant with a paved roadway between. I returned to the porter and told him to take my bags onto the train, find me a first class smoker, and wait there for me. I watched him onto the platform, then strolled casually towards the other, walked half way along it, then down onto the roadway and across. I gave the porter a good tip, and took my seat. So far, I had been very successful, and was getting interested in the game, though I heaved a sigh of relief as the train started.

At Southampton, the train ran onto the quay, and there was a general rush for the M.L.O.'s office. Men grabbed their kits and jumped to the platform before the train had stopped. I let them go, then, hailing a porter, I instructed him to put my bags on the ship. While he was doing so, I made another reconnaissance. The M.L.O.'s office was in quite a large building on the quay, with a huge counter in front, leaving only a narrow passageway each side, which again was blocked with a high picket fence guarded by a naval sentry with fixed bayonet. There was a seething crowd at the counter, elbowing and pushing to get in. A bold front seemed indicated, so I marched smartly up to the gateway, saluted, and said, 'Good evening, sentry,' and went straight through. The sentry replied,

'Good evening, sir,' and returned my salute. It was a reversal of the usual procedure, but it flabbergasted the sentry for a moment, and before he had time to think, I was gone and the crowd on my heels kept him busy. Once past the sentry, I was safe, as the ship was not responsible for checking warrants. Ascending the gangway without molestation, I found my porter, tipped him, and collected my luggage. I then sought a sheltered corner for the crossing.

In a few minutes, the troops were crowding onto the ship, and all was bustle and confusion — everyone looking for a spot to dump his kit, and endeavouring to remember where he had put it. Soon, we had our complement aboard, gangways were removed, the siren shrieked, and in the dusk of the evening we pulled slowly out from the quay. Another troopship joined us, and before we got out to sea we were met by three destroyers, who were responsible for our safe conduct to Le Havre. It was not a very comfortable journey. The ship carried no lights, and though not actually rough, a cold wind was blowing. There was, of course, no sleeping accommodation; it was only a small vessel, and packed to the limit with troops. Men put on their overcoats and lay on the deck, and slept or talked as the spirit moved them.

On arrival at Le Havre about eight o'clock next morning, there was another rush for the M.L.O.'s office, where everybody had again to present their warrants and sign a book.[2] But here, the quay was open and presented no difficulty. I engaged a taxi and drove to the Australian depot. My trouble with warrants was over, as the M.L.O. collected them. I reported my arrival, was allotted a bed, had a bath

---

2   According to military records, Barrie arrived at Le Havre on 10 June 1916.

and breakfast, and was ordered to report with other new arrivals in a lecture marquee at ten o'clock. Here, we were given certain instructions, the rules of the depot were explained, and we were notified of certain districts which were 'out of bounds' to the troops. Everyone was required to sign a book before leaving. Everyone did, except me. I mingled with the crowd for a minute, then walked out.

I have often thought that it would be a much wiser plan for the army authorities not to mention 'out of bounds' quarters to the troops, as the mere mention of it excites a natural curiosity in the individual as to the reason for it, and he immediately wants to see it for himself. If he did not know it was 'out of bounds', he probably would not bother with it. Soldiers are like children — they are not bad by any means, in fact 90 per cent of them are inherently decent, but they are curious and want to see the sights.

We had no duty at the depot, and in company with several others, I set off to see the sights myself. There was not much of interest to be seen in Le Havre. 'Out of bounds' quarters had no appeal for me. I had seen enough of them while on picquet duty in Cairo. We had lunch in the town, and spent most of our time at the English Officers Club. I was anxious to get away from the depot as soon as possible, and anyway before seven days was up, as I knew that if they were determined to chase me, a warrant could then be issued for my arrest, and I would not really be safe until I had joined my unit.

The Australian troops were arriving in France — the 1st Division being already there, but nobody knew where they were, and I could not go scouring the country to find them. My anxiety was relieved on the third day when the party of machine-gun officers was instructed to entrain that evening for the 1st Division depot at Étaples. We boarded the troop train at about 5.00 p.m., carrying two days' rations with us. The train consisted of cattle trucks each branded '8 Chevaux en long ou 40 Hommes'. As there were no 'chevaux', the 'hommes' piled in. We were not crowded, so we cleaned up the floor as well as we could, laid out our valises and made ourselves as comfortable as possible. The train arrived at Étaples at about 10.00 p.m. on the second day. I reported to headquarters immediately on arrival. The orderly room sergeant looked hard at me and said, 'I think the C.O. wants to see you, sir. Will you wait a minute?' and disappeared through a doorway. He reappeared a minute or two later and said, 'Will you go in, sir?'

I was prepared to hear the worst, but having got this far, I was not going back without a fight. I pulled myself together and entered. A major, wearing colours of the 2nd Division, was sitting at the table. I saluted and said, 'Good morning, sir. You wish to see me?'

'Yes,' he replied. 'Are you Lieut. Barrie of the 8th Battalion?'

I had to admit that I was.

'Where have you come from?' he asked.

'England, sir.'

'Yes, I know, but how did you get here?'

I told him I had travelled by the ordinary route. He said, 'Well, I have got a warrant here for your arrest as a deserter from Weymouth Depot, with instructions to return you to England under escort.'

The blow had fallen at last. I explained that I had left under instructions from administrative headquarters. Then he smiled and asked me what it was all about. I told him how I was stuck at the depot and how I had wangled my escape. Then he asked, 'But how did you get across?'

I explained how I had wangled that also. Then he smiled again and said, 'Well, it would be stiff luck to be sent back after all that, wouldn't it?'

I agreed that it would.

'Alright, I'll see you through. I will reply that your unit has asked for you, and will send you up as soon as I can.'

I could have hugged him. He was a good sport. I thanked him and left, feeling greatly relieved. I no longer felt the tapping of the A.P.M.'s fingers on my shoulders. I was free.

The depot was organised into headquarters, and three sub-depots, the personnel of the sub-depots comprising officers and men of the 1st, 2nd, and 3rd Brigades. Each sub-depot was organised in four companies, composed of officers and men of the four battalions. I went straight to the orderly room to report my arrival, and found a young reinforcement subaltern in charge. Bidding him good day, I enquired for the C.O. To my astonishment, he replied, 'I am the C.O.'

I was rather taken aback, but told him who I was, and that I was reporting for duty. He showed me my tent, and after a much needed wash I made my way across to the mess for lunch. On being introduced to the gathering, I found — with the exception of myself and one other, who had come over in the machine-gun party — they were all reinforcement officers, none of whom, including the C.O. and quartermaster, had yet joined their units or seen any service. This did not trouble me, but I thought it strange that the command of the depot would be left in the hands of such inexperienced youths, and wondered what training the troops were getting.

At 2.00 p.m., I wandered down to the 8th Battalion lines, where the troops were falling in, and was pleased to find several N.C.O.s whom I knew, from whom I got a very warm welcome. To my surprise, no other officers appeared, and on enquiring from the sergeants as to who was in charge, they informed me that they did not know. Officers did not attend parades — the senior N.C.O. took charge, and they carried on training between them. They then asked me if I would take charge and carry on the parade. I did so. I found to my astonishment that there was no organisation in the company. The N.C.O.s had no particular command; they just distributed themselves through the parade and did the best they could. We spent the afternoon in organisation, appointed N.C.O.s to definite jobs, to the satisfaction of all concerned, and the troops returned to camp happier than they had left it. They had begun to feel already that someone was taking an interest in them at last. It was a new experience for them. My friend of the machine-gun party, Lieut. Vinnicombe, had done the same with the men of his battalion.[3] At the issue of rations for the evening

---

3 This was evidently Lieutenant F.A. Vinnicombe, a 23-year-old farmer from Romsey with brown eyes and hair. A 6th Battalion original, initially a private, he had been commissioned just before the August offensive, but suffered a broken leg during it. Now recovered, he was, like Barrie, on his way back to the war. Vinnicombe was mentioned in dispatches, became a major in 1928, and died in a car accident in 1942.

meal, Vinnicombe and I were again the only officers present. We mentioned the matter to our C.O. that evening. He looked surprised, and told us we did not need to bother about parades — there were plenty of N.C.O.s to carry on. We remarked that we hoped he did not mind us 'butting in'. He missed the sarcasm and assured us we were welcome to, if we were looking for work. At reveille next morning, Vinnicombe and I were out, and attended morning roll call. There was no sign of movement from the officers' lines, and we were again the only officers on parade. We inspected the men's breakfast, then proceeded to the mess for our own. The table was not laid and there was no-one present. Seeking the cook, we enquired what time he served breakfast. He seemed surprised to see us and said, 'Well, you can have it in a few minutes, sir. Will you have it in your tent?'

'No,' I replied. 'We will have it in the mess.'

'Alright, sir. I'll get the table set.'

'Don't you usually set the table?'

'Not for breakfast, sir. The officers generally have it in their tents, and we are not allowed to disturb some of them until nine o'clock.'

'Hell!' I said. 'And this is war.'

We instructed him that we would take our breakfast at eight o'clock each morning, and left him to his cooking.

'What do you think of it, Vin?' I asked.

'I would like to see Pompey walk in,' he replied.

The same thought was in my head. However, it was not our pigeon. Though we were both senior to our C.O., it was his job, not ours. As we walked through the lines later on, on our way to parade, batmen were rushing back and forth with breakfast trays to the officers' tents. This was all happening in full view of the troops — there was no secret about it, and we had no authority to interfere. If this was the type of man the Australian Government were giving commissions to, it would be a poor look-out for the A.I.F. What leaders they would make. There was a rude shock awaiting some of them when they joined their units, if they ever did. It struck me that some of them were not too eager to do so.

The men in camp were a very fine type, mostly young

reinforcements, with a sprinkling of men returning to duty from hospital after wounds or sickness. I noticed on parade that their clothing was a bit ragged, but presumed that they were wearing old clothes for work and preserving their good clothing for use when they left for the front. I made no comment, thinking it was a wise precaution. A few days later, a draft was detailed to leave by train that evening. I instructed the sergeant to parade the men of the 8th Battalion for kit inspection, so that I could see that every man was properly clothed and equipped. To my surprise, they still wore their ragged clothing, some with the elbows out of their tunics, some with the seats out of their breeches — but worst of all for infantrymen was the state of their boots. There was not a good pair amongst them. In several cases the soles were worn right through, and in two cases the toes were protruding. I took the sergeant to task for not having them properly clothed, and said, 'They can't go in that state, Sergeant. They will have to go back to their tents and put decent clothing on.'

'That's all the clothing they have, sir,' replied the sergeant.

'What!' I exclaimed. 'Well, you had better parade the whole lot to the Q.M.'s store and get them fitted out and I will inspect them later on.'

I finished the inspection of kits and the sergeant marched them off. A few minutes later, the sergeant reported that the quartermaster refused to issue any clothing.

'Why?' I asked.

'He says they are not entitled to it, sir, but they can have what they want on payment.'

'Payment, be damned,' I said. 'What does he mean by payment?'

'Ten shillings for a pair of boots, ten shillings for a pair of breeches, and so on.'

'What is the idea, Sergeant? The clothing seems to me to be suffering from fair wear and tear.'

'So it is, sir,' said the sergeant, 'and when those men marched into this camp a few weeks ago, everyone was provided with a complete new outfit ready to march out at a moment's notice. Then one day a muster parade was ordered, and the whole camp sent on a route march, carrying a midday meal. While we were out, the quartermaster went through the camp and took every man's kit bag and put the contents into store, even to his underclothing. Naturally the men were wearing their old clothes, keeping their good things until they went to the front. He said they were not entitled to the second issue, but they could have what they wanted on payment.'

'My hat!' I said. I had heard of the doings of some quartermasters, and though I did not believe all the stories, this was the limit. I sent him back to his draft with instructions to tell them not to pay for anything, and to stand by until I came.

I reported the matter to our C.O. and requested him to give instructions to the quartermaster to make the issue. He did not appear interested. The quartermaster knew his job, and he could see no reason to interfere. The quartermaster obviously did know his job, and I suspected he had a partner in the business.

'Very well,' I said, 'but that clothing will be issued before the troops leave this depot.'

He reminded me that he was in charge of the depot and advised me to mind my own business.

'This is my business,' I replied, 'and I am going to see it through.'

Sending for two or three sergeants, I questioned them regarding the raid on the men's kits. They each corroborated the story. Instructing the sergeant in charge to march his draft to the quartermaster's store again, I preceded him and interviewed the quartermaster.

Bidding him good day, I said, 'I am parading the 8th Battalion quota of the draft for issue of clothing, and I'd be glad if you would fit them out as quickly as possible.'

'They have been here already,' he said, 'and I have told them they are not entitled to any free issue. They can have what they want on payment.'

I looked hard at him for a minute, and replied, 'I wouldn't raise the question of payment if I were you. These men are leaving for the front, and they have got to be clothed.'

'I'm running this job,' he blustered, 'and I would thank you not to butt in. I have got no clothing for them.'

'Who is all this for then?' I asked, pointing around his store, which was literally piled to the roof with clothing.

'That's my business. You've got no right here, and I would thank you to get out.'

'Now, look here,' I said, 'I haven't time to argue further. My men are here. You will either equip them at once to my satisfaction, or I will march the whole lot to division headquarters and make a full report to the camp commandant — including the method by which you stocked your store.'

His face turned white, then red, and he blustered again. Ignoring him, I said quietly to the sergeant, 'File your men in, Sergeant.'

When he quietened down again, I asked, 'Well, what is it to be?'

'Alright,' he said. 'I'll issue them, and if there is any trouble about it, you'll be responsible.'

He was furious, and I knew that was only bluff. I cheerfully accepted the responsibility and supervised the issue myself, insisting on every man getting clothing to fit him, and a full and complete issue, to the further annoyance of the quartermaster and his staff.

I became very unpopular over this incident, but that did not worry me. I was not seeking popularity in base depot.

A few days later, a 1st Division officer, Major Luxton of the 5th Battalion, arrived from the front to take over the job of camp commandant.[4] It was the practice to send officers of long service to this job, changing every six weeks, thus affording them a spell from front-line duty. I knew Major Luxton well, having served with him in a militia battalion at home before the war. We had been subalterns together. He had survived the Gallipoli campaign and achieved well-earned promotion. He was invited to dine with us on our guest night. Sitting next to me at dinner, he gave me all the latest news of the brigade. After dinner he excused himself on the plea of duty and said goodnight. Turning to me, he said, 'You had better walk down with me, Dan.'

---

4   D.A. Luxton, one of the 5th Battalion's initial lieutenants, was to become its commander in 1917 when only 25. A clerk from Hawthorn, he was awarded the DSO and CMG and mentioned in dispatches.

When we got clear of the mess, he said, 'I am not really in a hurry to get back. Come for a walk along the beach. I want to talk to you.'

It was a beautiful night. We lit our pipes and strolled along the sand.

'I suppose you are anxious to get back to the battalion, eh?'

'Yes, very,' I replied. 'I was going to ask you if you could fix it for me.'

'Well,' he said, 'I have just left the brigade, and your battalion is full. They have not been in action and can't absorb you yet. Now I want you to do something for me.'

'What is it?' I asked.

'I want you to take command of the 2nd Brigade Depot.'

I immediately lodged a vehement protest, explaining how I had been stuck at Weymouth, and if there was one thing more than another I wanted to dodge, it was another depot job.

He laughed and said, 'I expected that, but now listen, and I will tell you what it is all about. There has been some funny business going on here, and I have been sent down with instructions to straighten the show up. Drafts have been arriving from this depot with their clothing in a bad state and have had to be fitted by our units. C.O.s naturally wanted to know why, and the men all told the same story. You know what has been happening?'

I admitted I had certain suspicions.

'Well then,' he continued, 'these two fellows, C.O. and Q.M. have applied for leave to England. Having never joined their units, they are not entitled to it, but their applications will be approved. It is the easiest way to get rid of them and save a scandal. On their return, their jobs will be filled and they can join their units.

'We have definite knowledge that the Q.M. has recently sent home a draft for sixty pounds through a local bank, and there are other amounts as well, which didn't come out of his pay. Of course, he may have been lucky at cards, but we suspect it is the proceeds of the sale of clothing to the troops. The matter of a court-martial is left to my discretion. I think it better to get rid of them quietly, but you see, I must have someone here that I can depend on to straighten things up.'

Then with a smile, he finished, 'So that is why I am appointing you. And you needn't worry about getting stuck on the job. I give you my word that as soon as there is a vacancy in your unit, I will let you go.'

I accepted. I was apparently going to be appointed anyway, but that relieved my mind. Still, I stipulated that I be allowed to choose my own staff. This was readily granted, and I nominated Lieut. Adams of the 6th Battalion, commonly known as Bill Adams, who had just arrived, as adjutant,[5] and Vinnicombe as quartermaster. My selection was readily approved.

'That's alright then,' said Major Luxton. 'You can tell the other two all about it. And be ready to take over tomorrow. I will put it in orders tonight.'

I enquired as to how far my powers went, and got a ready permission to re-issue the troops with their clothing. After further instructions to 'shake these young officers up', and to see that they did not get breakfast in bed in future, we parted for the night.

Returning to camp, I imparted the news to my new staff. Like me, they were not over-keen at first, but when they heard the story and had Major Luxton's assurance, they were satisfied and agreed to their appointments.

Next morning, camp orders were issued notifying approval of leave for the two men, and our appointment to our respective jobs. This was rather a setback, as they had made their own arrangements for relief. However, they handed over in high glee, and spent the rest of the day cleaning and polishing in preparation for their departure in the evening. They both sewed their unit colour patches on their sleeves, to which they were not entitled until they joined their units.

---

5 Bill Adams, an orchardist, was an original 5th Battalion private, but became an officer at Gallipoli, where he transferred to the 6th Battalion and was evacuated twice, due to an arm wound and then illness. He was severely gassed in mid-1918, but almost half a century later was able to apply for his Gallipoli Medal at the age of 80.

We smiled, but said nothing — and after imparting instructions to us for the conduct of the job during their absence, they departed on the evening train.

Asking all officers to wait after mess that night, I told them what would be expected of them in future, and imparted the sad news that breakfast would not be served in bed in future, except on authority of the medical officer. All officers would attend early morning parade at 6.30 a.m. and breakfast in the mess at eight. Allotment of duties would be arranged and posted as soon as possible. The announcement was not popular, and one or two openly expressed their disapproval. I told them that although I highly approved the change myself, it was being made under instructions and they would be wise to obey, and closed the argument.

Next morning, two or three were absent from early morning parade and ordered breakfast in bed as usual. They were very annoyed when the cook refused to supply it. At 10.00 a.m., they were requested to appear in Orderly Room. They were still truculent. I told them I did not wish to take the matter further, but certainly would if my instructions were not obeyed. They seemed to have no idea of their duties or responsibilities, and still considered that we had no right to interfere with the routine of the camp. We decided there was nothing for it but to have an officer roll call also, and ordered that all officers report to Orderly Room at 6.15 a.m. We hated doing it, but while we did not want to run them into trouble, we could not allow them to defy us.

They were really good chaps at heart, but had been wrongly led and were unfortunate in being left at the depot for so long, without an opportunity to join their units. They soon came to their senses, the roll call was discontinued, and we became a happy family. We re-organised the depot, appointing all officers to definite jobs, and arranged a syllabus of training.

Having completed this, taking a company at a time, we re-issued the troops with clothing. The quartermaster sergeant made a vehement protest at this, stating that he had received definite instructions from the quartermaster that nothing was to be touched during his absence. I wondered if he was in the business, too, and after a five minute interview with him, he had a much clearer idea as to where he stood. He did not voice any more protests. Having cleared out the store, we then moved it to a more convenient position, as it was blocking one of the main camp roads where it was. After this, the work of the camp ran smoothly.

There had been an undercurrent of discontent before, which had disappeared, and everybody was happy. Even the officers began to take an interest in their jobs, and saw the error of their previous ways. It had been unpleasant in the beginning, but I knew I had a good solid backing with Bill Adams and Vinnicombe to support me. We were all members of the original division, and that is saying everything.

Chapter Eleven

Étaples itself is only a small town, known to history as Napoleon's headquarters when he was gathering his army at Boulogne for the invasion of England. It was now a big British training depot, of which the Australian depot was only a very small part. A big training school was attached to the camp, which all reinforcements had to attend for a special course of training in the use of gas, bombing, bayonet fighting, and the like. This was commonly known as the 'bull ring', and was presided over by a major of one of the guards' regiments and a staff of British regulars. It was supplemented by instructors from front-line units on the same principle as our camp commandant, changing every six weeks.

Two or three instructors called on us one evening and stayed to dine. They were members of various British regiments, and very fine chaps. One of them, known as 'Scotty', an officer of the Royal Scots, was very clever at card tricks, and bewildered us with his science after dinner. They invited us to dine on their guest night the following week. Official invitations duly arrived, and Bill Adams and I went. The major was a very austere person with a monocle, and the dinner was very formal and stiff. I sat next to Scotty, and I could see he was restless all through the meal. Their marquee was the biggest I have seen, with six-foot perpendicular sides, and the roof sloping up to a central pole about twenty feet high.

After dinner, the major and staff retired by one end of the tent, and instructors and guests by the other. It was a beautiful moonlight night. The party was standing in groups outside the tent, talking and smoking. Scotty, gazing up at the moon, which was just showing over the tent pole, said, 'It's a braw pole. I would like fine to climb it.'

'Are you any good at it?' I asked.

'Mon,' he said, 'I'm the champion tent climber of the British Army.'

'Splendid,' I replied, 'I'm the champion of the A.I.F.'

'The hell you are. Come on then, I'll race you to the top.'

Never thinking he would do it, I accepted the challenge. In a moment, he had announced the competition to the crowd, and to my surprise everybody took it up with enthusiasm. It was announced as a contest for the championship of the British Army. Judge, starter, and timekeeper were appointed, and we were each allowed a 'legger up'. I chose Bill Adams. I had started off in fun, but was now definitely committed. I could not withdraw. Bets were laid freely, and Scotty and I had a side bet between us. Conditions were announced and the judge ordered us to stations, one at each corner, so that each would have a clear run. The winner had to reach the top of the pole and sit astride it.

We went off to a good start and clambered up the canvas to the cheers and encouragement of our respective backers. It was a good race, and I managed to reach the pole about a foot ahead of Scotty, and duly sat on it to the satisfaction of the judge. As I reached the pole, Scotty said,

'Psht! There's the major. Get down' — and turning over, he tobogganed off the roof. I did the same on the opposite side, with less luck than Scotty. I landed in the middle of a group consisting of the major and his staff, who were loudly demanding to know who was on the roof. I knocked over the major himself and one other, then fled for my life while they were picking each other up.

The onlookers were shrieking with delight, but, anticipating ructions, they quickly dispersed to quarters, taking us with them.

Scotty appeared a few minutes later, and amid much laughter he formally handed over the 'belt', and I was duly acclaimed the Champion Tent Climber of the British Army. Bets were settled, then Scotty, remarking that discretion was the better part of valour, suggested a walk to give the major a chance to cool down. He preferred to postpone the forthcoming interview until the morning. We walked back to our lines, taking Scotty and a couple of his pals with us. Bidding them goodnight later on, I invited them to come again. They all said they would, except Scotty, who replied, 'You'll no be seeing me. I'll be away back to the line tomorrow.'

'Why?' I said, 'I thought you had only recently arrived.'

'Ay, so I have, but I'm no thinking the major will be over pleased at having his monocle knocked out of his eye tonight.'

We all laughed at the recollection, and I expressed regret that he should have to take the punishment.

'Och! It's not worrying me,' he said. 'I'd as soon be back with the brave boys.'

His anticipations were realised. He went the next day. They told me afterwards that his only regret was the loss of his title. He hoped he would meet me again and have the opportunity to retrieve it. I never met him again, and my claim was never challenged.

At the end of a fortnight, our heroes returned from leave. Adams and I were in the office one day when our ex-C.O. bounded in, full of vigour and vim.

'Hullo, you fellows,' he shouted. 'Just got back from leave. Had a great time in London.'

We were pleased to hear it.

'I'll take over now,' he said.

'Have you reported to Division?' I asked.

'No, not yet,' he replied. 'Plenty of time. I'll report later.'

'Better do it first,' I suggested. 'And we'll be pleased to hand over to you on your return.' (Which, I might add, we undoubtedly would.)

While he was still talking, in bounced the quartermaster in a towering rage.

'Who shifted my tent?' he shouted.

'I issued the instructions for it to be moved,' I replied quietly.

'You did, eh?' he fumed. 'What did you do with my stores?'

'I issued them to the troops.'

'Right,' he said, 'you'll hear more about this. I'm going straight down to Division to report it.'

'Do,' I said, smiling. 'Let us know how you get on.'

'I'll let you know, alright,' he yelled. Turning to his partner, he said, 'You'd better come with me and settle this.'

They went. They returned half an hour later, looking very crestfallen. I could imagine the result of the interview. Though I knew they deserved it, I felt sorry for them, and we did not open the subject again. Next morning, I received instructions that they were both to attend the 'bull ring' for training, and for a fortnight afterwards they marched out of camp every morning at 8.00 a.m. with the 'bull ring' squad, carrying a full pack on their backs, to the ill-concealed delight of the troops, and to their own chagrin.

In order to express their appreciation of the change in the administration of the camp, the sergeants invited me to dine at their mess one night. I gladly accepted the invitation. There were several amongst them from my own and other battalions from the brigade whom I knew well, and I was glad of the opportunity to fraternise with them off duty. They were wonderfully fine chaps, and I felt proud of the honour they had done me in inviting me to their mess. They spread themselves exceedingly for the occasion, and put on a very fine dinner. I have never seen so much champagne at a single function, before or since. Their hospitality was of no mean order. They had set themselves out to give me a good night, and though I thoroughly enjoyed the evening, I could never let it be said that the sergeants had seen me under the table, as I realised the necessity of adopting a passive resistance policy from the outset.

In accordance with custom when officers dine in the sergeants' mess, so as not to cramp their style and restrain the evening's pleasure, I rose to go at the conclusion of dinner. They would not hear of me leaving, as they said they had arranged for my return home later. So I stayed, and moved around the mess chatting to all the fellows I knew, and the evening proceeded merrily. At 11.00 p.m., the president rose and called the mess to order. There was instant silence, and my 'carriage' was announced. A sharp command was given by someone at the entrance, and in marched a stretcher party composed of four officers under the command of Bill Adams. The party halted in the centre of the mess, lowered the stretcher, and, after they had partaken of the hospitality of the mess, I was shouldered and laid carefully on the stretcher. Then, with proper ceremony, the stretcher was raised, and the party marched off to the accompaniment of cheers from the sergeants, and much laughter from everyone, including myself. It was a good end to a good evening, and though I was perfectly fit to walk home without any inconvenience, everybody joined in the joke and I was borne to the door of my tent.

Shortly after this, a call came from 1st Division for a number of officers to proceed to the front and join their units. Major Luxton was true to his promise. I was instructed to hand over my duties, and join the draft. At last, after all those months of striving and wangling, I was allowed to get back to the war. I could have yelled for joy. It appeared to me and the others situated like me, far harder to get to it than from it. Going to my tent to pack, after handing over my job, I found a deputation of half a dozen N.C.O.s — including Sergeant Major Baker of the 7th Battalion, Sergeant Maynard of the 8th Battalion, and Sergeant Young of the 6th Battalion, all of whom were well known to me — waiting for me.[1] They wanted to join the draft. They were frightfully disappointed when I told them that no troops were to go, but only officers and batmen.

'Couldn't you wangle some way for us to go?' they asked.

I was afraid it was impossible. I would gladly have done anything I could do to assist them, as I knew what splendid, solid chaps they were, and how welcome they would be with their units. As I have said, I knew Baker at home in the old militia days. Maynard had been in my company and had helped carry me out of the firing line when I was wounded at the Gallipoli landing, Young was of the original 6th, and the others were of the same type. They went off, looking

---

[1] Bill Baker, a 34-year-old collar-maker from North Melbourne, was widely admired for his bravery and conscientiousness. A 7th Battalion original, he was wounded at the Gallipoli landing. Having recently recovered from a bout of ill-health, he had just been transferred from hospital to the base at Étaples when he caught up with Barrie. Baker was awarded the MSM and was mentioned in dispatches, and survived the war. It has not been possible to identify Baker's companions in the deputation to Barrie at Étaples.

very downhearted. As they were leaving, I requested Sergeant Major Baker to send my batman to me to help pack. Having occasion to leave my tent for a few minutes, I returned to find my batman on his knees, packing my valise. Though I could only see his back, it struck me as being not quite familiar. When I spoke to him, he answered without raising his head. As I shifted my position to get a better look at him, he shifted his also and kept on steadily packing. Getting tired of this game, I asked him to give me a hand with something which necessitated his rising and revealing himself. It was Sergeant Young. His stripes had been removed from his sleeve. I looked at him a minute and said, 'So it is you, is it Young? I thought your back was unfamiliar. What's the big idea?'

'No, sir,' he replied. 'I'm Private O'Brien. You sent for me to pack your kit.'

I smiled. 'You can't get away with that,' I said.

'I don't understand you, sir,' he replied. 'I'm your batman.'

'You'll be caught, as sure as eggs,' I said.

'I'll have a darned good try for it, sir, if you don't put me away.'

My thoughts flew back to my own experience in Weymouth. How could I blame him for doing what I myself had done?

'Alright, O'Brien,' I said, 'Get on with your job, but I had better leave you to it. I don't want to know anything about it.'

A look of relief spread over his face. He smiled and said, 'Thank you, sir. You don't need to worry about your kit. I'll fix it up.'

I left him to it. I had hardly left the tent when Sergeant Major Baker appeared.

'About the baggage guard, sir,' he said, 'Do you think you could arrange for me to take charge of it? I would like to come to the station to see you off.'

'Oh, I don't think we will need a baggage guard, Sergeant Major,' I said. 'Each officer is taking his batman with him.'

'You can't trust the batmen, sir,' he said. 'They are mostly inexperienced young reinforcements. Better have a guard and make certain everything is right. Besides,' he repeated, 'I'd like to see you off.'

'Alright,' I said, 'I'll see if I can get permission.'

Permission was given, and Baker was instructed to detail four men and take charge himself. He thanked me and assured me he would pick a good team, and I need not worry about the baggage. He did. The train left at about 5.00 p.m. On arrival at the station I went along to the baggage van to make sure that the baggage was intact. It was stacked on the platform with the guard standing by. It was a good team alright, being composed of Sergeant Maynard and three other N.C.O.s, all of whom, like Sergeant Young, had temporarily and voluntarily reverted to the rank of private. Pretending not to notice, I spoke to Sergeant Major Baker, who assured me the baggage was intact, and he would see it loaded. I enquired for 'Private O'Brien'. He was in the van.

'There appears to have been wholesale reductions in ranks in the camp today, Sergeant Major,' I said.

He smiled. 'Well, sir,' he replied, 'they all wanted to come and see you off, and I thought you wouldn't mind.'

What could I say or do? After all, I had left the camp. It was no longer my job. I asked no further questions.

'That was very nice of them,' I said. 'Well, if you will see to the baggage, I had better say goodbye and get my seat.'

They all came and shook hands and wished me good luck, and hoped to see me soon. I had a feeling they would. I returned their good wishes, and boarded the train.

Horse trucks were again supplied for our accommodation. We spread our valises on the floor and made things as comfortable as possible. As the train started, I looked out the door to wave goodbye to Sergeant Major Baker and the baggage party. There was no sign of them on the platform. I wondered at not seeing them before I left. The train rumbled on all through the night. Everybody crawled into their valises and did their best to sleep. There was nothing else to do in a horse truck without lights. Shortly after daylight, the train stopped at a siding. I got out and went along to the baggage van to see how the batmen were fairing. As I boarded the van, the first person I saw was Sergeant Major Baker. I stopped dead and stared.

'Great Scott, Baker!' I said. 'What the dickens are you doing here?'

'Well, sir,' he replied, 'we were all in the van busy stacking the baggage when the train started off, and before we realised it was moving, it was going too fast for us to jump out.'

'Who do you mean by "all"?' I asked.

'All the baggage guard, sir.'

'Where are they?'

'They are all here, sir,' he said, pointing round at several recumbent forms. And out they all came from their various corners.

'By gum!' I said, 'You'll get me into a row over this. What are you going to do about your kits?'

'We'll take the blame, sir,' said Baker. 'But there won't be any row once we get back to our units. And by good luck, we brought our kits along with us, just in case of accidents.'

It was no good. I had to laugh. And I knew they were right about the row. Their C.O.s would cover them. I was not worried.

'Alright,' I said. 'But you will have to lose yourselves when we leave the train. We have to report at division headquarters, and you'll be arrested if you go near there.'

They assured me they would take care of themselves and find their own way to their units. And I knew they were capable of doing so.

Early that afternoon, we detrained at Vignacourt. We were still a long way from our destination. Leaving our heavy baggage to be picked up later, we started to walk. It was getting dark when we arrived at the village of Senlis, hungry, thirsty, and tired. A British cavalry regiment was billeted there, and they insisted on our remaining there the night as their guests. As we had only completed about half our journey, we gladly accepted their invitation. They gave us a meal, and went out of their way to do everything possible to make us comfortable.

There had been heavy fighting around Senlis in the early part of the war, and though the village was still standing, it was badly shattered by shell fire, and not a house remained intact. It was our first glimpse of the damage done in the war zone, and though it was bad enough, it was nothing to that which we saw later on. After an early breakfast next morning, we thanked our hosts for their hospitality, said goodbye, and started off on the tramp again.

We arrived at the 1st Division headquarters at about 11.00 a.m. The brigade was in the front line, and we were ordered to report to the officer in charge of brigade details at Albert. After a short rest, we set off again on another long tramp, and finally arrived there in the late afternoon. Major Hart of the 7th Battalion was in charge, with a reserve of officers and N.C.O.s of the 2nd Brigade.[2] We could get no definite information as to what has happening, except that the brigade had been in action, and though successful they had suffered heavy casualties. We were shown to our billets and ordered to stand by for a call to join our units. What had actually happened was that they had fought the first Battle of Pozières and were still in the front line.

We were kept at Albert for about three days. We had to stick pretty close to our billets all day in case we were sent for, and were only allowed to leave them for short periods. Albert was a fair-sized town, and though it had been held by the Allies from the beginning, it was within easy range of the German guns and was sadly shattered by shell fire. The civilian inhabitants had evacuated it in the first days of the war, and it had been used for billeting troops ever since. Big shells were falling at intervals in the town all day.

The outstanding point of interest in Albert was the statue of the 'Madonna and Child' on the steeple of a church, which was hanging over the roadway at an angle of about 135 degrees. The church was built close to the street, with a short flight of steps from the footpath to the main door. The statue was on a gilt dome at the top of the steeple, which was built straight up from the front wall. The dome was made of a steel network, covered with plaster. A German shell had cut through the dome on one side, and the weight of the statue had caused it to fall over, and hang in that awkward position. It gave the impression that it was liable to fall at any minute, and troops

---

2   Major A.G.C. Hart was an experienced militia officer and state public servant whose most recent position was Clerk of Courts at Eaglehawk. Now 49 years of age, he had been in charge of the 8th reinforcements batch of the 7th Battalion, and had served at Gallipoli.

passing along the road would look up and then involuntarily increase their pace when passing underneath it. I experienced this feeling myself many a time within the next few months, when passing along that road on our journeys in and out of the line.

The French people are very superstitious, and there was a belief amongst them that when the statue fell, the war would end. We laughed about it because we knew that British engineers had strengthened the part that was holding it, and there was little likelihood of it falling unless hit with another shell — and that was a very remote possibility. The Germans had retreated to the Hindenburg Line, after which Albert was no longer under shell fire, and many of the civilian population returned to their homes. Nevertheless, the belief persisted, and, strange to say, it came true.

In 1918, in the Germans' last effort to win, when they broke through the junction of the British and French lines and routed the British 5th Army, they advanced again across the old Somme battlefield, and were very close to Albert before they were checked. The inhabitants had to evacuate for the second time. The town was very heavily shelled and the church was practically demolished. The statue fell, and from that day the Germans advanced no further. The end for them was in sight. From then on, they suffered defeat after defeat until the end finally came in November — and when it came, the British Army was again at Mons, on the ground where it had first encountered the Germans in 1914.

On the morning of the third day, we got orders to join our units. Battalion headquarters were in the vicinity of La Boisselle, and we set off along the Bapaume Road. We had not very far to go. I found the 8th Battalion in the old German trenches near La Boisselle and reported my arrival at headquarters.[3] They had been relieved in the front line during the night, and were resting there for the day. They had had a gruelling time, having attacked and captured Pozières village, which the Germans had boasted would never be taken, and had held the captured position for five days and nights, during which

---

3 According to the 8th Battalion unit diary, Barrie rejoined on 27 July 1916 and was allotted to B Company.

time they had been subjected to incessant shell fire and practically no sleep. They had sustained about 300 casualties, and were too exhausted to move further.

I learnt what company I was allotted to, and where to find them, and went off to join them. I found them, almost to a man, sound asleep, lying on the floor of the trench, anywhere they could find room to lie down. Dixies of hot stew and tea had just arrived from the cookers but failed to interest them. The majority just grunted and rolled over, and went to sleep again. Very few came for their meal. I met a few old timers, some of whom came over from other companies on hearing of my arrival to welcome me back. After their meal, they went back to their rest again, and they looked as if they needed it.

Knowing the battalion would not move until dark, I went to look at the famous mine crater and trenches at La Boisselle, close by. The crater was caused by the explosion of a mine by the British troops a few weeks earlier at the commencement of the 'great push', and was intended to wreck a German strong point built of concrete in the trenches at La Boisselle. Unfortunately the British engineers miscalculated the distance, and the mine burst short of the objective, and did no damage.[4] It was an enormous crater; it looked to me big enough to contain the Melbourne Town Hall. The opposing trenches here were about five or six hundred yards apart on either side of a shallow valley, and the British troops had suffered tremendous casualties in the attack. Had the mine been successful, it would have lightened their task considerably. The strong point was built on a rise, and overlooked and controlled No Man's Land for hundreds of yards on either side as well as to the front. It was built entirely of concrete, with a breast-high wall all round for the protection of the garrison, with rooms and galleries three storeys deep underneath for their accommodation when off duty. On the outside wall could be

---

4 The tunnels did not quite extend to right under the German front line, but were close enough to do plenty of damage, obliterating various trenches and up to nine deep dug-outs, which usually accommodated about 35 infantrymen each.

seen the marks where our shells had hit, but they made very little impression. The underground rooms were also of concrete, and supplied with stoves for heating purposes.[5] Some were quite decently furnished. One room, evidently the officers' dining room, contained a good dining table with a cloth and the remains of a meal on it. The occupants had evidently left in a hurry.

On my way back to my company, I came across an old pal, Lieut. 'Puss' Catani of the 21st Battalion. Their brigade had relieved the 2nd the night before, and his battalion was in support of the front line, waiting their turn to go in. I stayed and talked with him for half an hour, and promised to look him up again if we were in their vicinity. He was a very popular chap, and I was very fond of him, but I never saw him again. He was killed a few nights later, when going up to relieve the front line.[6]

The troops were served their evening meal at about 5.30 p.m. They were all awake now, and I met many old friends, and received a warm welcome from them all. Many fellows I had known as privates were now N.C.O.s, and N.C.O.s were now officers — but there were big gaps amongst the old faces, filled by many new ones. At dark, the battalion fell in and moved off towards Albert, where we were to bivouac for the night. Looking back up Sausage Valley towards the front line, it was like a display of fireworks. The line was alight from end to end as far as we could see, with one incessant stream of flares shooting into the air and bursting over No Man's Land. It was a short march back to Albert. We moved straight on to an open field on the outskirts of the town known as 'the brickfields', formed column, and bivouacked where we stood. It was an unpleasant night; black, cold, and showery; but the troops had a lot of sleep to make up and were not long turning in. In company with another officer, I made a 'bivvy'

---

5   German positions tended to be constructed more thoroughly, with more extended occupation in mind than British equivalents.
6   Enrico Catani was a 25-year-old grazier. His sister stated in 1932 that their brother Ettore had 'never recovered' from Enrico's death. Their father, Carlo Catani, was an accomplished and influential engineer with the Victorian Public Works department.

by lacing two waterproof sheets together. We stretched our valises underneath, removed our boots, and turned in, too.

We had hardly got into bed when we heard the scream of shells approaching. We both sat up and listened. There were four of them, and they burst in quick succession, evenly spread from one corner of the field to the other. Fortunately, they missed us, and no-one was hurt, so we lay down again and tried to sleep. About half an hour later, another four shells exploded, and this kept up at half-hour intervals throughout the night. After about the fourth round, we heard cries for help from an artillery ammunition column in another corner of the field, and several of our people got out of bed and went to give a hand. One shell had burst very close to their horse lines, and scared the horses. They were afraid of a stampede, and were trying to move the horses in the dark. We did what we could to help. The next round came and did no harm; the horses took no notice of it, so the men decided to leave them where they were. We went back to bed and slept. Next morning, though everyone was cursing at having their rest disturbed, there were no casualties.

Up to this time I had not seen the C.O. He had been sleeping when I reported, and I had talked with the adjutant. I saw him during the morning for a few minutes, but he did not have much to say. He said he would see me again later on. I knew him well; he had been one of the original officers, but we had never been particularly friendly, and I was disappointed at finding him in command on my return.[7] Lieut. Col. Brand had been in command of the battalion, but he had recently been promoted to the command of the 4th Brigade.[8] Though everybody was pleased at his promotion, the battalion was sorry to lose him. He was a great soldier, and his successor was cordially hated by all ranks. He had been a shirker from the first, and had

---

7 Graham Coulter, a 36-year-old Ballarat accountant, commanded the 8th Battalion from July 1916 to April 1917 (and earlier at times in an acting capacity).
8 'Digger' Brand held a variety of significant positions in the AIF. He was 42 when he left the 8th Battalion in mid-1916. After retiring from the army in 1933 as a major-general, he became a senator for Victoria.

never done his job. Many a time in the early days in Broadmeadows and in Egypt, we had covered up for him when he had been lying in bed in the morning, still drunk from the night before, when he ought to have been on duty. The whole battalion knew that he had never reached the firing line at the Landing, and he had the reputation of never having seen the front line since, and when some months later he was relieved of his command and sent home in disgrace, that reputation went with him.[9] It did not take me long to sense that the battalion was not happy. The troops were seething with indignation at his behaviour during the recent fight. They declared quite openly that he had remained in his dug-out, drinking, during the whole time they were in the line, and the adjutant had conducted the fight, and organised the line afterwards.[10] Of course one cannot listen to that sort of thing, and I did my best to squash it. I mentioned the matter to some of the officers afterwards, and they all agreed that it was bad. They had the same thing in their own companies, they said, and the worst of it was that it was true.

I had often wondered whether that man realised and appreciated the loyalty of his officers, and the manner in which they covered up for him and carried him on their backs during the months that he held the command. Men like Mitchell, Yates, Catron, Traill, Lodge, Wallis, Mummery, and others like them who, while they held him in supreme contempt, were so imbued with 'esprit de corps', that, for the sake of the battalion, they would never let him down, while they themselves were held in such high esteem by the troops that the men would follow them anywhere. I felt that he was not pleased to see me return. He probably felt that I knew too much about him and when,

---

9   Military records confirm that, in November 1917, Coulter's services were declared to be no longer required in either the AIF's First Division or in the AIF's depots in the United Kingdom (then headed by General McCay), and he was returned to Australia. Two brothers of his died while serving in the AIF.

10 The adjutant was Captain Gus Lodge, who had enlisted at the start of the war as a 19-year-old coachman from Hamilton. Wounded at Gallipoli and again in France, he was awarded the DSO for bravery at Pozières, and was one of the 8th Battalion's most popular officers.

about three months later, Yates and Catron also re-joined, they met with the same cold reception, though he never had better officers in his battalion than those two.[11]

We left Albert in the late morning and bivouacked that night in a beautiful wood near the village of Warloy. Passing through Warloy village, the troops were delighted to see their old C.O., Brigadier General Brand, who with several other officers, was standing in front of the Hotel de Ville. As each company passed, they cheered him heartily. Hearing his old battalion was going through, he had come to see them, and to show his appreciation of their good work at Pozières. On a blackboard alongside him was written, 'Well done 8th'. It was praise well earned, but every man felt a thrill of pride at it coming from the 'Old Digger', as he was affectionately known by all ranks.

We remained in the wood for three days, and the troops were allowed a thorough rest. From there, the battalion moved by easy stages to the village of Canaples, which we reached at the end of a week. Canaples was a beautiful village, a long way from the front line and out of the sound of guns. We stayed a fortnight there to rest and refit. My company was bivouacked in an orchard, and the troops thoroughly enjoyed a well-earned rest. Batches of reinforcements joined us, and at the end of the fortnight we were more or less up to strength again. Then one day we packed up and started on the march back. We moved again by easy stages and were a week on the road. At the end of a month, the brigade, fit and strong again, was back in Sausage Valley.

The 5th and 6th battalions took over the front line, occupying trenches known as O.G.1 and O.G.2, near the Pozières windmill, close to Mouquet Farm. The 7th and 8th remained in support in old German trenches in Sausage Valley. About 100 yards behind

---

11 Despite Barrie's condemnation of Coulter's shortcomings — based on his own observations together with what he heard from other officers — Coulter was awarded the DSO and was mentioned in dispatches for his leadership at Pozières. According to the award citations, the battalion did well and he 'handled' it capably.

our position was a line of eighteen-pounder field guns, as far as one could see. Behind them were lines of sixty-pounders, 4.5 Howitzers, and 9.2s as close as it was possible to pack them. I had never seen so many guns before, and when they were in action the roar was terrific and the ground literally shook. The strange thing I noticed about them was that each line of guns had a breastwork of sandbags for protection against hostile fire, built in rear of the guns. I could not work out why, and on enquiry of the gunners, they told me they were using a good deal of American ammunition, and they were in greater danger from short bursts from the line of guns in rear than from the enemy's fire. I thought at first they were pulling my leg, but it was true.

Chapter Twelve

It was well known that the brigade had to carry out another attack, but as the 7th and 8th had done most of the fighting last time, the 5th and 6th were to do it this time — then we were to relieve them after the fight and hold the captured ground. The opposing trenches at this point were about 300 yards apart, which would render it too costly to launch the attack from the front line. It was therefore decided to dig a 'T' trench in No Man's Land to provide a jumping off place for the attack. Three parties were detailed for this job, to work in four hour shifts: Number 1 from 10.00 p.m. to 2.00 a.m., Number 2 from 2.00 a.m. to 6.00 a.m., and Number 3 from 6.00 a.m. to 10.00 a.m. The first two parties, working under cover of darkness, would have the job sufficiently far advanced to provide cover for Number 3, which would finish the job in daylight. The front-line battalion was to provide a covering party in No Man's Land for the protection of the working parties, and in the event of an attack the trench was to be held. I was detailed in command of Number 3 party, to consist of three officers, including myself, and 165 other ranks.

In the early morning, as my party was falling in ready to move onto the job, the adjutant came over with a message from brigade headquarters that I was to stand by for half an hour.

'Something has gone wrong,' he said, 'but I don't know what the trouble is.'

I checked and inspected the party, found them all present and correct, and sat down to wait further instructions. About twenty minutes later another message came, instructing me to report with my party to brigade headquarters. Brigade headquarters was in advance of our position in one of the old German dug-outs. The staff captain met me at the top of the stairs, and told me I was to stand by for a while. Enquiring the cause of the delay, he informed me that both the other parties had failed to reach their objective during the night, and the job had not been started. The brigade commander considered it too big a risk to send such a large party into No Man's Land in daylight without cover, and was in communication by telephone with division headquarters, asking for authority to postpone the job until that night. I hoped he would be successful. It was a nasty enough job in any case, but to climb over the parapet in a party of 168 and walk into the middle of No Man's Land in broad daylight was simply asking for it. The staff captain agreed with me, saying, 'They must postpone it. You would lose half your men getting there.'

After a quarter-of-an-hour wait, General Forsyth, our brigade commander, came up the stairs looking very worried. I knew him well. He was a staff officer of the Permanent Forces at home. I had met him in the days before the war, and he has visited my home on several occasions since. He was a man for whom I always had the most profound respect, both as a soldier and as a friend. The troops loved him, and they are very keen judges.[1] Bidding me good morning, he shook hands and said, 'Well, I am sorry, old chap, but I am afraid you will have to go up. You know the situation, I suppose?'

I replied that the staff captain had just told me the job had not been started.

'Yes, that is correct,' he said. 'I have been trying to persuade the division to postpone it until tonight, but they won't listen. They say if we failed during the night we will have to take the punishment and do it in daylight. They also say that the communication is partly dug, so that you can get in under cover, and the front-line garrison has a covering party in front of you.'

---

[1] Brigadier-General J.K. Forsyth had been a full-time soldier for decades after growing up in Queensland. Now 49, he had been commanding the 2nd AIF Brigade since July 1915.

'Well now,' he continued, 'I don't like it a bit. I am afraid you are going to have a bad time. I want you to keep me well supplied with information, and remember it is only a four-hour task. When your time is up, come home.'

'What about a relief, sir?' I asked.

'The front-line company will supply a garrison. Notify the officer in charge of the sector when you are leaving, and he will take over the trench and occupy it,' he replied. 'And in the event of an attack, you will hold it at all costs. That all clear?'

'Yes, sir,' I replied smiling. 'It sounds like the program for a pleasant Sunday afternoon to me.'

He smiled and said, 'I'm afraid you are not going to enjoy it half as much.'

After a few more parting instructions, and impressing on me the necessity for frequent messages, he enquired if there was anything further I wished to know.

'No, sir,' I replied. 'Everything's clear. I'll push off now.'

He shook hands again and wished me luck, instructing me to report on the way back.

Falling the party in, they filed past a heap of picks, and one of shovels, each alternate man taking one or the other. A guide was waiting to conduct us to the front line. Forming up again, we moved off at once. He took us by a rather round-about route, as the most direct communication had been knocked about by shell fire to such an extent that we could not get in without being observed. We reached the front line at a point about 200 yards distant from the job, near the old Pozières windmill, now a heap of rubble. It had been a very dirty night, and the garrison had suffered severely from shell fire. The shelling had ceased now, but they had not had time to bury their dead, and the floor of the trench for nearly the whole 200 yards we had to traverse it was covered with dead bodies. For the most part, there was not room between them to place our feet on the ground, and we literally had to walk over them. It was a gruesome sight, and a splendid introduction to the job we were undertaking.

Reaching the sector from which we were to work, I enquired for the company commander. He was in the line, and appeared in a few minutes in response to a message. It was Captain Lillie D.S.O., one of the original officers of the 5th Battalion, a splendid chap, commonly known to his intimates as 'Ginger'.[2]

'Hullo, Dan,' he said. 'What the devil are you doing here?'

'Morning, Ginger,' I replied. 'I have brought in a party to dig this "T" trench. Brigade told me to report to you, and you would show me where the job is.'

'My God! You can't get out there now.'

'Why not?' I asked. 'I have been ordered to do it.'

'Yes, but there should have been two other parties working on it last night, but they didn't get here.'

'I know that,' I replied. 'Brigade has reported that to Division. Division say we must take the punishment.'

'Oh hell!' he said. 'They're mad. I wouldn't send a dog out there now.'

'No,' I said smiling. 'But one gets unduly attached to a dog sometimes, don't you think, Ginger?'

'I get attached to my men, Dan, and I tell you it is impossible to take them out there in daylight. You can't do it.'

'Sorry, Ginger,' I replied, 'but I have been ordered to do it, and I am going to. Brigade informed me that the communication is sufficiently deep to provide cover going out, and that you have a covering party in front. Is that so?'

'It is not,' he said. 'I had a covering party out there all night, but then no-one turned up, so I withdrew them before daylight and I am not sending them out again for anyone. And as far as cover is concerned, there has never been a pick put in the job. Brigade has been misinformed.'

'Then how do I get out?' I asked.

'Step over the parapet and walk across the top,' he replied.

---

2 Cyril 'Ginger' Lillie was a 19-year-old red-haired clerk when he became one of the 5th Battalion's original lieutenants. He was a fine front-line officer despite his slight frame. Lillie survived the war, became a successful businessman in the wool industry, and was a lieutenant-colonel in World War II.

The situation was not improving, to say the least.

'Alright, show me where the pegs are.'

'Come on then,' he said. 'There's a short sap just here which you had better use if you are going out. If you come out to the head of it, I will show you the pegs.'

I followed him along a short sap running into No Man's Land for about fifteen yards. There it ended, and from there on there was nothing but shell holes. He pointed out a line of pegs extending into No Man's Land for about 200 yards, marking the line for the communication trench. The pegs for the main or 'hopping out' trench (the head of the 'T') were not visible, but he assured me they were there.

He again endeavoured to persuade me not to go. I assured him that I was no more eager for it than he was, but it had to be done. I asked him if he could do anything about a covering party. He refused to send a party out, for which I did not blame him, but he promised, as soon as we had sufficient cover, he would send me a Lewis gun and a team of bombers — and in the event of our being attacked, he would do everything possible to help. He disclaimed all responsibility for our going, and expressed his intention of ringing Brigade and informing them of the situation.

'In that case,' I said, 'you might tell them that I am starting out. The brigadier is rather anxious.'

He assured me that he would. Returning to the front line, he shook hands, wished me luck, and hurried off to the telephone.

Sending for my officers and N.C.O.s, I returned to the head of the sap with them, and pointed out the pegs. Of the two officers with me, one was Lieut. Scott and the other was Lieut. Rodda. Scott had been with the battalion a good while, and had proved himself a good and reliable officer. Rodda was fresh from Australia. He had only joined the battalion a few days before, and had never been under fire.[3] I

---

3 Lieutenant Daniel Scott, a 24-year-old engineering draughtsman from Heidelberg who liked practical jokes, was another Lillie — short and slim with a shock of flaming red hair. Of contrasting appearance was Errol Rodda, a tallish, dark-haired 27-year-old teacher from Maldon who had joined the

was angry at him having been sent on a job such as I had reason to anticipate this was going to be. I do not mean anything derogatory to him. From the little I had seen of him, I liked him, and he acquitted himself well that day, but it was not fair either to me or to the men, or Rodda himself, to send him on a job like that. Should Scott and I become casualties, which did not appear improbable, the command would devolve to Rodda. Moreover, he was of little use to me, being entirely without experience and unknown to the men. It was not his fault — he was only a youngster, and I believe he would have done well had he been spared. I sincerely regret that he was killed two nights later, in the attack from the trench we were digging. He was reported 'missing' and was never found, but we knew he died in No Man's Land, leading his platoon. He proved himself there, and died a soldier's death. His men had nothing but praise for him, and I know that several of them risked their lives afterwards searching in No Man's Land to try to bring him out, but they failed to find him. I suspected then and I knew later, that it was one of our C.O.'s little pleasantries to give me an inexperienced officer on the job. He was secretly hoping I would fail. Knowing that, I was all the more determined to succeed.

I issued final instructions to officers and N.C.O.s. Scott was to take the centre of the column, and to take command in the event of my becoming a casualty. Rodda was to take the rear and to be responsible that every man was clear of the front line, then follow, while I took the lead. The company sergeant major was to remain at head of sap and to be responsible for every man getting out as quickly as possible, so that there would be no gaps in the line to cause delay. The party was to follow me in single file along the line of pegs, using the shell holes for cover as much as possible. N.C.O.s were to take the head of their respective sections and to ensure that no man exposed himself unnecessarily. Two platoons were to work in the main trench on 'T' head, and two in the communication

---

8th Battalion three weeks earlier, when Barrie rejoined it. Although Barrie felt that Scott had been with the unit 'a good while', he had only been with the 8th seven weeks longer than Rodda.

trench. I would dispose the men in the main trench. Scott was to be responsible for the communication trench. Men were to work in the shell holes, two to a hole (one pick and one shovel) and connect up, and he was to impress on them that they must keep down.

Company headquarters was at the junction of the trenches. Company sergeant major was to report there as soon as possible, and also the stretcher bearers. We would move with bayonets fixed and rifles loaded, and in the event of attack the trench had to be held.

'All clear?'

'Yes, sir.'

'Right, file the party in. As soon as the sap is full, I am going. See there is no delay in the rear.'

The men filed in. When the sap was full, enquiring if all were ready, I bade them follow me as quickly as possible and climbed out. I made for a shell hole a few yards away, then over the lip and into another, vaulting from shell hole to shell hole, endeavouring to get as far as possible without being observed. The troops were following in good order, copying my example and using the shell holes as much as possible. We proceeded in this way for about 100 yards, then looking back I found I was outpacing the troops. I was three or four shell holes ahead of the nearest man. As one never knows what a shell hole may contain in No Man's Land, I decided to wait for him to catch up. We had met with no trouble so far, but I could see two German soldiers about 300 yards away, standing against the stump of a tree, watching. I stood up, the better to observe them. They waved their caps at me — quite a friendly gesture, apparently. I waved in return. They made no attempt to fire, but I kept an eye on them. My leading man, Private Forrester, had reached the hole next to mine.[4] Jumping into my hole he stumbled and fell against me, his left arm going round my neck and his right around my waist in an effort to save himself. As he struck me he let out a yell of pain, and fell.

---

4 This was presumably Private K.C.A. Forrester, a 23-year-old labourer from Maryborough. An original enlister in the 8th Battalion, he had struggled with dysentery at Gallipoli, like so many of his comrades. He returned to Australia in 1917.

'What's the matter?' I asked, bending over him.

'I'm hit, sir,' he said, to my surprise, and sure enough he was. A rifle bullet had hit him in the right elbow. While the two Germans were attracting my attention, a sniper in No Man's Land was taking aim at me. Forrester had intercepted a bullet which might have struck me in the stomach, and probably have dealt me a fatal wound. I was sorry for Forrester, but although painful it was not a dangerous wound, and I was grateful to a beneficial Providence that was watching over me. I tied up his wound, and told him to stay there until he could get out safely, and went on.

That shot was the opening of the party. Rifles cracked all around us. I gave them no more chances at me, and the men kept well down too. Progress was slower, but that way was safer. Proceeding carefully for another fifty yards or so, I stopped to listen to what seemed to be the sound of voices. Beckoning to the first few men to join me, I whispered to them to listen. They all agreed that there were voices, but none of us could distinguish any words. Cautioning them to be ready, I slipped into the next shell hole and listened again. I was certain now of the voices, but still could not distinguish any words. As far as I knew, there were none of our people out there, and I would surely have been warned if there had been. It could only mean one thing; there was a party of the enemy there, obviously unaware of our presence. There was only one thing to be done — rush them before they woke up. Beckoning again, four men slid into the shell hole. I whispered instructions to them, and drawing my revolver, gave the word 'go'.

We jumped out simultaneously and went for our lives. A few yards ahead of us was a small trench, and we made for it. Rifles cracked all round us. No Man's Land by this time was full of snipers. But we reached the trench without injury, and jumped in. To our surprise and relief we found there a party of Australian engineers, consisting of an officer and half a dozen men. We scared the wits out of them, so honours were even, and we all had a good laugh. Still, I had heard of enemy troops wearing our uniform before, and as there had been no mention of this party, I was not quite satisfied. Keeping them

John Charles Barrie.

The *Benalla* transported the 8th Battalion from Melbourne to Egypt. Some of the unit's officers signed the photo.

Barrie (on the right) was among many Australian soldiers photographed at this spot while the AIF was in Egypt early in 1915.

Anzac Cove, a considerable time after the fateful landing.

Barrie, wounded at the landing, receiving assistance.

Some of Barrie's fellow officers in the 8th Battalion, (from left) Dudley Hardy, Frederick Trickey, Graham Coulter, and Jack Mitchell. Barrie was scathing about one of them, but admired the other three. *(AWM C01197)*

Pompey Elliott (left) with George Wieck. Barrie esteemed both.

Joe Catron was one of Barrie's best friends in the 8th Battalion. *(AWM DA15235)*

Melville Roy Grinham was very young when he was recommended for the Victoria Cross. *(AWM DA10482)*

Gus Lodge was one of the 8th Battalion's most popular officers. *(AWM H06208)*

F.A. Vinnicombe, initially a 6th Battalion private, had become a lieutenant and a machine-gun specialist when he befriended Barrie. *(AWM P11400.001)*

After 'Mickey' Moon's extraordinary deeds at Bullecourt (when Barrie was nearby), he became the only soldier in the 15th Brigade to be awarded the Victoria Cross. *(AWM A02592A)*

Barrie's medals.

A locket containing photos of Barrie and his wife Daisy.

BARRIE.—Col. J. C., at R.G.H., Heidelberg, on Feb. 3, loved husband of Daisy and loving father of Isabel, father-in-law of Ken, grandpa of Ian and Graham. Late 8th Battalion A.I.F.

BARRIE.—On Feb. 3, at Heidelberg Repatriation Hospital, John Charles, beloved brother of Alice Kelly, dearly loved uncle of Max, Evelyn, Lindsay (dec., 2nd A.I.F.) and Noel (dec., 2nd A.I.F.).

Barrie died on 3 February 1957.

covered, I demanded proof of identification, especially as we were now closer to the German line than to our own. Being easily satisfied as to their identity, I lit a cigarette and sat down to wait for the rest of my party. The engineers had pegged the line the night before and were to supervise the digging of the trench. As no-one had turned up during the night, they had come out before daylight to wait for us, and had dug this little trench for cover at the junction of the 'T'. I remarked that they were pretty game, sitting out there on their own. They did not appear concerned. It was all in a day's work.

From here, I sent one platoon to the left and one to the right, along the line of the main trench, and by great good luck and extreme caution, succeeded in getting the whole line manned without further casualties. Rifle fire was increasing but I knew they could not do too much harm now as long as the men kept down. I could see the picks going up and down all along the line, but not a man exposed. Snipers were firing at the pick heads, but I was satisfied as long as that was all they had to shoot at. I was feeling very pleased at our success so far — we were on the job with only one casualty, and against all expectations. So far, there had been no shelling. The gunners were evidently resting after a busy night. I prayed that they would not be disturbed. The men were working like fury, and it was not long before the trench began to take shape.

A message came to me reporting Lieut. Scott wounded. He had been hit in the face by fragments of a bullet which had struck a pick head near him. This was bad; I had lost my only responsible officer. However, I had plenty of good N.C.O.s, and I did not change my organisation. Scott's sergeant took over his job, and Scott went down. Looking at my watch, I was surprised to find that our time had nearly half expired. It was 8.15 a.m. when I left the sap, and it was now ten o'clock. I sent my third message to Brigade. I had sent one by telephone when starting out, the second when work had started and reporting one casualty, now my third was to report the situation and progress, and two casualties. Sniping continued, but without further casualties, though several picks were struck, until consulting my watch again, I found it was 12.15 p.m. Our time was up and we had only two casualties, but the trench was not half dug.

The job was to get the men out. There was only sufficient cover for them to crawl on their hands and knees. The connection at the junction was not completed, as they were only working one way on that portion, and snipers were as thick as flies around a honey pot. As long as the situation remained as it was, we were safer where we were. I was never keen on exposing my men to undue risks — besides, I was wild at my company being ordered to take the punishment for someone else's blunder. It was not our fault the other parties failed, and I felt I would like to be able to go back and tell them we had finished the job on our own, and be damned to them. The C.S.M. agreed with me. I decided to put it to the N.C.O.s. Getting together as many as could reach me safely, I explained the situation.

'Now look here,' I said. 'We have completed our four hours and are now quite entitled to pack up and go home, but we haven't got much cover yet, and although we were lucky getting in, I am rather afraid we will have a sticky time getting out. Do you think the men can stick it out for a few hours longer and finish the job, when we will have a better chance of getting out safely?'

'Yes, sir,' they replied. 'The men are alright.'

'Well, what do you think?' I asked. 'Are you game?'

'Yes. That'll do us,' they answered. 'And the men feel the same. Let us finish the blooming job. They'll never say the 8th Battalion failed.'

'Right,' I said. 'That's the spirit. Let your men know then, and tell them to go for their lives, and we'll get out as soon as we can.'

They returned to their posts and spread the news. There was never a grumble. In fact, I think they worked harder than ever, and all felt the same as I did about it. I loved those fellows — they were wonderful. I sent a message to Brigade informing them of the situation.

At about one o'clock, the enemy started to shell one end of the main trench, where it ran out towards the windmill. This worried me a bit, but no casualties were reported, and the rest of the trench and the communications were unmolested. The shelling and sniping continued, but our luck still held, until about an hour later I heard a shout close by. Jumping up, I saw several men standing up, waving and yelling, and there was a man running across the top from the end of the main trench to the communication trench. He had evidently been wounded and was holding his left arm, which appeared to be broken. Running to the point he was making for, I joined in the chorus, shouting to him to get into a shell hole. Snipers were blazing at him all round, but he appeared to be in a panic, and kept on running. Then, to my horror, I saw another man jump out of the trench and chase him. It was Private Hunt, and the two were inseparable mates. Hunt, being unwounded, soon caught him up, and we shouted at him to get him into a shell hole, but he either did not hear us, or was too excited. He took his mate by the arm, and kept on running towards us, helping him along. And then the inevitable happened. I saw the impact of the sniper's bullet in the first man's stomach, and he fell. Hunt knelt over him, rolled him over, and proceeded to bandage his wound. We continued yelling to Hunt to get him into a shell hole, but he took no notice. By this time, everybody was up. I got a nasty jolt as a sergeant grabbed my leg and pulled me off the parapet. He apologised for being rough, but assured me I would be shot myself if I was not careful. I suppose he was right. I ordered those near me down, and sent people along the line to get them under cover. We were still yelling to Hunt, when a sniper's bullet hit him between the shoulders and they both toppled into a shell hole, but too late.[5]

Poor chaps; how silly to risk crossing there. They did not have a hope. Hunt had thrown his life away to help a mate, and now I knew neither could live. But that was the way of those men. Who could help loving them? And now they were both lying out there mortally wounded, and we could not get to them. The incident cast a gloom over the party, and for a few minutes work ceased and everybody was silent.

Then to my astonishment, I saw two men climb out of the trench with a stretcher. The first was Slattery, one of the gamest men that ever served under me, a quiet chap, ready at any moment to risk his life to help anyone, and taking it as all in a day's work, who served

---

5   George Hunt of the 8th Battalion was killed in action on 17 August 1916, aged 38. Born in London, diminutive with tattooed forearms, he had served in the Royal Navy for 12 years.

to the end, gaining the D.C.M. and Military Medal. With him was his mate Kennett, who was always ready to go with him.[6] They were two of the very best, but I am afraid I was rude to Slattery that day. Running towards him, I asked him where the devil he was going.

'We're going to bring those two in, sir,' he replied.

'You're not going to do anything of the kind,' I said. 'You get back in the trench.'

'Oh, I think we can get them alright, sir,' he said.

'Don't be a bloody goat,' I said, and grabbing his leg I pulled him in. This was where I hated being in command. I would have given anything to help those fellows, but I knew it was certain death to anyone who tried it, and I could not allow other lives to be sacrificed for no good purpose. I hated doing it, but I had to.

'Sorry, Slattery,' I said, 'But you could never reach them. You would meet with the same fate before you got half way out, and if you did reach them you would probably find them both dead.'

He agreed that I was right, though he hated not to go. We got the troops to work again, and proceeded with the job in hand. They were used to seeing men killed, and went on with the job as if nothing had happened. Though I know they never grew callous and hard-hearted as most people think, they simply had to put it out of their minds, else they would never be able to carry on.

Half an hour later, a sergeant reported to me that Hunt was coming in. Jumping up, I saw him there, sure enough, crawling towards the trench on his hands and knees. There were many willing hands to assist him. Slattery was over the parapet again and helped him the last few yards, and he was lifted carefully in and laid on a stretcher. Poor chap, it did not need a doctor to see that the end was fast approaching. We did all that was possible and made him as comfortable as we

---

6 Hugh Slattery DCM, MM was a 34-year-old labourer from Garvoc. He had blue eyes, sandy-coloured hair, and a shortish but sturdy physique. He was evacuated from Gallipoli due to illness, and was wounded and gassed in France. His stretcher-bearer comrade was evidently Les Kennett, a 22-year-old driver from Brunswick, who was awarded the Military Medal for bravely looking after the wounded at Pozières. Kennett died at Brunswick in 1969.

could. He was game to the last. His mate had died before he left him, and with his last remaining strength he crawled in. The trench was too narrow and too crowded to carry a stretcher, so we laid him on a waterproof sheet, and Slattery and Kennett carried him out to the first-aid post, but he died before they reached the front line.

It was now three o'clock. I went back to my post and despatched a runner with another message to Brigade. Though I felt very sad at having to report two killed, I could not help feeling that we had escaped very lightly. We had now been seven hours in No Man's Land, and our total casualties were four, of which two were not serious. The connection was completed at the junction, and it was beginning to look like a trench. I felt moderately happy. One could move about in the trench now with a reasonable degree of safety, and with no interruptions we would finish before dark. Captain Lillie had been true to his promise and had sent me a gun team and bombers.

As I was passing along the trench, one of his men caught my attention and with a smile asked if I remembered him. I didn't. He was a lad named Laugher from Kyneton, Victoria, where I had lived for a time before the war. He was a schoolboy in knickerbockers when I last saw him, and I little expected to find him sitting in No Man's Land.[7] I was standing talking to him when I received another jolt. Looking across No Man's Land, I saw another figure sliding into a shell hole, crawling out of it on hands and knees, wriggling like a snake to another hole, making towards my position. My first thought was 'another casualty'. The stretcher bearers had returned, but I ordered them to stay where they were. From his rate of progress he was obviously not too badly hurt. We stood by, ready to help him in. I was relieved to find he needed no assistance.

It was Corporal Inger.[8] He had been out amongst the shell holes

---

7 Private Charles Laugher, a 19-year-old clerk, was accidentally killed a month later when shot by an AIF sentry.
8 John Inger, a 23-year-old labourer, had been in the 8th Battalion since August 1914. He had brown hair, grey eyes, and a short, stocky build. Evacuated sick twice and wounded twice, he was promoted to sergeant, mentioned in dispatches, married an English bride, and survived the war.

for an hour trying to find Hunt and his mate, both of whom were in his section. He was very disappointed when he learned that his efforts had been in vain. I should have ticked him off for doing it, but how could I in a case like that? I was very thankful to see him unhurt. He had been 'potted at' several times, but was wise enough to keep very close to the ground. He returned to his post through the trench. I have heard some hard things said about soldiers, and I know from experience there were some wasters wearing uniform, but one did not find them in a fighting unit. I felt proud to be associated with the men under my command.

The shelling ceased, to my great relief, at about four o'clock, and though the snipers were still busy, we were now well under cover, and even the picks were no longer showing. Work proceeded quietly and without further incident until at 5.30 p.m. I decided that another half hour's work would suffice. I sent a message to Captain Lillie that I would vacate the job at six o'clock. He replied that he would have a garrison ready to take over when I got out. His men were to remain with me until relieved. I also sent my last message to Brigade. I instructed Rodda to find out the best route to return by, and to be ready to lead the way out in half an hour.

He discovered a much shorter route than the one we had come by. Having given instructions to the 5th Battalion party, at six o'clock I gave the word to pack up and file out. I was very pleased with the day's work. We had been ten hours in No Man's Land in daylight. The job was completed and our total casualties were only four, slightly over 2 per cent. Everybody, including myself, had anticipated 20 to 30 per cent, possibly more. I had reason to be pleased, though I knew our troubles were not quite over. We had yet to get out, but if our luck held, I did not anticipate much trouble there.

I waited at the junction and checked the party out of the main trench. When the last man was through, I followed in the rear. We reached the front line safely, where Captain Lillie was waiting to post his garrison. He expressed his surprise and congratulations at our success, said a cheery farewell, and I pushed on. A few yards down the trench, we turned into the communication and were headed for home. I could see the party stretched out in front of me in single file, making their way quietly down the trench, but it had been badly battered at the point where I was, and looking back I could see right across the German lines. I hurried on, hoping we had not been spotted, but we had. Almost immediately, a burst of gunfire came overhead, and from then on until we left the communication about two miles back, we ran through as nasty a barrage as I'd ever experienced. I shouted to the troops to run, and the word ran down the line, 'Go for your lives in front,' but they were already running. About half way down, I heard the scream of a shell coming straight towards me, above all the din. I stopped and listened. Yes, it was mine alright. What would I do? Stay still, run back, or go on? I ran on at full lick. I could still hear him coming closer, closer, closer, until it was on me. I dived, straight into a pool of water. One couldn't be worried about that. It burst straight above me about five feet over the trench. I was covered with dirt, but not buried. I had a splitting headache, and was half dazed with concussion. I was picking myself up when Slattery came running back to my aid.

'Are you hurt, sir?' he asked as he helped me to my feet.

'No,' I replied, 'I'm alright, Slattery. A bit of a headache, that's all.'

'By gum!' he said. 'I thought that one had you. I heard him coming.'

'So did I,' I said, 'and I ran like hell, but he was going faster than I.' He laughed.

'Well!' I said, 'I'm alright now; we'd better get on. Off you go.'

'You go ahead, sir. I'll follow you.'

'No fear,' I replied. 'I'm on the tail of this party. Go for your life.'

He went, but he adjusted his pace to mine, and was never more than a yard or so in front of me. Good old Slattery, he was not taking any chances of getting out without me. We ran out of the barrage at the end of the communication, where it ran into a sunken road near brigade headquarters. The party was waiting. To my intense relief, we had got through with only two men slightly wounded. Their mates had helped them out, and taken them to a dressing station. Total casualties were six. I was pleased, feeling that we had done a good job and were safely out at such a small cost; only 4 per cent and, with the exception of the two deaths, no serious wounds.

I instructed Rodda to take charge and report the party's return, and told him that I had been ordered to brigade headquarters and would make my report later. Setting off for brigade headquarters, I passed through the lines of the 7th Battalion. A sergeant stepped out from a dug-out, saluted and said,

'Excuse me, sir, you're wanted in here.'

'What for?' I asked in surprise.

'I don't know, sir, but I think it's important.'

Thinking that the brigade commander was probably in there, I followed him inside. There, waiting to greet me, were Sergeant Major Baker and Sergeant Rutherford, both ex-members of my old militia regiment,[9] and three or four other sergeants, some of whom I knew. They were all trying to shake hands with me at once. I wondered at the effusion.

'I hope you don't mind, sir,' Baker said, 'but we knew the job you were on today, and we've been looking out for you for hours. We thought a tot of rum would do you good.'

'In that case,' I said, smiling, 'I don't mind a bit, I quite agree with you.'

Rutherford handed me a noggin. It did me good too. I felt the need of it, for it had been a trying day. They were quite excited about our show, and would hardly believe me when I told them it was completed, and with so few casualties. It had created quite a stir. I had not seen Baker since his escape from the depot, though his C.O., Lieut. Col. Jess, had thanked me for bringing him back.[10] I had explained that it was nothing to do with me, that Baker had worked

---

9 Joe Rutherford and Bill Baker had much in common. Both were 34 and married. Both were respected 7th Battalion originals with extensive militia experience. Both were mentioned in dispatches, and both survived the war.

10 Carl Jess became commander of the 7th Battalion in February 1916 after Pompey Elliott was promoted to brigadier. Born in Bendigo, he had been a schoolteacher there before deciding in 1906 to become a full-time soldier. At Gallipoli, he was an impressive staff captain at Brigadier-General John Monash's headquarters, and an energetic brigade major in the 2nd Brigade.

his own passage.

'Oh well, Dan,' he said, 'Baker blames you anyway. It was a jolly good effort. I was very glad to see him back.'

I was very glad to see the old faces again, and appreciated their welcome. They had apparently been worried about me all day, but reminding them that I was still on duty, after a short rest, I continued on my way to brigade headquarters.

The brigadier welcomed me like a prodigal son, and his staff gathered around and joined in. I felt quite embarrassed. He shook my hand until it almost hurt, saying, 'By Jove, old chap, I'm glad to see you back. What kept you so long? I've been frightfully worried about you.'

'Well, sir, the situation was such, at the end of four hours, that I felt I couldn't get out without casualties and I preferred to stay in and finish it.'

'What state is the trench in now?'

'It is completed, sir, ready for use.'

'What?' he exclaimed. 'Do you mean to tell me it will not be necessary to send a party up tonight?'

'In my opinion, there is nothing more to be done, sir,' I answered.

'Oh splendid!' he said. 'I didn't expect anything as good as that. Now what about your casualties? Your last report gave only four.'

'They shelled us coming out, sir, after we left the front line. I had two more slightly wounded.'

'Yes, but your total for the day?'

'Four and two — total six,' I explained. 'Two killed, four wounded.'

'Do you mean to tell me you got through the whole day with only six casualties?' he asked, still not convinced.

'That's all, sir,' I assured him.

The old general hated casualties. He was as pleased about it as I was. Turning to his brigade major, he said, 'Bring me a map.' And to his staff captain, 'See there is an extra place set for dinner. And get out some wine.'

I knew then he was pleased with the day's work, because he never drank anything himself. To me, he said, 'You'll stay, of course.'

'Thank you, sir,' I replied. 'But I have not reported back to my battalion yet.'

'That's alright. I'll ring them up and tell them I am keeping you.'

So I stayed. Spreading the map on the table, and handing me a red pencil, he said, 'Show me exactly what is done.'

I sketched in a plan of the trench and gave a full description of the work.

'Splendid,' he said. 'Now, is there anything more of importance you can tell us?'

I hesitated. I had something in my mind alright, but I did not know whether I should let it out to a brigade commander.

'Well, out with it,' he said.

I looked up and smiled.

'Well, sir,' I said, 'if you will forgive me saying it, their snipers have been around us, thick as flies, all day. There is no question of us being observed. It strikes me that the Germans are no fools, and they don't imagine we have been out there for training. They have got all tonight to set a trap.'

Looking grave, he put his hand on my shoulder and said, 'I know. That is worrying me too.'

Then we went to dinner. During dinner I had to recount the day's experiences over again. I left soon after, and saying goodnight, the brigadier graciously told me he was very pleased with my work. The brigade major accompanied me up the staircase. He and I were old friends from the old militia days.[11]

Bidding me goodnight, he said, 'You'll get a decoration for this job, Dan.'

'Think so?' I said, feeling elated.

'Yes, I know,' he replied. 'The old man told me. He's recommending it himself.'

---

11 General Forsyth's able brigade major was T.F. Ulrich. A 25-year-old clerk when the war started, he was one of the 6th AIF Battalion's original lieutenants; he ended up in command of that unit for most of 1918. He finished the war as Lieutenant-Colonel Ulrich DSO & Bar, and was three times mentioned in dispatches.

I went home feeling very pleased. I reported at battalion headquarters. My C.O. was not interested, so I went to bed.

I never got that decoration. The brigade commander made the recommendation (he has confirmed this since), and in accordance with custom, forwarded it to our C.O. for his information and concurrence. He tore it up. Next morning, I handed in my own recommendations for Corporal Inger and Private Hunt (posthumous). They both met the same fate as mine. Splendid fellow.

Strange things happen. My wife interrupted me here to say there was a man at the door who wished to see me. It was Slattery. I had not seen him since I left France sixteen years ago. He was passing through the district and came five miles out of his way to see me. It is a long time since a more welcome visitor knocked at my door. And it's a strange coincidence that I should be writing about him. There are some things that are worth more than decorations. Much as I would like to have had it, I feel that the friendship and goodwill of the men, such as Slattery, who served under me, after all this time, is more valuable. It was certainly wonderful to see him.

Chapter Thirteen

Next morning, an item of pleasant news came to the battalion. Owing to the heavy casualties sustained by the front-line battalions (5th and 6th), they were not strong enough to carry out the attack. The 7th and 8th would therefore relieve that night, and the attack would be carried out by the 8th Battalion. We were always lucky. However, 'war's war', and we took it philosophically. What you lose on the roundabouts, you pick up on the swings. We spent a quiet day resting, if one could call it quiet with the thunder of the guns in our ears nearly all day. Still, one gets used to that. I felt very worried about the job ahead of us that night, and though I could not help feeling glad that my company was not to take part in the actual attack, but would remain in support, having done its task the day before, I could not help feeling concerned about those who were going in. I felt pretty certain that the enemy would have a surprise prepared for us. However, I kept my mouth shut on the subject. I knew nothing. It was only suspicions, and it was no use worrying the officers concerned about a thing I was not sure of. They had enough on their minds already.

We moved in early in the evening. The attack was to take place at midnight. The result was as I anticipated. Let us pass it over as quickly as possible. It was too terrible to dwell on, or to describe in detail. The Germans had prepared their trap under cover of darkness, quietly and unobserved, and our poor fellows ran into it with terrible results. They had dug a half-moon trench around our 'T', and caught them in front and flanks with machine guns, in this manner shown here:

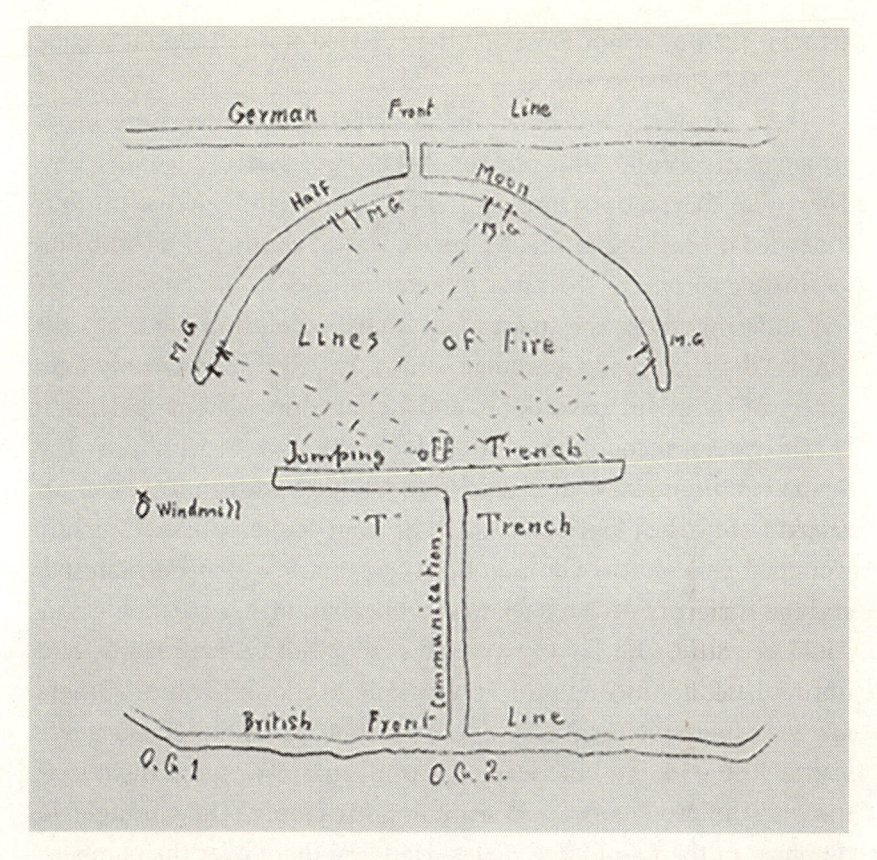

[Diagram: hand-drawn sketch showing German Front Line at top, with "Half Moon" formation of machine gun positions (11 M.G. and 13 M.G.) creating "Lines of Fire" with M.G. positions on left and right flanks, a "Jumping-off Trench" below, a "Windmill" marked on the left, a "T" Trench with "Communication" trench running down to the "British Front Line" at the bottom, marked with O.G.1 and O.G.2.]

Poor chaps! They never had a chance. They took the punishment, alright. We lost nearly 300 men and, of course, did not reach the objective. It was the only defeat the 8th Battalion ever suffered, and they were in no way to blame for it.[1] It had practically been arranged for them by higher authority on an open invitation. I have often thought since that the enemy allowed us to complete that job the day before in anticipation of a bigger prize. Much as I appreciated the good work of the staff, I think sometimes, through ignorance of the

---

1 Whether this was the 8th Battalion's 'only defeat' depends partly on one's point of view. As Barrie acknowledges elsewhere in his memoirs, 'according to all recognised standards of military ethics, we were licked' at the Gallipoli landing, despite all the dash and daring displayed by AIF units; a similar conclusion could perhaps be drawn about the charge towards Krithia on 8 May 1915 (which Barrie did not experience, having been wounded a fortnight earlier).

actual front-line conditions, that they carried stern discipline a trifle too far, as on this occasion.

The men of the 8th hated being defeated, but they were never ashamed of it, and had no reason to be. They behaved wonderfully. They were driven back to their trench, rallied, and tried again four times, led on each occasion by Captain Hardy. Hardy was a Duntroon graduate and one of the most popular officers in the battalion. He was suffering under the smart of an unjust accusation made against him by the C.O. Being a regular soldier, he felt it more keenly than others of us might have done, and he laid himself out that night to win special recognition, and so force the C.O. to withdraw. The whole battalion knew of it, and was seething with indignation on account of it. They loved Hardy. On the fourth attempt, he was badly wounded close to the German line. Our attack was again repulsed, and the survivors driven back to our line. No further attempt was or could be made. Our losses were too severe. But Captain Hardy had not returned. Someone said he was going to look for him. Others just went without mentioning it, in case it was forbidden. I never saw anything like it. Practically the whole garrison spent the rest of the night in No Man's Land searching for Hardy. They brought in numbers of their wounded mates. Handing them over the parapets, each would enquire if Captain Hardy had been found. On being told no, they simply wriggled away and continued the search.

After a couple of hours, one of the officers, Lieut. Goodwin,[2] came across a badly wounded man in a shell hole who had seen Hardy. He had crawled into the same hole, badly hurt. Being unable to assist him, Hardy had given the man his water bottle, expressed his intention of trying to crawl back to our lines, and promised if

---

2 Frank Goodwin was born and grew up at Colwall in Herefordshire, England. He was an unmarried 26-year-old farmer from Geelong when he enlisted at the start of war in the 8th Battalion. Wounded at Gallipoli on the first day, he was back with his unit two months later, and displayed consistently outstanding bravery. He was so extraordinary at Pozières in July and August 1916 that he was recommended for the VC, but ended up MC & Bar. On 4 October 1917, at the battle of Broodseinde, Frank Goodwin was killed in action by a burst of machine-gun fire.

possible to send him assistance. He showed Goodwin the way Hardy had gone. That was just like Hardy to give away his water bottle, the thing he needed most at the moment, to a wounded comrade. Goodwin got the man in and went back for Hardy, but although the search continued until nearly daylight, no further trace of him was found. The affair cast a gloom over the battalion for days. I never knew the men to take anything to heart so much as the death of Captain Hardy. Men cried that night. Their defeat and the loss of so many comrades was bad enough, but they all felt, and in some cases openly declared, that Captain Hardy's life had been sacrificed through an unjust charge laid against him by a man who was not fit to lick his boots. His name will never be forgotten by those who served with him.[3]

We also lost three other officers, Lieuts. Dabb, Rodda, and O'Kelly, all of whom, with Hardy, were reported 'missing — believed killed'. In spite of repeated attempts, we failed to obtain any information concerning any of them, and were forced to the conclusion that they had been killed. Dabb had been with his battalion a good while. I liked him very much, in fact he was very popular with all ranks.[4] Rodda and O'Kelly had joined together a short while before, and this was their first fight. Walking along a city street with my wife one day in Melbourne about three years after the war, a man stopped and addressed me. I did not know him. It took him a few minutes to convince me that he was O'Kelly. He had been wounded and taken

---

[3] Captain Dudley Hardy, a South Australian, was among Duntroon's first intake of cadets and its first batch of graduates. He was wounded on the first day at Gallipoli, but returned to his unit six weeks later. In January 1916, at Cairo, he married Lydia Kliaguina, a Russian resident of that city. The revered captain was killed in action exactly seven months later.

[4] Reginald Henry Dabb was another 8th Battalion original who had risen through the ranks to become an officer. A 19-year-old bank clerk from Camperdown with blue eyes and fair hair, he was evacuated ill from Gallipoli, like so many. He had been a lieutenant since April 1916. Dabb was taken prisoner by the Germans after being severely wounded on 18 August. His right leg, shattered by a shell, was amputated. He died of his wounds a month later.

in by the Germans. He was sent to hospital and then to prison camp.[5] He knew nothing of the others, nor was anything ever heard.[6]

The adjutant, Captain Lodge, again took charge of the operation and re-organisations. He was wounded during the fight. The C.O. was generous enough to secure for him the award of D.S.O., a well-merited distinction.

We were relieved after five days, almost exhausted. Shelling was practically continuous, and sleep was out of the question. In our two fights at Pozières, we had lost nearly 600 men, killed and wounded. Our strength now was a little over 300. The battalion was tired and sad. We slept in Sausage Valley, and next morning marched back to Albert, where we rested for two days.

The troops soon recovered their spirits and became quite cheerful on hearing the news that we were to relieve the Canadians in the Ypres sector while they took our place on the Somme.

Ypres previously had the reputation of being the worst sector on the British front, but the Germans were kept so busy on the Somme, that it was now comparatively quiet, and we were not likely to encounter any severe fighting. The troops were glad of the prospect of a spell for a while. A few days later we entrained for the north. We billeted in a standing camp known as 'Scottish Lines' at Reninghelst. Here, we filled up again with reinforcements, and enjoyed a couple of weeks' rest while refitting.

As we had not been in this sector before, company commanders took the opportunity during this spell to become acquainted with the

---

5 Leo O'Kelly had much in common with Errol Rodda. Not only did they join the 8th Battalion in France on the same day, but O'Kelly, like Rodda, was a tall schoolteacher in his late twenties who participated as an inexperienced lieutenant in the ill-fated attack on 18 August 1916, when they were both pronounced missing. However, whereas Rodda died in the operation, it eventually transpired that O'Kelly had been taken prisoner. O'Kelly's home address, duly noted in German military records, was Fish Creek.

6 Rodda's death was not the only calamity for his family. His younger brother, Fred, enlisted at 19, and suffered a compound fracture of his skull at Fromelles in July 1916; their sister stated in 1921 that Fred had never recovered, and was unable to continue with his pre-war post-office job as he was 'hardly responsible and wanders from place to place'.

land. Taking our horses, we rode up through Poperinghe to Ypres, and reconnoitred the routes leading to the various front line sectors. It was very interesting seeing for the first time the various places that had become so famous in the early part of the war and which still bore such a nasty reputation. Ypres had been a fine old town, and was sadly battered by shell fire. The cathedral and the famous Cloth Hall had been beautiful buildings, and it was a very sad sight to see them now just a heap of ruins. It was an old walled town surrounded by a huge moat on which families of white swans lived, reminders of peaceful days.

We went out past the gasometer to Dickebusch, where we saw some good examples of camouflage, disguising gun positions. Walls of houses that had been demolished by gunfire were replaced by painted canvas screens, which to the casual observer were quite hard to detect at a distance, thus rendering the gun inside secure from observation from the air. Leaving Dickebusch we rode back past 'Hell Fire Corner', along a road which was under observation from the front line with hessian screens strung between the poplar trees, and onto the railway dug-outs in front of Ypres, from where we could see the famous Hill 60 not very far away. We returned to Lille Gate, where the swans were swimming on the moat as we crossed the bridge, waiting for scraps from the passing troops.

At the end of a fortnight, we received orders to relieve the front line, and took over a sector on the right of Hill 60 in front of Dickebusch. The battalion went up by train as far as the Ypres Asylum, a big building outside the town which was as far as the train could go with safety. From there, we marched out through Dickebusch to the position of battalion headquarters, where guides met us to conduct us to the front line. Three companies were to go in with one in support: 'A' Company on the right, my company 'B' on their left, the sector next to me was suspected of being mined by the enemy and was unoccupied, and 'D' Company took the left, with 'C' Company in support. A battalion of The King's Liverpool Regiment was holding the line.

Beyond Dickebusch, we followed a duckboard track across open country which led us to the communication trenches in rear of our position. This country was under observation by the enemy in daylight, and the track was plainly visible, so the troops were warned not to waste time crossing it. As the track was narrow, we had to proceed in single file, my company being in the centre, with 'A' in front.

About half way across, for some unknown reason, the troops in front halted. We, of course, had to conform, and halted, too. I heard something 'plop' into the ground at my feet, then another and another, and wondered at first what the noise was. Then something 'zipped' past my ear and I woke up to the fact that we were under fire. Men were calling out to move in front but nothing happened, while bullets were plopping into the ground all round us. It was a pitch-dark night, and we could not see what was happening. It gave one a very uncomfortable feeling, standing there with bullets whizzing past. I said nothing, but, of course, the men knew as much about it as I did, and I was expecting any minute to hear a cry for stretcher bearers. I was very relieved when, after about ten minutes, the column moved on again without anyone being hit. A few yards along the track, we moved out of the line of fire, but the column behind still had to cross it, and did, fortunately, without casualties. It was long-range machine-gun fire, which the enemy played periodically on that track in the hope of getting a few stray casualties.

My guides were two Irishmen who spoke with such a broad brogue that I could hardly understand them. However, after a little hesitation and argument regarding the route, which they did not appear to be quite sure of, they got us in safely, and we completed the relief without trouble. The ground in this area was too wet to dig deep trenches, and the parapets had to be built up with sandbags, while for the most part they were quite open in rear, with communications built up in the same manner.

My company headquarters was a wattle-and-daub hut with three layers of sandbags on the roof, built at the end of a short sap at the end of the main communication, about fifty yards behind the front line and on the right of the company sector. I did not like the position, and on signing the certificate of relief for the outgoing company commander, I asked him if there was not a more suitable place that I could move to, nearer the centre of my sector.

He replied, 'I'm afraid there is not. We have been blown out of all the others. This is the only dug-out left standing.'

'Splendid,' I said, 'where do I go from here?'

'Well,' he replied laughing, 'I'm afraid I'll have to leave that for you to work out. I'm grateful it has seen me through,' and bidding me farewell he wished me luck and was glad to be gone.

Reporting by telephone the completion of the relief, I left an officer on duty and went to the front line. The situation was not pleasant, the trenches being only about thirty-five yards apart, and machine guns were rattling all up and down the line. One man, who became known to the troops as 'Parapet Joe', was making things very nasty for our observers. He was very clever with his gun, and swept along the line, making his bullets just skim the parapet all the way. The men soon got to know him, and ducked when he opened until he passed them by. I gave instructions not to use too many flares, as the less we used the more the enemy did, and as long as they were lighting up No Man's Land, we knew they were not up to mischief.

This sort of thing continued all night. It quietened down about daylight and finally ceased after 'stand down'. We had a peaceful morning. After breakfast, as things were quiet in the line, I decided on a rest. I had been in the line practically all night, and was feeling sleepy. I lay down on a bunk and dozed for an hour or so, when the signaller on duty shook me, saying I was wanted. Jumping up, I found three officers of the 5th Battalion wanting to see over the front line. I cursed them for waking me, but at the same time acknowledged that I was pleased to see them. They were all old friends, and the adjutant, knowing that they knew me, had sent them up to my sector with the request that I would conduct them through the trenches and explain to them the plan of defence. That was the end of my sleep. As my hat was the only article of clothing I had removed on retiring to rest, I was not long dressing and we started on the tour.

It was not mere idle curiosity on their part, as they, of course, would relieve us at the end of our tour of duty, which was to be fourteen days in this sector. By the time the inspection was completed it was nearly lunch time, and taking a couple of officers off duty, we went in search of a suitable place to rig a lunch table. There was no cover available. It was true what the Liverpool Regiment's captain had told me — all the other dug-outs had been blown in, and in mine there was no room for anything besides one bunk and the signaller with this table and telephone. We found a spot in the old support trench, now disused, and rigged a table in the open.

After lunch, finding things quiet in the line, I returned to company headquarters to continue my rest. I seemed to have hardly settled down when, at about three o'clock, I heard a tremendous crash. Going outside to see what was happening, I heard another crash. It seemed to be on the left of my sector. The company sergeant major came hurrying in and reported that the Huns were treating us to 'Minenwerfers'. The Liverpools had told them the Germans did this every afternoon from three o'clock to five o'clock. I instructed him to send an officer down, and I would come up to the line. It was a very strict rule that a company commander must not leave his headquarters without making his whereabouts known and leaving a responsible officer in charge.

'Minenwerfers' did not really do much damage, but relied more on moral effect. They were about the size and shape of an oil drum and filled with high explosive, and they burst with a terrific crash. They were fired from a mortar. We could hear the 'poof' of the gun, and then see them hurtling through the air until, at the top of their flight, they looked like a jam tin. Everybody watched and then, seeing where they were going to land, divided right and left, returning to their posts after the burst. I ordered everybody out of the firing bays except one observer in each to give them a better chance, and the game became quite amusing. When the gun 'poofed', there was a cry of 'Here she comes'. Everyone looked up, and those whose turn it was ran right and left out of the way. This continued until 5.00 p.m. and finished with a sudden round of 'whiz-bangs', a small, high-velocity shell which arrives without warning, the idea being to catch us out of the firing bays. Fortunately, they did no harm. We had had an amusing two hours for no damage and no casualties. Quietness reigned again, and we went to tea.

Half an hour before dark, I returned to the line for 'stand to'. There was a shell hole just at the back of the trench, and half a dozen of the biggest rats I had ever seen were drinking at the pool. The adjutant, who had come up for 'stand to' representing the C.O. (he being 'busy'), challenged me to a shooting match, and we enjoyed some good revolver practice shooting at the rats. There were no casualties amongst the rats, but we gave them a fright.[7] Just before dark, machine guns started up again, and as on the previous night, did not cease until daylight. I spent that night in the line also. Next morning, it was quiet again, and after breakfast I made another effort to get a rest. At ten o'clock, I was wakened again by another party of officers wanting to inspect the front line. There went my rest again. I managed to get an hour off after lunch, then 'Minenwerfers' started at three o'clock and kept me occupied until 5.00 p.m., then tea and 'stand to'. At dark, away went the machine guns again until daylight. Another night in the line. The war apparently went to a timetable up here. So apparently did my visitors. On the third morning at ten o'clock, another batch arrived and disturbed my rest. I went to bed straight away after lunch this day, determined to get a couple of hours rest. To my intense annoyance, I was disturbed at 2.30 p.m. by a loud explosion close by, and a shower of dirt off the roof falling on my face. Sitting up, I enquired of the signaller where that one went. He didn't know, but thought it was pretty close.

'I suppose the dirty dogs are going to blow over our last resting place,' I said. 'Have you located another spot to go to?'

'No, sir,' he replied, 'there is nowhere else to go as far as I can see.'

'Anyway,' I said, looking at my watch, 'it's only half past two. They are starting before time. You had better ring the adjutant and ask him to lodge a protest.'

While we were talking, another one landed closer still, and

---

7   With Captain Lodge wounded, the new adjutant was Captain Robert Wallis, a 27-year-old printer who had been an 8th Battalion original.

brought down another shower of dirt. Just to cheer the lad up, I said, 'By Jove, they are getting closer. I think I'll go for a walk and see what is happening. If they blow you up while I'm away I'll send a couple of the lads down to dig you out.'

'Righto, sir,' he replied, smiling and quite unperturbed.

I went out into the sap to have a look around, and met my company sergeant major coming in at the double.

'Hullo, Sergeant Major,' I said. 'What's going on?'

'Some stupid blighter is firing on us from behind, sir,' he replied.

'Oh rot,' I said. 'They must be coming from a flank, but not behind. There are only our own people there.'

'No fear, sir,' he said. 'They are coming from our rear. There you are sir, look,' and pointing upwards, 'There's another.'

Sure enough, there was a sixty pound 'plum pudding' bomb flying through the air from behind. It burst about half way between us and the front line. I heard the buzz of flying metal, the sergeant major shouted 'Look out,' and we both ducked as a piece of water pipe, three feet long, buried itself in the sand bags just above our heads. (The pipe is attached to the bomb and placed in the muzzle of the mortar when firing.)

This was a bit thick. One did not mind being fired at with 'Minnies' — that was what we were there for — but when our own people started too, we reckoned that was carrying the joke a bit too far. Telling the sergeant major to keep watch in case one lobbed on the huts, I instructed the signaller to ring battalion headquarters and get the adjutant. He had laughed at my remark about the protest, but I was making it alright.

The adjutant came, and I took the phone.

'That you, Bob?' I asked. 'Have you got a sixty-pound T.M. battery in your vicinity?'

'Yes, Dan,' he replied. 'There's one close by.'

'Well, look here, I want you to interview him. He has just poofed off three rounds, and they have all fallen in my front line, and I'm afraid he'll hurt someone if he's not careful.'

'What?' he said in surprise, 'You don't mean it, do you?'

At that moment, the sergeant major shouted, 'Another one coming, sir! Falling clear.' Then came a crash.

'Yes, I mean it alright, Bob,' I replied. 'His fourth has just lobbed, still in our line, so trot over and remonstrate with him like a good boy.'

'Righto, Dan,' he answered. 'I'll stop him,' and rang off.

After a couple more, the firing ceased. The adjutant rang on his return.

'I saw the T.M. man, Dan, and told him what you said. You are not making a mistake are you?' he said.

'Good Lord, no, Bob,' I replied. 'The first one landed within ten yards of my hut, and the rest were all in the vicinity. Why do you ask?'

'Because he was very indignant,' he said, 'and assured me that he could see the German line and observe his shots, and every one was a bullseye.'

'Better tell him to come up and make sure where the German line is before he opens up again,' I said. 'Every one of his shots lobbed in my line.'

'I told him that,' said the adjutant. 'He won't shoot any more today.'

We had no sooner settled this fellow than the Huns opened again on their daily 'Minnie' program, and I accompanied the sergeant major to the line for the afternoon's sport of 'Minnie dodging'.

At 5.00 p.m., they ceased again with the usual round of 'whizbangs', and fortunately again no casualties.

Three of my company officers had just retired to the dug-out, which like mine was a very frail affair, and the only one in the front line. The floor was dug out to about three feet below the trench level, with three steps down, and it had a narrow doorway facing the trench. Being satisfied the strafe was over, I was just leaving the line when I saw Lieut. Scott (who had returned after his wounding at Pozières) trundling an unexploded 'Minnie' along the trench. Scott was an engineer by profession, and had removed the detonator, but it was forbidden for anyone to interfere with them, and I personally treated them with the greatest respect. Scott was a good lad, but an inveterate practical joker. He was too far away for me to stop him, but I went back, intending to order him to desist. Before I could reach him, to my intense astonishment, he stopped at the door of the dugout and pushed the 'Minnie' in. Imagine the consternation of the three inside. They made a bound for the doorway, with the result that they all got stuck in it, and for a minute or so they struggled so hard they got stuck all the tighter and none could get out, while Scott was dancing with glee outside.

They finally extricated themselves and went for Scott, threatening murder. Scott took to his heels and went for his life. I never saw three wilder men. It was certainly funny, and I could not help joining in the general laugh, nevertheless it was too serious to pass over. High explosives were too dangerous to play with.

Sending for the four officers concerned, and finding the three victims still very wrathful, I made it clear to them that for the present they must forego their vengeance. They could deal with Scott when they were out of the line. As for Scott, if I caught him playing with live 'Minnies' again, I would report him, and ordered him to remove that one and take it away out of the trench. I returned to company headquarters, where I enjoyed an unrestrained laugh over the incident. By tea time, the three victims were beginning to see the funny side of it, and recounted their point of view, particularly while stuck in the doorway. I am afraid I laughed more than I ate at that meal time. But they still determined to get even with Scott.

Returning to the line for 'stand to', I found the same program being carried on as on previous nights, and again remained until daylight. This was my fourth night without sleep. I was getting used to it by now.

Just after taking over the sector, we had received a huge consignment of sand bags, with instructions to rebuild the parapets, and the intimation that we would occupy this area for the winter. The troops were kept busy on this job during the quiet parts of the day, so that they did not get much rest either, but they worked willingly enough, thinking they were building their winter home.

Next morning after breakfast, I lay down again, hoping for a few hours' rest, thinking surely I had done with visitors. At about ten o'clock, I was wakened again. I sat up and swore. A cheery voice hailed me from the doorway, asking me what I was annoyed about. It was Brigadier General Bennett of the 3rd Brigade, and his brigade major.[8] He also had been with my old militia regiment, and with the original 6th Battalion A.I.F. I knew him well enough to laugh about it, and tell him. He laughed, too, and off we went. He was pleased at the work being done in the front line, and assured me that this would be our winter home. At the end of my sector, I suggested that he should wait a few minutes before crossing the unoccupied part, as a patrol was just about due to start across. Both companies patrolled it at half hour intervals, but otherwise there was nothing to prevent a party of the enemy from jumping in, and I did not want to lose a brigadier while he was in my charge. There might be a fuss about it. We stood and chatted for a few minutes, then placing him in charge of the patrol sergeant, I sent him off under their escort. They delivered him safely. I returned for lunch and tried another sleep.

At half past two, our trench-mortar friend started again, still lobbing them in our line. The sergeant major came running in, but I was already at the telephone, demanding the adjutant to stop him. He ceased after half a dozen shots, none of which had gone over our parapets.

The adjutant rang again to ask if I was sure about his shooting.

'Of course I'm sure,' I said. 'Why, does he still think he is putting them in the German line?'

'Yes, he does,' he replied. 'He's more indignant than ever. He says he observed every one of his shots and can swear that they all fell in the German trench.'

'There is not one gone over our parapet so far,' I said. 'You had better both come up and see.'

'Alright. He won't shoot any more today, and has promised to check his range.'

I took my hat and strolled up to the line in time for the opening

---

8 Henry Gordon Bennett was to become a household name during World War II after his controversial escape from Singapore.

round of the afternoon's sport.

The usual program was carried out, without casualties. At 'stand to', machine guns started up as usual, and I remained again until daylight, spending most of my time on the left near the unoccupied sector, as I did every night. I did not like that place. We had a listening post in No Man's Land to give us warning of an attack, but beyond the half-hourly patrol, there was nothing to prevent a raiding party jumping in there, and they could probably scupper a couple of our posts before we could deal with them. I wanted to be on the spot if anything happened, and kept a small party handy to deal with the situation if it arose. This party was posted in a corner of the trench at the junction of a disused communication, and kept a sentry posted with instructions to allow no-one to pass without the password. As I was coming in that night after seeing the patrol off, the sentry scared the wits out of me. I had forgotten about him for the moment, and being pitch dark I did not see him, when I was suddenly challenged and felt a bayonet at my stomach. I did a record back jump, gave the password, and made myself known.

'Sorry, sir!' said the sentry. 'I didn't know it was you.'

'Sorry be blowed,' I replied. 'You were quite right. It mightn't have been me. But I'm glad you didn't push that bayonet any further. It would be a most uncomfortable thing to have in one's stomach.'

He was very apologetic, but I assured him he was quite right, and that was what he was there for. I was lax, and deserved the fright. And, indeed, he was right. He was on a dangerous post, and I was glad to see that he was up to his job. I approached that post very carefully afterwards.

Another night in the line. Another day without sleep. At 2.30 p.m. the trench-mortar battery opened. Another appeal to the adjutant succeeded in stopping him again after half a dozen shots, still very indignant and unbelieving. Three to five o'clock, 'Minnie dodging' — and so the routine went on. We got through the first week without casualties, and then one afternoon while standing at the back of the trench amongst a group of half a dozen men, watching for the next 'Minnie', a sudden and unexpected round of 'whiz-bangs' scored three casualties. Bad luck. However, I was relieved to find none killed. We rendered first aid and sent them down. We had really got off lightly for a week in a place like that.

Next afternoon — his fourth attempt — the trench mortar man opened again. I heard his first shot burst, followed by a rousing cheer from the troops. Enquiring the cause, I found he had at last succeeded in getting one over the parapet. I could not help laughing. They were great chaps. Much as they cursed the mortar man for his shooting, they could not resist a joke at his expense. But as I found he had lobbed this one in our own wire entanglements, and it would mean sending out a party after dark to repair it, it was not so funny.

I was beginning to be annoyed with him. Ringing the adjutant again, I reported what had happened, and threatened if he did not stop him I would take a team down myself and murder him. Though he had caused no casualties as yet, I predicted it was only a matter of time until he did so if he was allowed to continue, and it was not fair for my men to have to risk their lives in No Man's Land repairing the damage caused by him.

The adjutant was also serious about it and promised to settle him for good that day.

He rang me later and told me he had had a very serious talk with him, and threatened to report him if it occurred again, but though he related what had occurred, he believed that the officer was still unconvinced that he was bombing us.

I told him in that case, he had better take steps to convince him, or bring him up to the line and I would do it myself. If he killed any of my men I would make him answer for it, and I put the responsibility on to the adjutant to see that he did not. He assured me he would not fire on us again.

False hopes. Next afternoon, he opened up again as usual, and lobbed his first bomb right in the trench at the junction of 'A' and 'B' Company sectors, and succeeded in wounding three men of 'A' Company. While feeling glad my men had escaped, I had just as strong affection for the rest of the battalion. They were all the same to me. I was furious. Though the adjutant and I were the best of pals,

I rang again and reported the occurrence, telling him that I would stand no further nonsense, and if one more bomb fell in my line, I would make a written report on the whole affair, and I would not spare him. That was the end of it. We convinced him at last, but at the cost of three men wounded. The adjutant told me afterwards he took his revolver with him that day, and promised very definitely to shoot the officer in charge if he fired one more round. He then reported the occurrence to the artillery commander, with the result that the battery was sent out of the line for further training.

The usual routine proceeded, except in the second week my visitors were not quite so numerous, and I was able to snatch a few hours sleep in the quiet part of the day. We escaped further casualties until one afternoon, near the end of our tour of duty, a 'Minenwerfer' blew in a section of our parapet and buried two men. It was sheer bad luck. The 'strafe' had ended; we had our usual round of 'whiz-bangs'. I had ordered the troops back to their posts, and was just about to leave the trench myself, when over came another, unexpected one. It landed right on the parapet as the men were returning to the bay, and two observers were charging over. It blew an enormous hole in the parapet, exposing the trench to the enemy, who could have fired straight into it from any point over a couple of hundred yards of their front, and completely buried both men. I ran to the spot, but before I reached it, Lieut. Hickson and Sergeant (afterwards Lieut.) Errey were both in the breach digging for their lives. They were exposed to the German line for hundreds of yards either way. I pointed the fact out to them suggesting that they would be safer digging from the bottom. They replied they were alright and went on digging. Ordering the people in the vicinity to man the parapet and watch for snipers, I got up myself, feeling very worried at the risk of these two getting hurt. Both Hickson and Errey were splendid fellows, of long service, absolutely reliable, and game as lions. I let them do the job in their own way, praying for nothing to happen. Nothing did. It is hard to say why. I can only think the Huns had no observers up, and had not seen the effect of their shot. After about twenty minutes digging, they succeeded in extricating the two buried men, without a shot being fired at them. They were both alive, and we got them away at once, but unfortunately one man died on the way down to the first-aid post. The other went to hospital and recovered.

I expressed my appreciation of their bravery to Lieut. Hickson and Sergeant Errey, and made a report to the C.O. It went the same way as the others had done. I was annoyed, as they both deserved recognition, but what could I do? One can't go over the head of his commanding officer. I feel it might be some little recompense to pay them this tribute now. Both, I regret to say, have since lost their lives. Lieut. Errey was killed in action later in the war, while Hickson, after surviving the war, had the extreme misfortune to die of ptomaine poisoning shortly after his return to Australia.[9]

Their memories remain green with me. I never had two more loyal and reliable men under me.

We were relieved at the end of fourteen days, and went into reserve. We had escaped lightly, but it was a nasty sector, and for the whole of the fortnight, except for an occasional change of socks, I had not even had my boots off. I enjoyed the luxury of a bath and a change of clothing.

---

9 Frank Hickson was a recent immigrant from England when he enlisted in September 1914, describing himself as a 22-year-old 'horse driver'. Short and stocky, he had brown eyes, dark hair, and a ruddy complexion. Illness caused his evacuation from Gallipoli, but after returning to the 8th he progressed from private to lieutenant in seven months. He was wounded, gassed, awarded the MC, and invalided with trench fever. Having returned to Australia in mid-1919, he died on 17 April 1920, and was buried in Brighton Cemetery.

Len Errey, a short and slight Camperdown carpenter, also enlisted early in the war. Recognition was slow to come his way, but in February 1916 he became a corporal. Seven months later, in a rapid ascent rather like Hickson's, he was a lieutenant. Errey was recommended for the Victoria Cross in 1917 after successfully attacking a pill-box, but had to settle for the DSO; he was also awarded the MC for an exploit earlier that year. As the 8th Battalion's intelligence officer, he laid out the marker tapes before the battle of Broodseinde on 4 October 1917, but later that day Errey died of wounds, aged 25.

Chapter Fourteen

Our reserve position was at Chateau Segard. The trenches were dug in the grounds of a beautiful old chateau, now sadly damaged by shellfire, and the bottom storey barricaded by sandbags, relics of the fighting of the early days of the war. We had a quiet, restful time here for a fortnight, but it seemed almost like sacrilege to be living in trenches in the beautiful grounds of this lovely old home.

While we were here, a new brigade commander arrived to take over the brigade. General Forsyth had left us, to the great regret of the whole brigade. He was very unjustly treated. Higher authority had required an explanation of our failure at the second Pozières fight. Division passed the blame down. General Forsyth was far too honourable a man to do likewise, and he could not pass it up where it belonged. So he was made the scapegoat. Division had ordered him to get the jumping-off trench dug in daylight as a punishment for the failure of the two parties at night, in spite of his advice and protest, and his warning of the probable result. His warning had come true, but somebody had to pay.

Our new brigade commander had just arrived, and had not previously held any command in France.[1]

He inspected the battalion at Chateau Segard. The adjutant sent me a message warning me to prepare for his inspection, and to

---

1 Brigadier-General J.M. Antill took over command from Forsyth in mid-September 1916. His previous AIF service had been in the Light Horse — at Gallipoli and Palestine — and he was new to the Western Front.

'stand to' in the trenches. He also gave me the tip that rifles were his particular fad, especially the cooks' rifles. Every exalted person has his own particular little idiosyncrasy, and I was glad of the tip. I was not worried about the rifles of the fighting troops — they were under my eye, and the men themselves realised the importance of keeping them clean. But the cooks' rifles were the bane of a company commander's life. He never saw his cooks while he was in the line, and though all the cooks were armed with a rifle, they were never called upon to use them, and looked upon them as so much superfluous hamper.

After issuing the necessary instructions to my company, I visited the cooks and warned them to prepare for the inspection, and gave the sergeant cook a special warning in regard to his rifles. Hurrying back, I was just in time to meet the inspecting party entering my sector. I was duly introduced, presented my officers, and accompanied the brigadier through the trench. He inspected an occasional rifle, found it in good order, and congratulated me on my splendid company. He then demanded to see the cooks. The cooks had fixed themselves up very well in a corner of the grounds, with a tea-tree screen around the cookers. The cookers, I knew, were in good order, as I kept my eye on them as far as possible, and made it the duty of the company orderly officer to make a daily inspection when out of the line. The brigadier was full of praise for them. Then he asked to see their rifles. I wondered what he would find. The rifles are carried on the cooker in a place arranged for them, but to my surprise the sergeant cook said, 'Yes, sir, the rifles are here,' pointing to a row of rifles neatly arranged against a fence in an improvised wire rack, and looking very clean outside. Knowing the wiles of a cook from long experience, I thought to myself, 'Hullo, what's this?' I stood back and left it to the sergeant. The brigadier was quite taken with the display and remarked, 'Ha, that's the idea. Let me see one, Sergeant.'

The sergeant handed him one. Opening the breach, he looked through the barrel and remarked, 'Splendid! Have a look at that, Colonel,' and passed it over to the C.O. Turning to the sergeant, he asked, 'How often do you clean your rifles, Sergeant?'

'Once a week, sir,' the sergeant lied without a smile.

'Good. When were these cleaned last?' asked the brigadier.

'This morning, sir,' replied the sergeant.

'Splendid,' said the brigadier. Then, turning to the C.O., he said, 'That's what I like to see, Colonel. Show me the cooks' rifles in good order and I will show you a good battalion.'

Once more he congratulated me, and moved off. I saluted and remained behind.

'Let me have a look at that rifle, Sergeant,' I said.

He handed it to me. It was in very good order. Looking hard at him, I said, 'Where did you get this from?'

'Oh, I borrowed that for the occasion, sir,' he replied with a grin.

'Thought so,' I said. 'How are the others? They look alright outside.'

'Yes, sir,' he said. 'We just had time to give them a rub over with a drop of oil, and fix up the rack. I thought that would take the old man's eye.'

It did. They were not good inside.

'And I suppose the spiders have been living in your own barrels so long, you thought it would be a shame to disturb them, eh?'

'Well, sir, we have become sort of friendly,' he replied.

I could not help a laugh.

'Oh well, you had better eject them now,' I said.

I couldn't be angry. His resourcefulness and bluff had saved me as well as himself, for after all it was my responsibility. As an afterthought, I said, 'Suppose the brigadier had asked to see another rifle — what were you going to do about it?'

'Well, sir, I had thought of that. I reckoned I could manage to hand him the same one again.'

I had to laugh. And I knew he would have done it.

My company headquarters here was quite a comfortable and roomy sand-bag shelter, which had been used as an artillery ammunition store, now empty. One night, Lieut. Hickson, who before his promotion had been scout sergeant, asked my permission to invite one of his scouts, Private Grinham, in that night. It was not strictly in accordance with military etiquette, but I, of course, knew Grinham. He was only a lad, and one for whom I had a great affection.

He was full of wit and humour, game as a lion, and one who could be depended on to produce a joke when it was most needed. Hickson was also very fond of him and took a fatherly interest in him. He explained that he had a couple of cakes which had arrived in parcels that day, and as Grinham was celebrating his eighteenth birthday, he would like to give him a birthday party. I was astonished at the news. I knew he was young, but he had been with the battalion quite a time, and as eighteen was the minimum age for enlistment, I had put him down at about twenty. He had actually enlisted at sixteen, and added two years to his age.[2]

I gave Hickson permission to arrange the party, provided he invited me. He assured me that I was on the guest list. Grinham came and we had a most amusing evening. At about nine o'clock, I heard a very familiar Scottish voice at the door enquiring for me. Going to the door I found, to my great astonishment and delight, Sergeant Harris, one of the original members of my platoon in 1914, and one whom I had missed in my battalion on my return. He was the first N.C.O. I made in the original company, and he proved my judgement good. He was an ex-British regular, having served in the Seaforth Highlanders. After the evacuation of Gallipoli, thinking, like so many others, that the A.I.F. was to be left in Egypt on garrison duty, he had volunteered for service with the Camel Corps in Tripoli. When the A.I.F. left for France, he immediately applied for transfer back to his unit, but his application was refused. He was too good a man to lose. On the first opportunity, he deserted from the Camel Corps,

---

2 Melville Roy Grinham, a groom from Merino, enlisted in June 1915 with his parents' consent. His age on enlistment was officially recorded as 18. He arrived at Gallipoli shortly before the evacuation, and continued with the 8th Battalion until stricken with rheumatic fever in November 1916. After being away from the 8th for nine months while he recuperated, he distinguished himself at the battle of Menin Road east of Ypres on 20 September 1917. Advancing alone as a scout 200 yards ahead of his company under heavy shellfire, Grinham silenced a machine-gun nest by killing four Germans and capturing another four. Recommended for the VC, he was awarded the DCM. Later that same day, he was wounded (with shell fragments in his left buttock); he was evacuated to England, and then home to Australia.

got to Alexandria, stowed away on a troopship, and made his own way to England. From England, he made his way to France, located the battalion, and had arrived half an hour before. The adjutant had welcomed him as warmly as I did. He was taken on strength at once, but to my regret he was posted to another company. On finding his quarters and dropping his kit, his first enquiry had been for me, and here he was. I brought him in to join the party. On hearing the story of his adventures, I was more than ever glad to see him, because I knew the great risk he had taken to get back to his mates. He was safe now. But had he been caught on the way, he would have been charged with one of the most serious offences a soldier can commit, and punishable in the British Army by death. I gave him a noggin from my reserve rum issue. It was a truly wonderful effort, and I think he deserved it.[3]

While we were in Chateau Segard the battalion carried out a raid on the German line. The raiding party were chosen from volunteers and sent away for a fortnight for special training. The party was commanded by Captain Hurry, who had with him Lieut. Evans and Lieut. W.D. Joynt (afterwards Captain Joynt V.C.). Captain Hurry became ill during the training and the raid was carried out with Lieut. Evans in command. It was very successful. Our casualties were remarkably light (three wounded) and they brought back two prisoners, who were required for identification purposes.

At the conclusion of the brigade tour, we moved back to a standing camp in the vicinity of Poperinghe, where we were able to reconstitute the officers' mess. There was a building in the camp for the purpose, and the officers foregathered once more. Some of us had not seen each other for quite a time, and we spent a happy week together there.

One night, while the colonel was away on two days' leave, we set the mess gramophone going and had a dance. In the absence of

---

3 According to military records, George Harris rejoined the 8th Battalion on 10 September 1916. Like Grinham, Harris was awarded the DCM for bravery at Menin Road on 20 September 1917, and was sent back to Australia after being wounded during that offensive east of Ypres.

ladies, we had to dance with each other, but we made the best of it. All our officers were there, with a few guests from other battalions. During the evening, I noted the absence of Lieut. Scott. I always became apprehensive when he was missing from a party, and wondered what mischief he was brewing now. None of my officers knew anything about him. The party proceeded. A quarter of an hour later, Scott entered the ante-room, looking perfectly innocent. I was relieved to see him back and was no longer concerned about him, when suddenly, in the middle of a dance, with everybody singing to the music, there was a loud explosion. Master Scott was at it again. I might have known. He had a flare pistol this time. Extracting the fireworks from the cartridge, but leaving the charge intact, he had filled the cartridge with flour. He made an awful mess of several of the fellows in the vicinity. Everybody jumped and cried, 'What the devil's that?'

Then they all went for Scott. Scott went for the door. Finding his exit blocked, he turned in his stride and went straight for a window, taking a beautiful header straight through it. It was a canvas window, so it split easily, and he sailed through without touching the frame. That gave him the start while everybody else went for the door, with the three 'Minenwerfer' victims calling loud for vengeance.

Then followed an exciting twenty minutes of 'hare and hounds'. Scott was finally run to earth and escorted back to the mess. They came in puffing and laughing. Scott had put up a good run. The senior officers present decided on a drum-head court-martial. The charge was duly framed, the court-martial constituted, prisoner's friend and prosecuting officers appointed, and the case opened. I was asked to appear for both sides, but in the circumstances decided to remain neutral. It was a most amusing case. The evidence brought forth many touches of humour, causing great difficulty in preserving silence in the court.

The sentence of the court was that Scott should get down on the floor on his hands and knees, and submit himself to be kicked in the seat of the pants by every officer present. In default, he would be held in position and kicked three times. Scott was a good sport. He submitted and duly assumed the required position. The punishment was administered in order of seniority. I was not concerned about any physical hurt to Scott, as I knew the kicks would be very light ones, except in the case of the three victims, whom I could see were itching for their turn. I interviewed them before they got to him and warned them to go easy. Scott had been a good sport and was taking his punishment — and, after all, he had caused a lot of fun. They let him down fairly lightly, telling him what they would like to have done if I had not been present. He emerged from the ordeal laughing, and the party proceeded, after taking precautions to ensure that Scott did not leave the room again. It was the best night we had had for a long time, and everybody retired happy, still laughing over the incident.

After a week or so in this camp, we moved into billets in Poperinghe. It was quite a fine town, and though subject to long-range shell fire, with many of its houses more or less damaged, it was not destroyed, and a large proportion of the population still remained. It was the home of 'Toc H'. I remember the place well. I was billeted with some of my company officers, at an estaminet near the cathedral. Our landlady was quite a fine woman, and looked after us very well. We remained there a week, and then came our turn for the front line again.

The line ran along the top of a well-defined and fairly steep ridge. A deep railway cutting ran through the ridge, with a single arch bridge spanning it and held by us. Hill 60 was a huge mound on top of the ridge, formed of earth excavated from the cutting. It dominated the whole line and was held by the Germans. There was a similar mound in our territory on the opposite side of the cutting, but of little tactical importance, and used as cover for a trench mortar battery.

Our battalion sector was on the left of the railway cutting, directly underneath Hill 60, and on the left of the sector there was a gap of 600 yards between us and our next brigade sector, their right flank being a good deal in advance of our left. In this gap, we had to supply a standing patrol, consisting of one officer and sixteen other ranks. We also had a forward bomb post in No Man's Land, occupied by an N.C.O. and half a dozen men. This was built up with sand bags, and was reached by crawling on hands and knees through a hole in a front-line parapet and along a sand bag communication. As the trenches were very close, being not more than thirty yards apart, this was a very nasty post, and not particularly popular. Looking over the top, it seemed as if one could almost shake hands with the German observers.

In the cutting on our side of the bridge, our people had built a high wall of sandbags to prevent the enemy from firing down the cutting. We had a ration dump at the end of the cutting, and they were very fond of sniping at it at night, and got quite a number of casualties until the wall was built. On the enemy's side of the wall, the cutting had filled with water, and we posted a guard between the wall and the bridge to prevent raiders coming through. This guard was officially known as 'the submarine guard' because one night the enemy had sent a raiding party down the cutting in a boat, and, after throwing a few bombs at our people, had been hauled home again by a rope attached to the boat before our fellows could get at them. Taking it altogether, it was a very sad and unpleasant place.

The battalion moved out of Poperinghe the next afternoon and marched to Ypres. We were instructed that our tour of duty would be fourteen days in the front line, as before, and fourteen days in reserve.

Saying goodbye to our landlady, we thanked her for looking after us so well, and promised to call and see her on our return from the line. She shook her head and said, 'No, you will not see me again. In six days you will be relieved and will return to the Somme.'

We laughed. What could a civilian woman know about it? Our C.O. had told us definitely that we would remain here for the winter. Brigadier General Bennett had confirmed this during our last tour. And we were instructed this time that we were to carry on with repairs to the front line, to make our winter quarters comfortable. We assured her she was mistaken. We would come and see her again in a month or so. She shook her head again, and said, 'We will see.'

She wished us luck and said goodbye. The relief was carried out quietly and without trouble, and we passed a fairly quiet night, though the position was such that extreme vigilance was essential, and I remained in the line until daylight. Our quarters here were more comfortable than in the previous sector, and we were able to get a certain amount of rest in the daytime. The standing patrol was not relieved until twenty-four hours after the front line, owing to the risk of getting in and out. Their relief was carried out safely the next night. The German line ran back almost at right angles opposite the left of my sector. Our trench conformed, but was unoccupied except by two posts enfilading No Man's Land. At the second post, a track ran across the open to the patrol's position in a disused trench about 200 yards out on our left front. In our unoccupied trench opposite the patrol post, the Germans had established a machine gun post, so that it was necessary to proceed with caution going to and from the patrol. The following day, two officers of battalion headquarters 'Bombs' and 'Intelligence' notified me of their intention of visiting the standing patrol that night, requesting me to give the necessary authority to my left post to allow them out and in again. I agreed to go with them. They joined me in the front line during 'stand to'. After 'stand down', nothing out of the ordinary occurred, and we started off. It was a beautiful moonlight night, though moonlight nights at the front are not so popular when one has to move about without cover.

I stopped a few minutes at my left post talking to the corporal in charge, when I suddenly realised that the other two had gone on, and prepared to follow them, when the corporal, with an anxious tone in his voice, said, 'What about those other officers, sir? Where are they going?'

'Out to the patrol with me,' I said. 'They have gone on.'

'My God, they haven't!' he cried. 'They went in this trench. They will walk straight into the German post up there.'

'Hell! We had better go after them.'

And we started off at the run. Stopping a couple of times to listen, we called softly, but could hear nothing, and ran on again.

We were more than half way out when we met them coming back at the double. They were relieved to see us, but not half as much as we were to see them. They had got to within a few yards of the post. Hearing voices, they thought it was our patrol and went on, until they suddenly realised the voices were German, and they turned and bolted without being discovered. They had a narrow escape.

Returning to the post, and pointing out the track to the patrol position, we climbed out of the trench and started across. We reached the position safely, lit cigarettes, and smoked while the officer in charge gave us the details of his post. After a quarter of an hour or so, we started on the return journey. Goodwin climbed out first, followed by Foden, then me. As soon as I was out, a machine gun opened on us from the German post. I dived into the trench again, with the other two on top of me. The firing ceased. We waited five minutes and started again, Foden going first this time, followed by me, with Goodwin last. The same thing occurred as soon as Goodwin was up. We dived again, and fell in a heap. After another five minutes, we tried again. I took the lead this time, with Foden last. The same thing happened immediately the third man got out. Again we dived for the trench. We had escaped injury so far, but decided it was no use tempting Providence any further. The post was only about 100 yards away, and they could see us plainly in the moonlight.

The O.C.–Patrol advised us to follow the trench that he was in until we got out of sight of the German post, then we could get back over unoccupied ground and reach the front line from the left flank. We agreed to do this, but the trench had been badly damaged. After going about thirty yards under cover, we were forced to get out in the open again to get around a block in the trench. Thinking the Germans would not be looking for us here, we climbed out quite unconcernedly, when bang went the gun again, with bullets whizzing all around us. We wasted no time getting in to the trench again, fortunately still unhurt. Twenty yards further on was another block. We decided that a display of caution was indicated. Making sure how far we had to go, we each made ready to jump, and on the word sprang out and ran for it. We were hardly on our feet when the gunfire opened again, but again we beat it. This happened five or six times, until we apparently got too far away for them to see us — but we decided to go a bit further so as to make sure before taking to the open again.

To our surprise, we heard voices ahead of us. Not knowing what to expect, we proceeded with extreme caution until we were certain that they were talking English, when we let our presence be known and entered their post. They were a 2nd Division working party under the command of Lieut. Wertheim. They gave us our bearings and directions for getting back. We were about to leave them when Wertheim and Foden suddenly fell on each other's neck with exclamations of surprise and joy. They had been classmates at school and had not met since. We gave them a few minutes to chat before we had to drag Foden away.[4] It was time we were back. Getting out in the open again, we made our way across the top without further incident, and finally reached the line in safety.

Nothing beyond the ordinary trench routine occurred for the next couple of days, except that Division sent up a tripod, suggested for use with the Lewis gun, and I was asked to test and report on it. Fixing it in a good position and placing one of my best gunners in charge, I tried it out that night and fired a few drums myself. As far as the tripod was concerned, I liked it. It was very light, yet strong, and greatly improved the shooting of the gun — but in my opinion it robbed the gun of its greatest value, its mobility, and reduced it to the status of a fixed armament. I reported accordingly. I never heard any more about it, but the tripod was never used.[5]

---

4 Lieutenants James Clement Foden and Rupert Carl Wertheim had both attended Melbourne Grammar School. They left in the same year, 1910. Soon after their impromptu school reunion in no-man's-land, Foden resigned from the AIF and joined the Royal Flying Corps. Both survived the war. Wertheim played Davis Cup tennis for Australia. Foden became a Wing Commander in World War II.

5 This was not the only time Barrie's specialist expertise was put to good use. In November 1916, while the battalion was having a spell from the front, he delivered a lecture to the 8th Battalion's officers on the 'Lewis gun in co-operation with infantry'.

Early in the afternoon of our sixth day in the line, company commanders were instructed to report to battalion headquarters. We were all full of conjectures as to what was in the wind now. We expected a raid at least. To our surprise, we were told that we were to be relieved that night and would return to the Somme, where it was expected we would be required to carry out another attack. Receiving directions for battalion rendezvous and billeting area, we returned to our companies and made the necessary arrangements for relief. Our landlady was right. She knew more than our brigade commanders and C.O.s.

A battalion of 2nd Division relieved us that night. The relief had apparently been hurriedly arranged, and company commanders had no opportunity for inspection beforehand. There was, consequently, some confusion amongst the incoming troops. The communication trench was packed with them, and apparently not realising the close proximity of the German line, there was a good deal of noise going on. We warned their officers of the danger, but we were too late to avert trouble. They had evidently been heard by the Germans, for almost immediately shelling started straight down the trench from one end to the other, and they suffered quite a number of casualties before we could get them out.

Completing the relief, I kept my company in the front line until the shelling had ceased, and eventually got them out without casualties. The C.O. was a bit querulous when I arrived at the rendezvous for having kept him waiting. But I was used to that, and did not let it worry me. I was more concerned about the safety of my men than the strain on the colonel's nerves through waiting half an hour in the open, and I did not consider his personal comfort was worth the possible sacrifice of half a dozen good men. We marched through Ypres, and camped in a field beyond the town until the next afternoon.

Next morning, all mounted officers of the brigade were ordered to report, mounted, at 11.00 a.m. in an adjacent field for instruction in equitation by the brigade commander. This rather tickled us, for being recruited from country districts, most of our fellows were fair riders, while we saw so little of our horses in trench warfare that those who were not had little opportunity for learning. I personally had ridden from my earliest youth. It was my favourite recreation, and I had always kept a horse at home and in the country.

We assembled at battalion headquarters and rode to the appointed spot, where the brigade commander himself delivered a lecture on the points of a horse, then instructed us in the art of mounting and dismounting, after which he formed us into a ride and sent us round a circle at the walk, trot, and canter. There was a spirit of levity in the class, and nobody seemed to be taking the lesson seriously. I am afraid that our new brigade commander had not impressed us with a feeling of confidence. While cantering round the ring, one officer whom I knew to be a good horseman, having left his place, cantered past me with one foot out of the stirrup and hanging on to his horse in a most amateurish manner, while obviously kicking him along with the other foot. Two others were following him. As he rode alongside, I enquired what was up.

'My horse is bolting,' he said. 'I can't hold the brute. Kick yours up and bolt too.'

One of our officers moved up on my inner side and said, 'Come on, bolt, Dan.'

I kicked my horse up and joined them. Presently it looked as if half the class had lost control of their horses, though none actually had. The brigadier fumed and swore, and eventually halted the ride and ticked us all off in good style. He knew we 'damned infantrymen couldn't ride', and we continued to let him think so. He eventually sent us home, disgusted with our efforts, but swearing to make horsemen of us before he was done with us. But that was our only lesson.[6]

We left our bivouac that afternoon, and moved by two or three easy stages to the vicinity of St Omer, with the 8th Battalion billeting

---

6 Brigadier-General Antill was notoriously abrasive and authoritarian. He was known as 'Bull' or 'the Bullant'. Antill had been in the Light Horse throughout the first two years of the war before joining the 2nd Brigade, and it was characteristic of him to assume that a blunt lesson in how to ride a horse was appropriate.

in the village of Éperlecques, where we rested for a week.

While here, the battalion was ordered one day to parade just outside the village under the command of the regimental sergeant major, it being specifically stated that no officers were to attend the parade — the object being to give a labour politician the opportunity of addressing the troops on the question of conscription.

A referendum was to be held in Australia, and the troops were required to vote also.[7] The order annoyed everybody, as the troops, both officers and men, were fed up with politics and especially politicians, and deeply resented being asked to vote on the conscription question, and did not desire to be lectured about it. They had their own views and very definite ones at that.

I heard many a discussion in the billets, and the general opinion seemed to be that it was a matter for the politicians to decide, and they had no right to drag the troops into the matter.

They felt that conscription was the fairest method of raising reinforcements, and though they were doing their share in the war, they should not be asked to say that other men should be forced to come. I could see that, as far as the A.I.F. was concerned, the referendum was not going to be a true vote, as the outstanding point of view was that 'if they didn't want to come they could go to the devil and we would fight it out on our own.' They were too proud to demand the assistance which was promised them and should have been given voluntarily. Therefore, when the vote was taken, a great many men who were really in favour of conscription voted 'no' out of personal pride; and though the A.I.F. returned a 'yes' majority, the margin was small, and unscrupulous politicians at home jiggled the result and announced that the soldiers had voted 'no', making political capital out of soldiers to serve their own rotten ends. The troops were

---

7 Prime Minister Billy Hughes, sensing he did not have the numbers in parliament to introduce conscription via legislation, opted to hold an indicative plebiscite on the controversial issue. Assuming that the AIF would be strongly in favour, Hughes arranged for the soldiers' vote to be conducted early enough for him to be able to trumpet this anticipated large majority before polling day in Australia.

disgusted with the whole proceedings and those who ran it.[8]

The mere mention of politics reminds me of the man with the muck rake. Let us go back to something clean. We will return to the soldier.

We had a very happy week in Éperlecques, and the troops enjoyed a complete rest. Goodwin and I billeted together, and our billet became the regular meeting place for the officers in the evenings, especially the original 1914 men, amongst whom there was a very strong bond of comradeship. We enjoyed many happy evenings there.

At the end of a week, we packed up again, marched to Arques, and entrained for the Somme.

---

8   With the AIF's narrow margin in favour much less than Hughes was expecting, he cancelled the advertising he had booked, and refused to reveal the figures for five months, which fuelled rumours that the soldiers had voted against. Voting motives within the AIF varied. Barrie's assessment was accurate for some soldiers. Others voted against conscription because the Western Front was so ghastly that they were not prepared to compel relatives and friends to endure it against their will.

Chapter Fifteen

Arriving in the Somme area, the 5th and 8th billeted in Vignacourt, and the 6th and 7th in an adjacent village for three or four days before taking over a front-line sector.

I could sense a sort of nervous tension in the atmosphere. Commanding officers were conferring together, and I wondered what was afoot. I knew that the prospect of an attack would not cause them any undue anxiety in the ordinary course. That was part of our job. I discovered that they were nervous of going into action under our new brigadier.

They had all been ordered to report at brigade headquarters the day before we left Hill 60, when the brigadier had disclosed the news that we were to carry out another attack on the Somme.

He then proceeded to outline his ideas on the conduct of an attack. They were of such an astounding nature that all C.O.s were really alarmed. He proposed, for one thing, to revolutionise the methods of communication. Normally the method of communication is by telephone from battalion headquarters to artillery, thence to brigade headquarters. The artillery has to work in such close co-operation with the infantry that direct communication is essential. During the fight, the shelling is so heavy that telephone wires are generally destroyed, and communication has to be maintained by runners. The brigadier's idea was that telephone wires should be laid direct to brigade headquarters.

'Never mind the artillery,' he said. 'I'll let them know all that is necessary.'

And as far as runners were concerned, we need not bother about them. He had a better idea. Each company in the attack would carry a flag, and immediately they gained their objective it was to be planted on the parapet. He himself would be watching through his field glasses from the roof of his dug-out, with his staff captain alongside with a map. As soon as he saw the flag he would know the objective had been carried, and the staff captain would mark it off on the map. And that would be quicker than telephone or runner. One C.O. with a sense of humour asked, 'But suppose the flag is destroyed by shell fire, sir?'

'Well,' he replied, 'I will give you two flags to make sure.'

Splendid. They all wanted to laugh, but could not. They said no more. But they realised it was no laughing matter for the troops to go into action under a man so inexperienced, and they were really worried. Moreover, a point quite overlooked by the brigadier, was that his headquarters may be anything up to five miles away, and there might possibly be two or three hills between him and the front line.[1]

On our first night in Vignacourt, I had occasion to visit battalion headquarters. On leaving, Lieut. 'Tas' Mummery (intelligence officer) accompanied me, suggesting that I should walk as far as brigade headquarters with him, where he was going on a matter of duty.[2] It

---

1 Antill, opinionated as ever, was characteristically disinclined to defer to those much more familiar with Western Front conditions than he was. At Gallipoli, where he had been culpably involved in the slaughter of the Light Horse at the Nek, he had insisted that the futile charge had to continue (as depicted in the celebrated film *Gallipoli*) because a marker flag had allegedly been spotted in the Turkish trenches. Antill had planned that disastrous operation, and his insistence on continuing it when it had clearly become suicidal escalated the casualties. He claimed in 1916 that 90 officers had served at Gallipoli in his Light Horse brigade, and he was the only one who went right through the campaign; it evidently escaped him that he had wiped out a lot of them himself.

2 Tas Mummery was a tall, dark-haired, 19-year-old Wonthaggi clerk who enlisted in the first month of the war. He was wounded at Gallipoli, but rose through the ranks and became an officer in February 1916. His intellect was impressive, and his courage consistently outstanding. He was awarded the MC & Bar for his bravery at Pozières and Menin Road. Mummery was killed in action in October 1917. Among his admirers was Will Dyson, Australia's

was a fine night. Having nothing to do, I went with him. It is strange how fate arranges things. I started off with no ideas other than a pleasant walk and yarn with Mummery, one of the finest of our young officers, and one of the most popular in the battalion, amongst all ranks. That walk resulted in my being drawn into and taking part in the enactment of a little drama, which, though I think to this day is unknown except to the half dozen actors, is nevertheless, in my opinion, one of the epics of the war.[3]

Brigade headquarters was situated in a red-brick building on the corner of the street. Entering by the back entrance, I waited at the back door while Mummery transacted his business. Shortly afterwards, our C.O. entered. A good many people at this time were suffering from colds, and I could hear the brigadier coughing and spluttering inside. The C.O. emerged, and enquired if Mummery had left. Hearing he was still inside, he said, 'Good! I'll wait for him.' Then, 'What are you doing?' he asked of me.

Explaining that I had walked up with Mummery and was waiting for him, he said, 'That's alright then. I want you to walk back with me. I have a job for you.'

'Very good, sir,' I replied, wondering what it was all about.

Presently, Mummery appeared, and we all set off towards battalion headquarters. On the way, the C.O. explained to Mummery that he had been nominated as a staff learner. That is, for appointment as assistant staff officer on brigade or division staff, for instruction in staff duties. Mummery was a very smart officer, and had been with the battalion since August 1914, gaining his commission in the field. He would have made a good staff officer, and his duties would have been a deal less dangerous than as a battalion officer. The C.O. explained to him that he had taken upon himself to refuse

---

first official war artist, who dedicated one of his drawings to the 'Memory of Tas M—'.

3 It is indeed a remarkable story, but it seems that Barrie may have been mistaken in referring to Vignacourt. When the 8th Battalion arrived in the Somme area on 21 October 1916, their base for a few days was Yaucourt, not Vignacourt.

the appointment on Mummery's behalf, 'knowing' that he would not leave the battalion. Mummery received the news in silence. What could he say? Had it been left to him, he would have jumped at the chance. The real secret was, of course, that the C.O. could not spare him. He was a valuable officer, thoroughly game and dependable, and one of those who was taking a large share in carrying the C.O., who, though shrewd enough to know who was doing the work for him, had no recompense to offer Mummery for the sacrifice he had made on his behalf. I knew Mummery was furious, but could do nothing. I was sorry for him and just plain disgusted with the C.O.

On arrival at battalion headquarters, we entered the regimental office. Requesting those present to retire, the C.O. locked the door, and explained that he wanted our assistance in a plot which he would divulge to us under an oath of secrecy. We took the oath. He then confided in us that we would move into the line in a few days, and the attack was to be carried out by the 8th Battalion. He told us of the fears of the battalion commanders, and how on his visit to brigade headquarters he had found the brigadier suffering from a cold, and had endeavoured to persuade him that he looked ill, and should go to hospital.

'I can't go to hospital, Colonel,' the brigadier said. 'What would the brigade do without me?'

'Well, sir,' the colonel said, 'If you get really ill, we will have to do without you. At least, you had better see a doctor.'

'Doctor!' he snorted. 'What's the good of doctors? You haven't got a decent doctor here.'

'Oh yes we have, sir. The doctor I have in mind is one of the best men in Melbourne.'

The doctor he had in mind was indeed one of the best in Melbourne and a highly respected battalion medical officer. I will protect his reputation here by calling him Captain Clear.[4]

---

4 The identity of 'Captain Clear' remains unclear. It can hardly have been the 8th Battalion's doctor, Captain George Heydon, as Barrie described 'Captain Clear' as one of the best in Melbourne and relatively new to the Western Front. Heydon was based in Sydney and not new to the front.

Still protesting that the brigade could not do without him, after some further argument, the brigadier gave a grudging permission to send the doctor around.

'Now,' said the colonel to us, 'This is our chance to evacuate him. First, I want the other three C.O.s here, when I will explain the situation to them; then I want Captain Clear.' Turning to me, he said, 'I'll leave it to you to get them here as quickly as possible. Don't tell them anything, but say it is urgent. Mummery will remain on duty in the passage and see that no-one enters until the conference is over. When you return, remain on guard at the door of this room and admit the C.O.s as they arrive, but no-one else. Keep Captain Clear in the passage until he is called. Are you game?'

'Yes, sir,' we both replied. We were prepared to sink our feelings and join the plot for the sake of the brigade, and there was, moreover, a spice of adventure in it.

Securing two reliable runners, I sent them post haste to the C.O.s furthest away. I then delivered the summons myself to the third and nearest one, and warned the M.O. to attend in half an hour.

Returning to headquarters, I took up my station at the door. In an incredibly short space of time, the three C.O.s arrived, and the conference proceeded.[5] It did not take long. The decision was obviously unanimous. The door opened, and I was instructed to admit Captain Clear as soon as he arrived. He arrived almost immediately, and I admitted him at once. The four colonels were sitting at a table, looking very solemn. A service revolver was on the table in front of the chairman. The M.O. had not been long at the front, and did not know quite what to expect, but he was a good sport. He was first sworn to secrecy, and warned 'on pain of death' not to divulge any secrets which might be disclosed to him. The situation was then explained to him.

The brigadier's cold, which was not thought to be very bad, was to be made bad enough to send him to hospital, and it was the

---

5   Besides Coulter, at the helm of Barrie's unit, and Jess, who was still in charge of the 7th, the other battalion commanders in Antill's brigade were John Walstab of the 5th and C.W.D. Daly of the 6th.

bounden duty of the M.O. to evacuate him within twenty-four hours. In default, he would incur the everlasting displeasure of the whole brigade.

He agreed to carry out his instructions, and left immediately for brigade headquarters.

The rest of the story, as told to me afterwards, was as follows:

Arriving at brigade headquarters, the doctor announced himself and asked to see the general. The general was coughing as he entered.

Doctor — 'Good evening, sir. Not too fit?'

General — 'Oh, a bit of a cold, Doctor. Nothing much.'

Doctor — 'Hmm, I don't like your cough, sir. There are some nasty colds going about. Regular epidemic. I have had to evacuate quite a number.'

General — 'Well, you can't evacuate me.'

Doctor — 'I hope that won't be necessary, sir, but I would like to take your temperature.'

The thermometer showed normal, but the doctor assumed a grave expression.

Doctor — 'I'm afraid you ought to go to hospital, sir.'

General — 'Can't do it, Doctor! Can't do it! Why, we are going into action in a few days. What is the brigade going to do without me?'

Doctor — 'Well, of course I realise that it is bad for the brigade, sir, but it would be worse if you became seriously ill, and I'm afraid I couldn't take the risk of allowing you to go into the line in your present condition. However, we won't decide anything tonight. I will see how you are in the morning. In the meantime, you must get to bed, and take these pills I will leave with you.'

General — 'Alright, if you think that will do me any good, but I am not going to hospital.'

Doctor — 'Well, I will see you in the morning, sir, about ten o'clock. Better stay in bed until I come.'

Interviewing the staff captain, the M.O. left instructions that the brigadier was to be kept in bed, and if no better in the morning he would have to go to hospital. He advised that his batman have his kit packed, just in case.

Returning to his quarters, he arranged for an ambulance to report to him at nine o'clock next morning. Driving in the ambulance, the M.O. instructed the driver to wait for instructions in the next street, while he proceeded on foot to brigade headquarters. On being admitted to the general's room, he said, 'Well, sir, how are you feeling this morning?'

General — 'Much better, Doctor. Much better.'

Doctor — 'Let us see your temperature, sir.'

Again the thermometer showed normal.

Doctor — 'Hmm. Sorry, sir, but I am afraid I will have to evacuate you.'

General — 'But I can't go away, Doctor, I told you that last night.'

Doctor — 'Sorry, sir. But your condition is such that I couldn't take the risk of allowing you to go into the line.'

General — 'Rubbish, man! I am going into the line. How will the brigade get on if I am away?'

Doctor — 'I'm afraid I'm not concerned about that, sir. It is your health that concerns me, and I am sure you will pardon me if I remind you that even generals must bow to a doctor's orders. I will have an ambulance here for you in half an hour.'

General — 'Oh well, if you think so, I suppose I will have to go.'

Doctor — 'I'm afraid it can't be helped, sir. I would never hear the end of it if anything happened to you. I couldn't risk it.'

General — 'Alright, alright.'

Interviewing the staff captain again, the M.O. advised him that he was sending the brigadier to hospital. He was to be ready to leave in half an hour, when an ambulance would arrive to take him.

Returning to the ambulance, he instructed the driver to wait for half an hour, then drive to brigade headquarters and say he had been sent for the general. His instructions were duly carried out, and half an hour later our brigade commander was driven away, and we never saw him again.

Our C.O. was not popular, but I must give him due credit for the way he stage-managed that little act. The brigade heaved a sigh of relief when they knew that the brigadier was not to be allowed to risk his health in the line. The senior C.O. was appointed to command temporarily,[6] and shortly afterwards Brigadier General Heane took over the brigade.[7]

A couple of days after our brigadier's departure, we left Vignacourt. We were to travel by bus, and were ordered to rendezvous at 10.00 a.m. at a point about two miles out of the village where the buses would be waiting for us. It was a bitterly cold morning. Snow was lying thick on the ground and still falling occasionally. There was no sign of any buses. Something had gone wrong. We had to wait for two hours for them to arrive. I will never forget that wait; it was one of the coldest I have ever experienced. It was open country, with no shelter of any description. I thought we would freeze. Eventually, they turned up, we climbed aboard, and they drove us as far as Albert. From there, we marched to Pommiers Redoubt on the Montauban Road, where we were to camp for the night. It was almost dark when we arrived there. The battalion was halted in an open field, ankle deep in slush, with six bell tents erected in it. This was our accommodation for the night. We had some pretty rough billets, but this was about the roughest — and to make things worse, it was raining. However, it is astonishing what one can put up with when there is no alternative. It was not long before the troops had some sort of 'bivvies' erected, and though it could not be said by the greatest stretch of imagination that we passed a comfortable night, we still passed it. But I do not think anyone was sorry to see daylight.

---

6 The senior CO who became acting brigadier after Antill's departure was Jess.
7 An intriguing aspect of this arresting anecdote is that the first reference to Antill's ill-health in the official records is dated 26 November. There was often a delay before the record-keeping system caught up with events, but a gap of a month is unusually long. Coulter went on leave to London on 17 November (and was away more than a fortnight), so what Barrie described could not have occurred after that date. According to the records, Antill was in various hospitals with 'bronchitis' (one labelled it 'influenza'), and he was eventually sent to England. He returned to Australia in 1917, and his AIF. involvement ended, although the conclusion of the war was still a year away.

Next afternoon, we moved into Bernafay Wood, two or three miles further on. All traces of a wood had disappeared, and as we marched in off the road we went down to our knees in mud. This was a comfortable camp later on, but at this time it only contained about half a dozen Nissen huts. It was situated on the side of a hill forming one side of a long valley, with railhead just below us. The main accommodation was in holes cut in the side of a hill, the sides of which were built up with sandbags, and tarpaulins stretched across the top. It was not very comfortable, but better than Pommiers Redoubt.

The officers of my company and another shared a Nissen hut. The weather was bitterly cold and wet, with mud everywhere. Each hut was fitted with a brazier, and a ration of coke to burn in it was authorised, but never appeared. That coke ration was one of the mysteries of the army. I do not know whether it was ever discovered what became of it, but the soldiers looked in vain for it, until eventually in desperation they stripped the inside timber lining off the huts and burnt that.

While we were here, I discovered a clue as to what became of some of it. Early in the evening, with a couple of companions all clad in overcoats, I was pacing the floor trying to keep warm. Several others had crawled into their valises with the same object, while an enthusiastic bridge four were endeavouring to play at one end of the hut on an improvised table made of petrol cases with a steel helmet for a candlestick in the centre. They were having a very trying time, and pouring periodical torrents of abuse on all and sundry. What with three people tramping the floor, and everybody talking, and the poor light, it was difficult enough to concentrate on the game, but their patience was absolutely torn to shreds when a six-inch naval gun a couple of hundred yards away started to shoot at five minute intervals — and every time it fired, the concussion knocked their candle over. The wilder they got, the more amused everybody else became. They were four very wild men. I could not understand how they stuck to it. They were real 'fiends'.

While this was going on, a knock came to the door, and somebody asked for me. A corporal and two men of my company were there. They wanted two hours leave. The request astonished me. There was nowhere to go. It would take more than two hours to reach the nearest inhabited village. Moreover, we were, to all intents and purposes, in the line, as this was a reserve position. I refused the request. But knowing the corporal was a good lad, his request intrigued me, and I enquired what he wanted to do. His reply was evasive, but he assured me he would return on time if I let him go. I regretted it could not be done. He then tried another tack.

'Have you got any coke, sir?' he asked.

'No, of course I haven't,' I replied. 'I am not likely to have coke when the troops haven't got it.'

'If you give us leave, sir, I think I can bring you back a sand-bag full.'

'Where are you going to get it?' I asked.

'Well, sir, it's a cold night. I don't suppose you would worry where it came from if you had a fire, would you?'

'Not a bit. But I don't want you to get into trouble. You can't get near the railway coal dump, you know. There are too many sentries around that.'

'I know,' he answered. 'We are not going there, and we won't get into trouble. If you let us go, I will bring you back a bag of coke.'

'Alright,' I said. 'Report to me when you're back, and if you bring a bag of coke, I will give you a tot of rum.'

Away they went. In less than two hours, they returned and asked for me again. It was a pitch black night. I enquired who wanted me.

'It's Corporal Smart, sir,' a voice said. I have changed his name to protect his integrity. 'We have brought your coke.' They handed me a bag full.

'Good Lord!' I exclaimed. 'Where the devil did you get it?'

'You said you wouldn't ask any questions, sir,' said the corporal.

'Alright. I also promised you a tot of rum. Come in.'

The excitement over that bag of coke was intense. Even the bridge four ceased their game and came to see the magicians who had procured it. We soon had the brazier going and everybody gathered round to enquire where they got it, but they would not divulge the secret.

I gave them their tot of rum and tried to bribe the secret from them with the offer of another. But it was no good. They wouldn't tell. So I gave it to them anyway, and sent them off home to their mates with the two other bags they had brought.

Next evening, having used all the coke, we were pacing the floor again, trying to keep warm, when the same trio appeared, asking for me again.

'How's your coke, sir?' asked the corporal.

'I'm afraid it is all gone,' I replied. 'Haven't you any left?'

'No, sir. Would you like some more?'

'Rather, but where do you get it?'

Again he refused to tell.

'You said you wouldn't ask any questions, sir,' he said. 'If you give us two hours leave, I will bring you back a bag.'

'Alright. Go on. I will give you another tot of rum if you do.'

In two hours they were back with the coke, and received their tot of rum. But in spite of our combined efforts, we failed to discover the source of supply. They had brought an extra bag this night, and the corporal said, 'You can have the extra bag, sir, if you don't ask where we got it.'

'Alright,' I said. 'Fair thing. No questions, but you had better keep that bag. One will do us.'

'That's alright, sir. We brought it for you. We have plenty.' And he handed it over.

I gave them another issue, and they retired.

Next night, we moved into the line. The following morning while inspecting my posts, I met the corporal and his two confederates. Bidding them 'Good morning', I inspected their post, and after satisfying myself that everything was in order, I was preparing to move on, when looking hard at the corporal, I said, 'I say, Corporal, I am still rather intrigued about that coke. Where the devil did you get it?'

'Oh, now you said you wouldn't ask questions about that, sir,' he replied with a smile.

'I know, but you see, the situation has changed. Here we are in the line, and life up here is more or less uncertain. We may return. We may return to Bernafay one day and want more coke. It would be a frightful thing if anything happened to you while we are in, and we lost the secret.'

He laughed and said, 'Alright, sir, I'll tell you. I know you won't give me away.'

I assured him he need not fear that. He proceeded to explain.

'You know the A.S.C. camp and Willow Siding, near Fricourt, sir?'

'Yes,' I replied, 'but you surely didn't get it there. That is too well guarded.'

'No, sir, but opposite that, there is a German prison camp.'

Yes, I knew it well. It had an eight-foot barbed-wire fence all around it, and was also well guarded. They admitted it was.

'But on the corner of the road, there is an Armstrong hut with geraniums growing round it, and a path lined with white stones leading up to it from a gate in the barbed wire.'

Yes, I knew it.

'Well,' he said, 'that is occupied by the O.C.–Camp, and there is no sentry on that gate.'

'Well,' I said, 'what about it?' I still did not grasp the plot.

'Well, sir, the garden path was paved with coke, so we shook his garden path.'

I roared with laughter. It was one of the best pranks I had heard for a long time. I gave him full marks for initiative.

Chapter Sixteen

The battalion was not happy. We were occupying trenches known as 'Grease Trench' and 'Cheese Trench', with battalion headquarters in a sunken road known as 'Bull Run' in front of the village of Flers. The winter had set in. The trenches in places were waist deep in slush, and No Man's Land was a sea of sticky mud, in which men sank to the tops of their thigh boots, and had to use both hands to pull each boot in turn out of the mud as they advanced. It was in these conditions that we were ordered to carry out an attack. Our objective was a German strong point which had resisted many previous attempts at capture.

If other troops had failed to capture it while conditions were good, we realised that we had a very frail chance under the existing conditions. In fact, we knew that we would be nothing more than glorified 'Aunt Sallys' for the German riflemen and machine gunners, and would be shot down while floundering in the mud, without the slightest hope of ever reaching the objective.

The 8th Battalion always prided themselves on the fact that they never 'squealed', but we knew that any attempt at attack under these conditions could only end in another disaster such as had occurred at the Pozières windmill. Company commanders reported accordingly.

Under instructions from the C.O., the adjutant came up to verify our report. He supported it strongly. Representations were made through Brigade to Division to postpone the attack. Without seeking to obtain any first-hand knowledge, Division again refused the request — the attack must be carried out.

Realising the utter stupidity of the order from Division, company commanders made a further protest. Pointing out the impossibility of success and the certainty of heavy casualties, we requested that, before the attack took place, the brigade commander or his brigade major should make a personal inspection, so that the blame for failure this time could be fixed in the quarters where it belonged. Our suggestion was adopted, and the brigade major inspected the position. He returned fully convinced that we were right. The outcome was that the brigade commander paid a personal visit to Division, and insisted on postponing an attack. Grudging permission was given by division headquarters, with the intimation that when the weather cleared we would have to return and do it. This did not worry us, but the implied suggestion that we were 'squealers' annoyed us tremendously. However, our men were saved from the consequences of another blunder, and that was the main thing — but the battalion's back was up.

Next afternoon, Lieut. Bill Goodwin, bombing officer, visited the line. Taking a long look at the German strong point from one of our observations posts, he expressed the opinion that it was not manned during the day, the garrison coming in after dark and retiring before dawn. He decided to investigate. A sunken road ran through our line, across No Man's Land and into the German line past the strong point, and he decided to crawl along this road, and if as he suspected it was empty, to jump in and inspect it. No amount of argument could stop him, so our posts were duly notified that he was going and not to fire on him, but to be prepared to open on the strong point if he was caught and had to run for home.

He crawled out into the sunken road, and we anxiously watched his progress and for any sign of activity amongst the enemy. He made his way cautiously along the road. Nothing happened, until to our great surprise he reached the strong point. He peered cautiously in and then to everybody's astonishment, disappeared into it. Everyone was anxiously watching and listening. We heard nothing. After a few minutes, he reappeared and came back along the road. There was no-one there. It was an old dodge of the Germans. Knowing that any attack on a place like that would be made under cover of darkness, they withdrew the garrison to rest during the day. We were, of course, ordered to attack at night. Goodwin returned to battalion headquarters and reported his discovery. He then proposed to the commanding officer that he would take the strong point the next day, stipulating that he be allowed to make his own arrangements. The C.O. asked for his suggestions. He asked for two sections of riflemen, two Lewis-gun teams, and a team of bombers, to leave the front line at 4.30 p.m. without artillery preparation.

His idea was that he would be able to occupy the post unknown to the enemy, and surprise the garrison when they came in. It sounded simple enough, but we all knew that, though the capture might be easy, it would be a different matter to hold it, and the Germans were certain to make a desperate effort to retake it during the night.

Goodwin's proposals were submitted through Brigade to Division, and given approval. Next afternoon, he arrived in the line with his party drawn from the supporting companies, and at 4.30 p.m., just at the onset of dusk, he led them cautiously out along the sunken road. The front line garrison was standing to, ready for emergencies. The party reached the strong point without opposition, jumped in, and took possession. Unfortunately, they lost one man, Corporal Sack, who was accidentally killed by a premature burst from our own artillery.[1]

It was a wonderful effort, but we were all still very anxious, wondering what was going to happen when they were discovered. We fully expected the strong point would be blown to pieces during the night.

We had not very long to wait. After half an hour or so, though we could see nothing, we heard the explosion of a few bombs and some rifle fire, then silence. We knew the enemy garrison had made their appearance, and had been driven off. 'Now for it' was the thought in everybody's mind. Everyone thought that, as soon as the garrison reported the loss of the strong point, the Germans would

---

1 James Sack was a 23-year-old watchmaker from Hamilton. He died on 9 November 1916.

turn every gun they could bring to bear on it, and then launch a counter attack. We were ready to help as far as possible. Time went on. Nothing happened, but we did not allow their silence to deceive us. Everybody was alert and watchful, expecting hell to break loose at any minute. At midnight, the front-line garrison was relieved, and the battalion moved out to rest. But Goodwin and his party had to remain and hold their post for twenty-four hours, to be relieved by the incoming battalion the next night. We hated leaving them, being still certain that something was brewing. Imagine our delight and astonishment when Goodwin turned up the next night with his party complete. The Germans had accepted the loss of their post, and made no attempt to recapture it, and after driving the German garrison off they had not been molested.

It was a wonderful show. Goodwin, by his bravery and resource, had captured a post which had previously cost us hundreds of casualties, with the loss of one man accidentally killed, and had saved the battalion from an estimated loss of 200 to 300 men. In addition, the loss of this post to the enemy neutralised another known as 'Fritz's Folly', which also had cost us hundreds of casualties and defied capture, and which they soon afterwards evacuated. It was a feat well worthy of the D.S.O., but Goodwin's only recognition was the distinction (if any) of having his name inscribed on the map. The place was thereafter officially designated 'Goodwin's Post'.

Everybody expected that he would get some decoration for such a splendid job, and the whole battalion was properly indignant at his being overlooked. Unfortunately, our C.O. was not sober long enough to attend to such trifles. The battalion got credit for the job, and it was a large factor in gaining for the Commanding Officer the award of the D.S.O. in the New Year's Honours list. He became a very proud man. His battalion scoffed. It was incidents such as this that cheapened, in the eye of the soldier, that which should have been a great honour.

On our next tour, we went into 'Fritz's Folly'. This was, I think, about the worst sector we ever occupied, as far as conditions are concerned. We had two companies in the line and two in support.

The left company was fairly comfortable in a fairly dry trench. The right company, mine, was distributed in a series of posts in old German trenches in what was, to all intents and purposes, No Man's Land, with a garrison in 'Fritz's Folly' itself.

Company headquarters was in an old German artillery dug-out on the side of a sunken road, running out of Gueudecourt village. A hundred yards to the left, this road turned at right angles and ran through the German line. Round the corner of this road was a row of dug-outs which had been used by the German garrison of 'Fritz's Folly'. Between the two rows of dug-outs, there were barbed wire entanglements. It was a very uncomfortable place while the Huns were still in possession of the strong point. The distance from battalion headquarters to company headquarters was about 800 yards through a communications trench which it was impossible to keep clear of mud. As fast as it was dug out, the mud oozed in again, and it took the strongest of us a good two hours to traverse the distance, pulling each leg in turn out of the mud with both hands, and at the end stumbling and falling from sheer exhaustion. Men could not carry anything in their hands, so special containers strapped to their backs had to be devised for the ration parties, in order to leave their hands free for pulling their feet out of the mud.

Company headquarters was comfortable enough, being a deep dug-out with fifteen feet of earth on top, but it was under direct observation by the German artillery, and as we had no trenches and our only method of communication was across the top, all movement was forbidden in daylight. This was not only on account of the risk of casualties, but also to ensure that the position of our posts should not be given away to the enemy.

The situation was quiet during the day as a rule, but as soon as it got dark, shelling started, and company headquarters was under almost continuous shell fire until daylight. The ration party arrived each night about 6.30 p.m. very fatigued, and it was always an anxious time until we got them away again.

I used to start the first round of my posts as soon as it was dark enough to move in safety, and get back in time to receive the rations and superintend the issue.

There was an element of sport getting in and out of the dug-out once shelling had commenced. The entrances, of course, faced the German line, and there was quite a good chance of a shell bursting in the doorway, which sometimes actually happened. Climbing the staircase, one waited for a shell to burst, and estimating his chances of getting out before the next one arrived, dashed out through the entrance and made for the opposite bank of the sunken road, crouching there until the next one burst. Then up and run for it along the road, keeping as close to the bank as possible and flopping down when necessary, until clear of the line of fire. Then out across the top to two posts on the right of my sector. These were situated in an old German trench which had filled up with mud in the same way as the communication trench. There was no cover of any sort, not even a place to sit down, and for four days and nights those men stood in mud waist deep — except when each man took his turn on observation, he climbed on to a petrol case on the floor of the trench, and so got out of it a few inches. How they stuck it, God only knows. But during the whole of the time, when I visited them as often as I could, I never heard one breath of complaint from any of them, except that there was no rum issue.

I almost felt ashamed at having to tell them that I could not get it. If ever rum was needed it was there, but as I have explained, the conditions were such that the ration parties could not carry it. They could not even bring us water, and though at my request they made a special effort to get some up to us in two-gallon petrol tins, every tin was lost on the way. We badly needed water for washing and shaving as well as drinking, and our only way of getting it was to dip it out of shell holes. This was a risky procedure, because as soon as anyone moved out of the doorway they were liable to be fired on, and the enemy did not miss many opportunities.

I saw him one day chase two officers with shrapnel for a quarter of a mile along the communication trench, when only their heads were visible. The only thing to do was to wriggle out of the doorway on one's stomach, and across to the nearest shell hole, fill the can, and then run for it on the way back. The water was too dirty to drink, so we boiled it and made tea, and issued the balance out carefully for washing and shaving. I did not like the taste of the tea, but said nothing until others began to remark on it. It certainly had a horrible taste. We decided to investigate. Crawling out cautiously, two of our officers probed around the hole and discovered a dead German in the bottom. After that, we went without water, and saved what we could of our ration tea to shave in, and then washed in it with the aid of a washer.

It was recognised that the conditions in this sector were particularly bad, and the tour of duty was reduced to four days, to be done in two tours of forty-eight hours each. But it was such a frightful job getting in and out that the troops themselves asked to be allowed to remain in and complete the four days and be done with it. Their request was granted, though I began to seriously wonder whether they could possibly stick it out. It seemed to me to be beyond the powers of human endurance for men to stand for four days and nights waist deep in slush, soaked through from the waist down, without sleep, their only rest being to lean against the parapet into which they sank until only their faces and the front of their tunics were visible. This is no exaggeration. It is perfectly true. And they did it without a grumble. I used to dread going to their post each evening, wondering what I would find, but always I found them on their job and they met me with a smile. All they asked for was rum, and I always had to tell them there was none. What would I not have given for it then? And even then they did not grumble, for I think they knew that if it was possible I would have got it for them. I could not help feeling proud to command such men. They were wonderful. If only we could infuse their spirit into our national life, what a wonderful world it would be. At the end of their tour, they came out and carried on with their ordinary routine without any special recognition nor even special thanks, and they did not expect it. It was their job. But I did not fail to let them know that I appreciated them and what they had done.

During our tour of duty here, I made a report on the plan of defence, and requested permission to move a Lewis gun team. No alteration is permitted in the plan of defence without the permission of higher authority. One of my Lewis guns was occupying a post on the right of my sector, where it did not appear to be particularly advantageous, while the sunken road which ran through the German line and presented a perfectly good and safe approach for a raiding party was entirely unguarded. I therefore requested permission to move the gun to a position where it could control that road. My suggestion was approved. On my first visit to his post that night, I notified Corporal Gates, who was in charge of the gun, of the change of position, and instructed him to get his team out, and I would visit him on his new post at the conclusion of my tour. Gates was a 1914 man and a good, solid, and reliable N.C.O. He proceeded to pack up while I moved on to the next post. Soon after, to my surprise, I saw him and his team climbing over the parapet into No Man's Land. I enquired what he was doing. He assured me that he knew a way across the top which was shorter and easier than by the usual route. As it was almost dark and I knew I could trust Gates, I left him to it and proceeded on my tour of the other posts.

On completion of my tour, when returning to the sunken road by the track I always used, I heard voices in a place where I knew there was no post. I stopped and listened. Then I heard someone call my name. I went to see what was up, and there was the gun team standing on the parapet of an old German trench which they had all successfully jumped across, except Corporal Gates who had slipped on the top and fallen in. He was buried to his armpits in mud of such consistency that he could not extricate himself, and the united efforts of his mates failed to move him. Telling them to stand by, I went across to where I knew a party of engineers were working on trying to drain some of these trenches, and asked for the loan of a shovel, explaining what had happened. Two of their men came back with me. Handing Gates the shovel, we told him to dig himself out as far as he could, then we would try to pull him out. He dug down to his waist but could get no further, as the mud oozed in as fast as he dug. Then, two straddling the trench and the rest on either side, six men heaved on the shovel handle while Gates hung on from below. At first, they failed to move him — then gradually he came, and with one final heave they got him out. He had been wearing boots and puttees, but he came out of the mud barefooted, leaving them behind. His ankles and knee joints were almost dislocated and his thigh joints nearly pulled out of their sockets. He could not walk for twenty-four hours afterwards, and we had to put him to bed in the dug-out.[2]

Although our dug-out was a good one as regards construction, it was a very uncomfortable one to live in. Owing to the difficulty of getting in and out of the sector, we could not get our kits up, and were consequently without blankets. Thus we were forced to use some which had been left behind by the Germans. They were quite good blankets, but were literally crawling with lice, and though for some reason for which I was duly grateful, lice never troubled me, my companions had a frightful time with them. Added to this, the Germans, as well as splattering shrapnel around our doorways all night long, were lobbing H.E. on the roof with monotonous regularity and were gradually blowing the roof away — and each night we could feel them coming closer and closer, and began to make calculations as to how many nights it would take them to get one through and blow us up. On the fourth night, my company was relieved. I also was relieved to see them get out safely for a well-deserved rest and clean up. But I did not go with them. To my surprise, I was ordered to stay in for the remainder of the battalion tour, to supervise the guns in this sector and report further on their disposition for defence.

I did not have so much to do during the next four days, and in addition to my own duties I gave a hand generally with the ordinary trench routine. My two pals of 1914, Yates and Catron, came in with the relieving company. They had both recently re-joined on their return from Australia, and had met with the same cold reception that I had done. We had not seen much of each other, and we enjoyed our little reunion in spite of conditions. Each night, the shelling seemed

---

2   Stan Gates of Ballarat had been wounded and then evacuated sick from Gallipoli. On 12 March 1917, at the age of 28, he died of cerebro-spinal fever in France.

to become worse. A shell burst right in the doorway one night and wounded a sentry on the staircase, and the H.E. on the roof was getting deeper and deeper, until the last couple of nights the timbers began to shake with the concussion, and we knew they would get one through eventually if they kept at it. At the end of another four days, we were relieved by another battalion, and I was not sorry to see the last of that sector.

I had spent a very uncomfortable eight days covered in mud, continually wet, shaving, and doing my best to wash in what I could save of my tea — and I was looking forward to the prospect of wangling a bath somehow. I had been for longer periods in the line without a bath, but never so dirty.

On handing over, we warned the incoming people of the danger of the dug-out being blown in. The shaking of the timbers was very ominous to us, and was nightly getting worse. But they apparently did not realise the extreme danger of the situation, and continued the occupation. Before the completion of their tour, the enemy succeeded in penetrating the roof and bursting a shell inside, wrecking the dug-out and killing or wounding several of its occupants.

Our estimate of the time had proved correct, but we regretted that our friends had not taken our warning seriously.

After this tour, the brigade returned to Vignacourt and St Vaast, where we had a fortnight's rest and clean up.

On the way down, we halted for a day, and the battalion, one company at a time, visited the divisional baths, where everyone enjoyed the luxury of a hot bath and the troops were issued with clean underclothing. It was badly needed. We had been weeks in the line without the chance of a change.

We had a quiet time at St Vaast, with occasional leave to Amiens. Then back to the line again. We halted at Buire a couple of days on the way up. There was a German prison camp close by, and each morning a party of prisoners marched through the village on their way to a road-making job they were employed on. They were in the charge of one of their own N.C.O.s, with a Scottish private with fixed bayonet as escort. Prisoners of war were given the option of going to England or remaining in France and working on the roads, for which they were paid four and a half shillings per day. They were never employed under fire as ours were by the Germans, and many of them elected to stay.

Walking down the village street one evening to my company billet, I met this party of prisoners returning from their day's work. The German N.C.O. called the party to attention and saluted as he passed. I returned his salute — then, to my surprise, I noticed that the escort was missing. I wondered, but as they were walking in the direction of their camp, and I had no authority to interfere, I did not stop them, and proceeded on my way. Presently, I heard in the distance a Scottish voice singing 'Scots Wha Hae', and here was the escort being escorted home himself by two hefty Germans, one on each side holding his arms, and one of them carrying his rifle. Jock was singing at the top of his voice, as tight as a lord. What had happened was that Jock, doing duty in the prison camp while convalescing from wounds, had met his battalion on the road and, unfortunately for Jock, they had halted for the midday meal in the vicinity of his job. He was naturally excited at meeting his mates, and had lunch with them. Some of them were obviously carrying in their water bottles something stronger than tea, and Jock had imbibed well, but not too wisely. It was a humourous sight to see the prisoners conducting their escort home. I don't know what happened to Jock, but I was sadly afraid that he would be on the mat in the morning.

From Buire, we moved up into the front-line area again. And for many weeks afterwards were never out of it. We were in and out between front line and reserve, always in the mud, our feet continually wet, clothing covered in mud, and everybody filthy but happy. The weather conditions had put an end to active operations, and we were restricted to short tours of garrison duty. Our heavy baggage was left at the wagon lines, and we could not get a change of clothing or wash what we had. I always took the precaution of carrying a fair supply of socks in my pack, and changed them frequently, but my boots were never dry — they were wet inside and out, and within five minutes of my sock change, my feet were wet as ever again.

I have often wondered what would have happened if we had encountered those conditions in ordinary civil life. I feel quite sure many of us would have been down with pneumonia. But our sick list was remarkably small. It was a hard life, and everybody was perfectly fit. I can only think it was our fitness that saved us. Personally, I was never more fit in my life than during that period, though I suffered great discomfort from the lack of bathing facilities and clean clothing. We were relieved about the middle of January, when I received the welcome news that I was to go on leave. Then, as I was preparing to depart, I received a message stating that my leave was cancelled. A general order had come out stopping all leave. My luck! Everyone began to wonder what was on now. It sounded ominous. However, a couple of days later, just as we reached our billets in a comfortable little village, I was notified that I could now proceed on leave. Leave had been stopped on account of congestion at the base caused by German submarines in the Channel.

I suggested that I should wait until the next day, as the baggage would be up that night, and I badly needed a change of clothes. I was advised to hop it while my luck was in, in case I missed it altogether, as the situation in the Channel was somewhat uncertain. A leave train was due to depart that evening, and I would just have time to catch it. I caught it. And then ensued one of the most tedious train journeys I have ever experienced. It took us forty-eight hours to reach Le Havre. We were accommodated in dog-box compartments packed to full capacity, but the fact that we were going on leave kept everybody more or less cheerful.

Every time I think of that train, Bruce Bairnsfather's description of a train flashes through my mind. It was rather good. First, the spider spins a web from the buffer to the rail. The train starts. The cobweb stretches further and further until it finally snaps, but it must have taken the train at least a week to reach the breaking point of the cobweb. Then the dashing young subaltern catching the train, full of glee at the prospect of leave in London, leaves the train at the base a decrepit old man with a large crop of grey whiskers. Bairnsfather had a wonderful sense of humour and the ability to put it on paper.

His drawings, though necessarily exaggerated, were true to life. There was more humour in an infantry battalion than in any pantomime.

On arrival at Waterloo, my first thought was clean clothes. I was in a filthy state, having been without a change of clothing for nearly eight weeks, and being blessed with a tender skin, I was a mass of blotches from head to foot. I had all my life been in the habit of taking a daily bath, but now I could hardly remember when I had had the last one. I was frightfully uncomfortable and felt ashamed to come in contact with people. I hired a taxi and drove first to a store where I purchased a new outfit, then to a hotel, where I booked for a week. Mrs Midwood had invited me to spend my leave at 'The Grange', but I felt I could not possibly go to a private home in my present state. Procuring the services of a valet, I ordered a hot bath at once, and gave him a good tip to take my clothes away and burn them. Oh, the luxury of that bath. I just wallowed in it until it was almost cold — then, in clean, fresh clothing, I felt a new man. Proceeding to the basement, I sought the services of the hotel barber for a shave and haircut. Taking my seat in the chair, he proceeded to lather my face, and then I remember no more. I fell fast asleep. When I awoke, he presented me with a bill for seven and sixpence. He had been through the whole gamut of things a barber does. At least, he said he did. I didn't know. I could only smile and pay. The days of Richard Arkwright were gone for ever. I spent the first week of my leave in London, at the end of which, by the aid of three hot baths each day, my skin returned to normal and I felt comfortable again.

I went up to Cheshire for the second week, and spent a very happy time at 'The Grange'. It was like going home. The time went all too quickly, and I seemed to have hardly got there when the last day arrived and I had to return to London to catch the leave train for Southampton. Meeting some friends in London, I was persuaded without great difficulty to overstay my leave a day and have one more night in London. We went to a show and supper, and I enjoyed the night immensely, perhaps the more so because it was stolen. The brigade had been promised three months' rest before I left, so I knew that an extra day would not matter, and after my previous experience I was not worried about being caught. In fact, I enjoyed the adventure. Adopting the same tactics as I employed on the previous occasion, I had no difficulty in reaching Le Havre without being questioned, and from there I went by train to the front. I travelled in company with one of the medical officers, and we decided to detrain at Amiens, where we arrived about 6.00 p.m. and spent one more comfortable night at a hotel in preference to going on to Albert, where the accommodation provided for us was a bell tent in a miserably cold and muddy camp. We were well enough versed in the ways of the army to know we would have no difficulty in wangling a ride by motor transport next day.

I had always put up at the Hotel Universal on my previous visits to Amiens, but we found to our disappointment that it was full. The 2nd Division was resting in the vicinity, and their people on leave had taken up most of the accommodation. We finally secured rooms in a small hotel almost opposite the Universal. We spent a comfortable night and stayed to lunch the next day, which was Sunday. After lunch, we secured a lift in an ambulance as far as Albert, where we had to report ourselves and find the address of our units. I learnt weeks afterwards that my younger brother was on leave that weekend and was staying at the Universal, within a couple of hundred yards of our hotel.[3] I was frightfully disappointed at not seeing him. Though I knew he was in France, I had not seen him since I left Australia. It was hard luck to be so close to each other and for neither of us to know. We did not meet until about three months later.

On enquiry at Albert, I was astonished to find that the 2nd Brigade were in the line again. The promised three months' spell was all a myth. The 8th Battalion was at Bazentin with two companies in the line at 'Factory Corner'. I went up at once, regretting the stolen day in London. Finding the reserve companies at Bazentin, I discovered that my company was in the line. I left my bag and went to battalion headquarters.

On reporting my return, I was received with exclamations of

---

3 His younger brother was Sydney William Barrie of the 23rd Battalion.

surprise, and enquiries as to why I had returned so soon. I explained that my leave was up, and confessed that I had stolen one extra day as it was. I was advised not to mention the matter, as the M.O. and another officer who had gone four days ahead of me had not yet showed up. He asked if I had seen them. I hadn't.

'Well, anyhow,' I was told with a grin, 'you are soldier enough not to give your pals away like that. Didn't you like London?'

I assured them I did, and I certainly would not have come back out of my turn had I known, especially as I expected to find them still in rest billets. I was forgiven, and left to join my company.

It was a peculiar situation here. The front line ran parallel to and at the foot of a steep ridge. There was no communication trench. A duckboard track ran from battalion headquarters straight down the face of the ridge and into the trenches at the bottom. This was alright at night, but not so good in daylight, as all the way down the face of the ridge the track was exposed to direct fire, and one could see for miles over the enemy territory. Making my way down the track, I found my company at the bottom, where I received a welcome home with more exclamations of surprise. It was a beautiful moonlight night, and the whole country was white with snow and ice. It was a welcome relief from the mud. I started almost immediately on an inspection of my posts. On the left of my sector, a Lewis-gun post was forward in No Man's Land, and a shallow trench leading out to the post. I followed this for some distance, until I began to wonder if I was on the right track. I stopped and listened, but heard nothing, and was considering returning to make sure, when I heard a hiss not far off, then a voice calling softly to me to get down and come on. The trench was only waist deep. I got down and proceeded. A few yards further on, I entered the post. They explained to me in a whisper that they were very close to the German line, and I could be plainly seen against the snow.

I spent about ten minutes there, endeavouring to get the hang of the situation, then returned to the line, being warned to keep down on the way back. About half way back, thinking I was safe by then, I straightened up, then stopped, and leaning on my arms on the parapet, looked out over No Man's Land, admiring the scene and thinking of my last night in London. Presently, I heard the crack of a rifle and the smack of a bullet against the angle iron on the wire not a foot away. Realising then that the warning had been well warranted, I proceeded on my way with my head well down, and reached the line in safety. Beyond the beauty of the scene, I appreciated the ice that night, as I was all dressed up in a brand new outfit, just as I had left London. I would have hated the mud worse than ever in my new clothing.

I did not stay at 'Factory Corner' very long. About midday the next day, I received a message to report to battalion headquarters. I did not like the look of that duckboard track in daylight, and it looked worse from below. It ran straight up the hill, exposed to the whole world, and seemed impossible for anyone to reach the top, if a single German rifleman decided that he shouldn't. However, it was no use standing looking at it. I had to get to the top, and the sooner the better. I started off, feeling I wanted to get my head down and run for it. Pulling myself together and assuming a nonchalant air, which I did not altogether feel, I lit a cigarette and strolled quietly out on to the track and up the hill. I will never forget my feelings as I slowly climbed the hill with my back to the enemy. I could feel thousands of pairs of eyes looking over their rifle sights, boring into the middle of my back, and expected every second to feel the impact of a bullet. I badly wanted to look back, but refused to allow myself to do so. I kept my eyes fixed on the point where the track disappeared over the top of the hill. With every step, it was coming closer. I was half way up, and nothing had happened. I began to think I might reach it after all. Three parts of the way, and I was still going strong. The last few yards took a frightfully long time to cover, but at least I was at the top and over safely. Then I stopped and looked back over their lines for miles to the rear, and right and left along the front. Not a shot had been fired at me for some reason, but I could not imagine for a second that I had not been seen. I could see no reason why I was not shot at, but I was very grateful for the result. I went on to battalion headquarters and duly reported myself.

I was informed that my application for transfer to the 60th Battalion had been approved, and was instructed to report to 15th Brigade headquarters. I felt a pang at leaving my old battalion and particularly my company, more especially as I had had no opportunity of bidding them farewell. I left at once and made my way back to the headquarters of the 15th Brigade.

Chapter Seventeen

I had met General Elliott of the 15th Infantry Brigade one day a few weeks previously. His brigade headquarters happened to be situated a mile or so away from where the 8th Battalion was camped. I had not seen him since my return to France, and took the opportunity of calling on him. I found that he was ill. He was confined to his bed with an attack of influenza.[1] I left a message to say that I had called to see him, and was leaving again when his staff captain called me back, saying the general wished me to come in. I was admitted to his room, where I found him in bed. I was very glad to see him, though sorry he was ill. I always had a great admiration for Pompey, and I believe he was just as pleased to see me. I felt that he was too ill to be bothered with visitors, but he insisted on me sitting down and talking to him.

His brigade had suffered severely at Fromelles six months before, and had not yet fully recovered.[2] In fact one of his battalions, the 60th, which had come out of that fight with only one officer and sixty-two other ranks, had never since been sufficiently strong to take its place in the line. He was endeavouring now to build it up again, but was worried by the lack of experienced officers. The 8th were always interested in the 60th, as it was our sister battalion. The

---

1 Pompey Elliott was confined to bed for several days early in December 1916.
2 The disaster of Fromelles remains the worst 24 hours in Australian history. The AIF casualty toll at Fromelles — 5,533 in one night — is equivalent to the entire Australian casualties in the whole of the Vietnam War, the Korean War, and the South African (Boer) War put together.

nucleus of the 4th and 5th Divisions, which were formed in Egypt after the Gallipoli campaign, were obtained by splitting the 1st and 2nd Divisions in half, and then all four divisions were filled up with reinforcements, thus giving every battalion a stiffening of service men. Those taken from the 8th Battalion became the core of the new 60th Battalion.

I made a tentative suggestion to the general that he might find a job for me. To my surprise, he jumped at it.

'Of course I'll find a job for you,' he said. 'Why the devil didn't you come to me months ago?'

'Well,' I said, 'I didn't like leaving the old battalion, you know, sir.'

'I know that,' he replied, 'but you haven't been very happy there, have you?'

Surprised that he should know, I admitted I had not. I suggested that perhaps he had better make some enquiries first, and satisfy himself as to the cause, before he offered me an appointment.

'That is alright,' he said. 'I've made all the enquiries I want to make. You have never been to see me, but I have kept my eye on you. I am perfectly well aware of the situation in the 8th Battalion, and who and what is the cause of it. I have been hoping you would come and see me for months. If you want to come over, there is a job waiting for you, but I couldn't go ask for you, you know.'

I thanked him, and told him, if he was satisfied with me, I would apply.

'I am perfectly satisfied,' he said. 'I trained you, you know, and I have watched you as well as I could. You put in your application, and I will push it from this end.'

I was committed now, and though I did not like leaving my company, I had certainly not had a fair deal from the C.O. I agreed to apply, and bade him goodbye for the present.

I duly made my application, and though it met with some opposition, it was finally approved through the efforts of General Elliott. And now I was on my way to join him.

Arriving at brigade headquarters, I reported for duty and was told the general wanted to see me. I was shown to his room. He welcomed me kindly, and then proceeded to tell me what he expected of me.

His brigade was filling up with reinforcement officers and others promoted from the ranks who, he felt, while having nothing derogatory to say against them, were lacking in training and experience.

'And I will expect a good deal more from you than I do from them, both in and out of the line,' he said. 'I trained you, and you know what to expect. I will expect you to set an example to them at all times, and I won't spare you.'

'Very good, sir,' I replied. 'I will do my best.'

I was not under any illusion as to what to expect. It was not Pompey's way to give preferential treatment to those he knew, except in the way of hard work. The better he knew one, the more he expected, but he was always just.

I was appointed to the 60th Battalion and to command of 'B' Company.[3]

I was not an entire stranger, as several N.C.O.s were old 8th men, and one officer, Lieut. Richards, though not of my company, had been a corporal in my company in 1914.[4]

I received a warm welcome from them all. The battalion was in a low state, but was now rapidly filling up. The C.O., Lieut. Col. Duigan, also an old friend of mine, was absent in hospital, and I regret did not return.

Shortly after I joined, the battalion took its turn in the line again, the first time for months. We were not yet up to strength by any means. My company strength was two officers and seventy

---

3 The official date of Barrie's transfer to the 60th Battalion was 24 January 1917. He became a captain on 1 March.
4 Harry Richards was a 20-year-old motor mechanic from Stawell when he joined Barrie's 8th Battalion company in August 1914. He was promoted through the ranks while at Gallipoli. When the AIF was expanded after the evacuation, he was among the veterans transferred to form the experienced core of the 8th's newly created sister unit, the 60th Battalion. He was awarded the DCM for his brave rescuing of numerous wounded comrades from no-man's-land in the devastating aftermath of the Fromelles fiasco. Richards was out of action for months in 1917 after being gassed, but he survived the war and returned to Australia. He died in 1963.

other ranks, against an establishment of six officers and 220 other ranks, and my one subaltern, as I soon discovered in the line, was worse than useless. He was a newly arrived reinforcement officer who not only did not know his job, but was thoroughly unreliable and lacking in courage, principle, and morals. Although he doesn't deserve it, I will now protect his identity and just call him 'Dozer'. It is beyond me to conceive how such a person should ever have been given a commission while the ranks were full of splendid men, many of whom, with the necessary training, would have made excellent officers. He must have had a political pull somewhere, for I am certain that he was never chosen for his ability. Thank goodness I had some good N.C.O.s — and the troops, though new and inexperienced, were wonderful chaps.

On our first tour of duty, immediately after the relief was complete, my noble subaltern complained of indisposition. Unsuspecting, I suggested that he remain at company headquarters, which was in the front line, and stand by the telephone while I did duty in the line. Lieut. Richards, who was on battalion headquarters as bombing officer, had his bombers in the line and elected to camp with me. He was a splendid chap, and suggested that I should allow him to take a turn of duty for me. I thanked him, but refused, thinking my subaltern would be alright in the morning. But I was wrong. Next day, he was still bad, and spent the day resting and mostly sleeping.

I spent that day and all the next night in the line. During 'stand to' at daylight, we observed quite a large party of the enemy emerging from a communications trench behind their line, and turned a couple of Lewis guns onto them. It was quite amusing to see them scatter and run for cover, but they evidently got annoyed about it, for soon afterwards they shelled us, and things were quite lively for half an hour or so. Fortunately, their range was not so good, and we escaped casualties. They finally landed a shell right in their own line, when immediately a flare went up and shelling ceased. After 'stand down', I went to enquire about my subaltern's health. It had not improved. He was still not fit for duty, though I noted at breakfast his appetite did not seem to be affected.

I had been forty-eight hours without sleep, and felt I would like a rest, but I carried on until lunch time. After lunch, Richards suggested that he should take a turn in the line and allow us both to have a rest. He suspected that our patient was not as ill as he would have us believe. My own suspicions were aroused by this time, and after some argument I finally ordered him on duty.

Leaving instructions to call me if anything started, Richards and I both lay down as we were and slept a couple of hours. About 4.00 p.m., I woke and got up. I did not feel satisfied. Richards heard me sit and jumped up too, enquiring what was wrong. I assured him I was only going to have a look around, and he had better go to sleep again. He insisted on coming too. We went to one end of the sector and, though we found everything in order, there was no sign of the subaltern, nor had anyone seen him. I was not unduly concerned as he was probably at the other end. On my return at company headquarters, I met Company Sergeant Major Calder, a splendid fellow who later gained his commission.[5]

'Where have you been, Sergeant Major?' I enquired.

'Along the other end of the line, sir,' he replied.

'Is Dozer up there?'

'No, sir,' he answered.

'How far along did you go?'

'Right to the end post, sir,' was the reply.

'Well, that's strange,' I said. 'I have just been along this end and he is not there. Where is he?'

He looked a trifle sheepish as he replied, 'I don't know, sir.'

'Well,' I said, 'I want to know and I am going to find out. You had better come with me.'

'Very good, sir,' he replied. Then with an angry flush, 'Do you want to find him, sir?'

---

5 Roy Calder was a shortish 22-year-old carpenter with hazel eyes from Murphy's Creek. Like Richards, Calder was promoted to lieutenant and awarded the DCM after transferring from the 8th Battalion to the 60th when it was formed. Calder was severely wounded in August 1918: his left arm was fractured, and his right arm was amputated. He died in 1962.

'Yes, I do,' I answered.

'Very well, sir,' he replied. 'I will take you to him.'

I knew then that his patience had given out.

'Why did you say you didn't know where he was?' I asked him.

'You will see when you get there, sir. He's my officer,' he replied.

I did not quite know what he meant, but I sensed there was something wrong. I said no more.

He led us back the way we had come, and stopped at an observation post. Lifting up a waterproof sheet covering a ledge in the parapet dug out by the troops and used by them for their resting place, he exposed the officer in charge of the line, sound asleep. I was so enraged and disgusted, that I seized his belt and pulled him out. He dropped with a thud on to the floor of the trench, where Richards administered a good solid kick in his rear end. He picked himself up, whining and complaining. I ordered him back to company headquarters. I should, of course, have placed him under arrest at once and charged him. Had I realised what an unmitigated waster he really was I would have done so, but I still thought he might really be ill. Richards swore that he was simply a waster. The sergeant major would not say anything, for which I secretly admired him. Dozer swore that he felt so ill he had to lie down, and did not realise he was committing a crime. I gave him the benefit of the doubt, even though his crime was one of the most serious a soldier can commit. But I began to realise that I could not trust him, and carried on the remainder of the tour with the aid of Richards and the C.S.M.

On the fourth night, we were relieved. The relief was completed at midnight, with the exception of four posts which had somehow gone astray on the way in. The usual procedure in this case is to leave a junior officer in the line to bring the men out when the relief turns up. As I only had Dozer, I decided not to take the risk. Instead, I instructed him to take the company out and see them into their billets, while I remained for the completion of the relief. We were only going back as far as 'Switch Trench', near Delville Wood, and I could not conceive him making a mess of that job. There was nothing that I could see to go wrong. The missing posts eventually turned up, and I left the line about 2.00 a.m. with the balance of my company.

It was a moonlight night, but cloudy. As I reached 'Switch Trench', I found the duckboards blocked with troops. I enquired what they were doing.

'Waiting to find where we are to go, sir,' someone answered.

'Who are you?' I asked.

'60th Battalion, sir,' someone replied.

That was strange. I thought they were all down long ago.

'What company are you?' I asked.

Imagine my surprise when a man near me said, 'Your company, sir.'

'What? But I sent you down two hours ahead of me. What is wrong?'

'Don't know, sir,' they answered.

'Where's Dozer?' I asked. 'Send him along here.'

'He isn't here, sir. We haven't seen him since we arrived.'

My hat! How lovely. Telling them to stand by for a few minutes, I went to enquire what the delay was. I found a cupola close by, where some of our officers were sleeping. Upon entering, I found the officers of one of our companies and some of the relieving battalion. I enquired for the location of my company billets. The incoming people explained that there had been a mix up. They were instructed to camp here and had apparently taken the billets allotted to us. They expressed their regret, but my company had been put in somewhere else. When I explained that they were standing on the duckboards, waiting, they thought I was joking. I assured them I was not, and asked for Dozer. He had been in bed a couple of hours, they said, and must have seen his company right first.

'Where is he?' I enquired.

'There he is,' pointing to a form curled up in a valise. He was sound asleep. He had a rude awakening. Ordering him to dress and follow me, I went in search of the sergeant major. He had just returned from an unsuccessful search for accommodation. We started off again. Dozer joined us, but I could not stand his whining. I am afraid I was rather short in the temper. I sent him back to bed. He was more useful there.

A quick glance at the trench, and Calder's assurance, satisfied me that there was no accommodation there, but not far away was an old artillery position now vacated, and there we found ample room, and in a quarter of an hour or so we had the troops well on the way to bed.

On my return to the cupola, someone suggested a nightcap. I was tired and angry, and wanted a drink. Our guests produced a bottle of whisky and we had one; in fact I had two, and felt better.

When I returned the bottle, they said, 'Oh, leave it there, we'll get it in the morning.'

It was three-parts full. I put it under the head of my valise for safety and turned in, looking forward to a late reveille in the morning.

At 6.00 a.m., I received a message instructing me to provide a working party of one officer and sixty other ranks to report to brigade headquarters at 8.00 a.m. Rousing Dozer, I warned him for duty and gave him his instructions. He was still too ill to go. I was fed up with his whining by this time and told him so — also that if I had any more nonsense from him, I would place him under arrest.

I went to warn the C.S.M. to detail the party. On my return, I met the M.O.[6] Here was the chance I was looking for. I asked him to certify to Dozer's illness and to state whether he was fit for duty. He made his examination and reported that he did not seem too good. Then he asked him to sit up and show his tongue. Dozer sat up and immediately became violently ill. I relented at once, and regretted that I had perhaps been a bit harsh with him. There was nothing for it but to take the party myself. Remembering the whisky, I went to get it to return it to its owner. It was gone. Nobody knew anything

---

6 Captain Keith Doig was the 60th Battalion's 25-year-old doctor. He was brave, capable, selfless, and widely admired. Tall and solidly built, he had played 44 matches for University in the Victorian Football League. Enlisting after completing his degree at Melbourne University, he served with the 60th from December 1916 to June 1918, and wrote superb letters about his experiences to his fiancée, Louie Grant. Major Doig MC survived the war, married Louie, and settled in Colac, where he became a revered GP. His funeral in 1949 was one of Colac's biggest.

about it. I looked at Dozer and wondered; then, feeling in the head of his valise, I found it, empty. I showed it to the doctor. It assisted him materially in his diagnosis. The infernal waster — he had not only stolen the whisky, but had drunk the whole lot himself during the night, and was now too drunk to go on duty. He was a bright example of political influence.

I was very grateful when another officer offered to take his place. At first, I refused his offer, but he insisted, pointing out that he was not making the offer out of any affection for Dozer, but he knew what had happened in the line. He had not been in this time, but he had had a good job in charge of a ration dump. After some argument, I gratefully accepted his offer, and having seen the party off, went back to rest.

Next day, we moved to Bernafay. On the last night of the brigade tour, a few nights later, I was ordered to take a working party of 100 men to the front line to complete the laying of an underground cable. Another party of the same number was to go from another company. The brigadier was very keen about this job, and, after battling to get it done, wanted to complete it before he left. We were given a task and instructed to complete it, and we would return as soon as the job was done. Large bodies of troops were forbidden to move forward of Delville Wood before 4.30 p.m., as the country from there to a point just in the rear of the front line was exposed to the enemy's view, and we were liable to be shelled. We arranged to be at Delville Wood in time to leave there at 4.30 p.m. A little before then, I considered it was dark enough to escape observation, and we decided to take the risk. Two tracks ran parallel from Delville Wood to 'Needle Trench', the close support position, and we decided to use them both, my party taking the left, and the other the right.

We started at once. It was nearly dark, and normally quite safe. I was at the head of my party, and could just distinguish the other party keeping pace on my right. All went well until we were about 150 yards from 'Needle Trench', when an aeroplane flew over us, flying towards the German line. He came down very low and right above us, but it was too dark to distinguish his marks. After crossing the line, he fired a flare, which was followed immediately by a hail of shrapnel and gas shells straight up each duckboard track. He was a German alright. Almost immediately, the gas alarm sounded from 'Needle Trench'. I ordered gas masks on. Not having adjusted them, we could not see where we were going, so I took mine off and sniffed. My eyes were running, and I felt sure it was only lachrymatory, so I ordered masks off and run for it. We could not stay there. Stepping off the duckboards, I shouted to the troops to run, telling the sergeant to see the masks adjusted as soon as they reached 'Needle Trench'.

Shrapnel was falling in a regular hail; a nose cap landed at my feet, and I felt very uncomfortable standing there in it. I was very glad when I saw the last man of the party coming. On the tail of the party, two men were helping another along, but he had only a slight wound in the foot, and they kept going, so I followed. By a stroke of luck, we reached 'Needle Trench' and got safely under cover without further casualties. Making certain that all gas masks were adjusted, I went to see about the wounded man. I found him in a small dug-out with half a dozen others, then went in search of an M.O. I found one at battalion headquarters. It was an amusing sight to see everybody there, from the colonel down, with tears pouring down their cheeks, crying as if their hearts would break. The doctor came with me at once. They were still shelling heavily. One landed on the parapet just over our heads. We both ducked. I smelt a sickly odour and the doctor shouted, 'Get your mask on quickly. That is phosgene.'

I slipped on my mask, and we proceeded. It was a clever trick. The shrapnel was covering up the gas, and the tear gas was covering up the phosgene. I was somewhat worried, not knowing what damage had been done, as the effects of the gas would probably not show for some hours later.

After half an hour, the shelling ceased, and we moved out of 'Needle Trench' and on to the job. The task was completed at about 4.00 a.m., and we returned to camp. At about seven o'clock, the M.O. appeared and wanted to sound me. I assured him I was alright, but he had a different opinion. He had been instructed to overhaul everyone who had been with the working parties the night before. I submitted to an examination, and to my surprise he informed me that I was suffering from a slight dose of gas, and was to remain in bed for twenty-four hours. Several numbers of the party were suffering from the same effects, fortunately with no serious results.

I was not very pleased with the condition of the Lewis guns in my company, and took the first opportunity out of the line to make a complete and thorough inspection. The result astounded me. The guns themselves were in bad order. Most of them were minus the barrel, and almost entirely devoid of spare parts. In addition, there was only one man with each gun who knew how to handle it. This state of affairs was liable to land us in trouble in the event of an attack. If the gun itself broke down in a fight, it simply meant that it was out of action, as there were no spare parts to repair it. If the gunner became a casualty, the same thing happened, as there was no-one trained to take his place. Making out a complete list of spare parts required, I sought out the C.O., made a verbal report to him on the state of my guns, pointing out the risk of going into the line with guns in that condition, and requested him to requisition spare parts immediately, and also to permit me to depart from the syllabus of work for the purpose of training extra gunners.

Major Trickey, one of the original 8th Battalion officers, was acting in command.[7] Knowing him well, I was able to impress him with the seriousness of the case, and he readily agreed to my request, promising to send for the spare parts at once. He then asked me what the state of the guns in other companies was.

This, of course, I could not tell him. I had no authority to interfere with any guns outside of my own company.

'Well,' he said, 'it's a pretty serious job if they are all in that state. You had better inspect them all. I will put it in orders tonight, and instruct company commanders to send their guns to you for inspection, and men for training.'

---

7   Frederick Victor Trickey was an experienced officer who had served in South Africa as well as in the militia. Married, and employed as a public servant, he had a dual celebration when the Armistice was declared — it was his 34th birthday.

I suggested that company commanders might resent me butting in on their job.

'Never mind that,' he said. 'I am going to order it. None of them understand the gun like you do, and while I am in command of the battalion I want to know they are fit to work. It's too serious to be worried about that. I want a full report.'

'Alright, sir,' I replied. 'I quite agree. I will inspect them and report accordingly.'

Instructions were issued in orders that night, and the next day I made my inspection. I found the guns all more or less in the same condition as mine, and no spare gunners. I reported the situation as I found it, accompanied by a list of spare parts required.

It was a formidable list. I completed my report by stating that the condition of the guns was more the result of circumstances than anyone's fault, and was due to the state of the battalion during the last few months. This was correct, and I did not want to land anyone in trouble. Nevertheless, one officer in particular took my report very much to heart, and refused to speak to me in consequence. It was very silly, as there was no blame attached to him, and the ultimate result was that his guns and teams were brought up to a state of efficiency, with spare parts complete.

The C.O. thanked me for my report, but was very worried at the reply from the ordinance department that there were no spare parts available.

'What are we going to do now?' he asked.

'Well, if you will leave it to me, sir,' I said, 'I will get the spare parts. There are hundreds of guns lying about on the battlefield. If I can have half a dozen men for a couple of days, under Corporal O'Connor, I think he can find enough parts to fit out the battalion.' Corporal O'Connor was a good man and my best gunner.

The C.O.'s face brightened. 'Do you think you can?' he asked.

I assured him it could be done.

'Alright,' he said, 'I will leave it to you. Do what you like, and let me know how you get on.'

In two days, we had more spare parts than we knew what to do with. Every gun was complete with equipment even to spare barrels, and at the end of a week each gun had a full team of six men, each one with a working knowledge of the gun.

Personally, I felt much more comfortable about going into the line again. The C.O. was also very pleased, and most of the company commanders realised the position now, and were also pleased about it. Only one man still had the 'huff' and never spoke to me again. His was a brand of mentality that I could not understand. However, I was not worried about him, and as he left us soon after, it did not matter much.

I had a nasty experience coming down from the line one night about this time. The ground had thawed. The snow and ice had gone, and the mud had resumed duty. It was a pitch-black night, I think the darkest night I have ever experienced. There had been a good deal of rain, followed by two days of sunshine, and the shell holes were full of thick, sticky mud. We had come down via Delville Wood at about 2.00 a.m., and I took the head of the column to make sure of the track. Approaching the Bernafay Road, the duckboards petered out about 300 yards from the road, and from there on a track wound between the shell holes.

I had traversed it so often, I did not think it possible to go wrong, but owing to the darkness it was impossible to distinguish it. I strayed a little, and walked into a fifteen-inch shell hole. Floundering in the mud in an effort to extricate myself, I found I could not move my feet and I was gradually sinking. Making a desperate effort to get one foot out of the mud, I failed and fell forward. I knew I was gone if I got under the mud. Jerking my head forward, by a lucky fluke (or was it an act of Providence?), my steel helmet flew off my head and landed upside down in front of me. I struck it with both hands as I was falling. It was not much support, but it helped me, and I was able to keep my head out, though I could feel my body going gradually down. I was waist deep by this time. I had called to the men behind me to look out. They stopped on the brink. Realising what was happening to me, six of them, each seizing hold of the belt of the man in front, came after me until the first got within reach.

Grabbing my belt, he hung on, while the rest pulled, and eventually extricated the two of us. I cannot tell how grateful I was when I was standing on solid ground again. I had had a very narrow escape from a particularly nasty death. From there on to the road, the whole party linked up and proceeded with caution, eventually reaching it safely, to my great relief.

At the end of February, I was notified that I had been nominated by Brigade to attend a course at the 4th Army School at Domart-en-Ponthieu. I did not particularly wish to attend this course. My company was building up. I had three subalterns now, and I was more interested in training and building up my company. But I had to go. It appeared that the brigadier himself had nominated me. I had had something of a reputation as an instructor in the old days at home, and he desired to send officers with the ability to impart the instruction gained on their return to their units. So, in company with a party of officers and N.C.O.s from other units of the brigade, I left for Albert one afternoon to entrain next morning for Domart.[8] I spent the night at a house in Albert which was run by the Y.M.C.A. as an officers' club, and next morning repaired to the station to catch a train which was scheduled to depart at 10.00 a.m. The party was complete, but there was no sign of a train. Enquiries from the R.T.O. elicited no information. That did not altogether surprise us, as I have never yet discovered an R.T.O. who could give any information about his job. The most we could discover was that he thought there might be a train going about midday, but he did not know where to. There was nothing to do but wait. Four hours later, the R.T.O. announced that our train was standing in the yard and we could board it now. We formed up in the yard only to discover that the train was composed entirely of horse trucks.

Our party clambered aboard these dirty horse trucks, but the train seemed to be in no hurry to depart, and it was late in the afternoon when we finally pulled out.

We passed through Amiens that evening at 6.00 p.m. There

---

8 According to military records, Barrie left his unit on 25 February 1917 to attend the course.

being nothing else to do, we spread our valises out and turned in. At midnight, we ran slowly into a large, but dimly lit station. Getting out of bed to see where we were, I was astounded to find we were at Amiens again. Lord knows where we had been in the intervening six hours, but there we were. Being acquainted with the vagaries of troop trains, we turned in again and tried to sleep, while the train rumbled slowly on. Early in the morning, the train stopped at a wayside station. Getting out to enquire if we had reached our destination, we discovered we were at Abbeville. Nobody knew how long we would be there, or why we had stopped, or anything at all about us. We stood by, expecting to start at any minute. At nine o'clock, there was still no sign of moving.

Having no rations, everybody was hungry, so we took the risk and set out in search of food. Finding a shop, we bought a supply, and returned to the train for breakfast. It was a cold morning. We borrowed a sheet of iron which was lying on the platform and laid it on the floor of the truck, then borrowed some coal from the dump and soon had a fire going, which made things cheerful, even if it was against regulations. After breakfast, there being still no sign of moving, some of us decided to go for a walk to get some exercise and warmth. We were afraid to go far, in case the train crew suddenly decided to go somewhere. Approaching midday, we made a further effort to get some information regarding our movements. Again, we failed. Nobody knew anything about us, nor was anyone sufficiently interested to find out. We took a risk and went out in search of lunch, which we procured at an estaminet close by.

Not wishing to be left behind if the train did start, we returned and sat round the fire in the truck, taking the precaution of laying in a further supply of coal to last us through the night. Finally, at about 6.00 p.m. we noticed signs of activity amongst the train crew. The whistle blew, a few strays came running back, and we started off again. We had been nearly twelve hours lying at a siding and nobody knew why. We travelled all that night, and at about 6.00 a.m. the train stopped again at a wayside station. Again, we could discover no information. Nobody knew why we had stopped, nor when we would start again, if at all, nor whether we had further to go, nor anything about our trip. So we just strolled about the platform and waited.

At about 8.00 a.m., we managed to extract from the driver the information that he would not be starting again for some time and we would have time to get breakfast. He also promised to give us a signal before starting. We arranged breakfast at an estaminet close by. A little before 10.00 a.m. the whistle blew, everyone climbed aboard, and off we went again. Not far this time. The train pulled out of the station, shunted on to a branch line, and went backwards for about a mile, then stopped at another station. Here we were instructed to detrain for Domart. Enquiring about transport, we were informed that we were expected the day before. Transport had been there to meet us yesterday, but there would be none today. What were we to do? There seemed only one thing for it — to walk. There was no possibility of hiring a vehicle there. The distance? Twelve kilometres. Splendid! A nice little stroll before lunch. It seemed the only thing to do. We enquired about the route. The road crossed the railway at the station we had just left and where our train, for some unknown reason, had been resting for four hours. Time enough to have walked the distance, and the mile they had pushed us back was now added.

Troop trains are a wonderful institution, but I think this was the best example I had met with. We had been forty-four hours in a horse truck, to accomplish a journey of thirty-five miles.

Leaving our baggage at the station, we set off on the tramp to Domart, where we arrived in the early afternoon. We were paraded before the commanding officer (a colonel of the Rifle Brigade) to show cause why we should not be returned to our units for being twenty-four hours late in reporting. We were evidently suspected of joy-riding on the way. It was not worrying me to any extent, and I almost wished that the threat would be carried out. I afterwards regretted very much that it was not, for it was during the course of this school, which lasted a month, that the Germans commenced their retreat to the Hindenburg Line.

However, our explanation was accepted, we were duly allotted syndicates, and transport sent for our baggage.

I enjoyed the school well enough, though I felt constantly that I was wasting time. Except for a few new drill movements and the latest ideas in bayonet fighting, I did not learn much. It was nevertheless a good school, but mainly intended for the instruction of N.C.O.s and officers promoted in the field, whereas I had passed examinations at home of a higher standard. However, it brushed me up on instructional work, and I felt that I was up-to-date at the end of it.

During the course of the school, we were treated to a lecture by a Professor Atkinson on 'The Russian Revolution and Its Possible Effect on the Allies'. Professor Atkinson was a very clever man, and delivered a very interesting lecture. He had been sent to France by the British Government to help qualm the fears of the troops and prevent a panic in the British Army. The British Army was not particularly interested. They realised that the revolution would possibly make their job a bit harder, but they went quietly on with it, ready to meet the trouble when it came.

The lecture was admirably delivered, calculated to inspire those who heard it with confidence. The revolution was the best thing that could have happened for us, and would hasten the end of the war in our favour. The lecturer was apparently sincere in all he said. He had to be, of course, but it was so obviously political propaganda that I am afraid the lecture defeated its own ends, and merely increased our contempt for the tactics of the politicians. Soldiers may be simple, but they do not swallow everything. We were left with the feeling that the politicians were panicky, but did not take it as a compliment that they should class the soldiers in their own category.

I was not sorry when the school ended. We heard rumours of happenings at the front, but could get no detailed information. The Germans had evacuated their position on the Somme on 17th March, and were retiring on the new position on the Hindenburg Line. The 15th Brigade were allotted the job of advance guard for the 5th Division, though as I said, we did not know then what was happening, and our pals were too busy to write and tell us. It was our first experience of open warfare, and I was sorry to have missed it.

Chapter Eighteen

Upon reporting our return to duty at brigade headquarters, we found that the brigade had just been relieved of front-line duty, but was still up in support. The 60th were billeted at Haplincourt village. I made my way up at once, reported, and took over my company.[1] The Germans were still holding a line of villages in front of the Hindenburg Line, and we had not yet actually settled down to trench warfare again. Cavalry patrols were working in the front-line area, and it seemed quite strange to see them moving about. It was the first time that our own mounted troops had an opportunity of getting into action in France. Our casualties had not been severe during the advance, and the troops appreciated the change from the monotony of trench warfare. It was also a pleasant change to get into good country again that had not been churned up by shellfire. But the wilful damage done by the Germans as they retired was appalling. There was not a single house left standing in any one of the numerous villages between the old Somme battlefield and the Hindenburg Line. They had been systematically destroyed by explosives before being evacuated. This was done, of course, to prevent us from using the villages as cover for our troops.

In every case where the demolition was not complete and there was any possibility of our troops finding shelter, the place was either fouled by the Germans or else they had laid a booby trap. Such things

---

1 Barrie rejoined the 60th on 30 March 1917.

as a stove pipe lying on the floor with a wire attached which would explode a mine, so that when our troops attempted to replace a stove pipe preparatory to lighting a fire, the mine would explode and blow up the house and all who were in it.

In some cases, the most notable one being the Bapaume Town Hall, mines were laid with a time fuse. Bapaume was a big town, and the town hall was, I think, the only building in the town that was not damaged. The town hall was occupied by the Town Major and certain headquarters details for about a fortnight before the explosion occurred. It must have been terrific. There was nothing left but a heap of rubble, under which were buried the mangled remains of all who were in the building at the time. I saw it a few days later, when men were still searching for bodies. They located some and were shovelling the pieces into sandbags. Mines were also laid at road junctions, so arranged that they would not explode until a load of a certain weight passed over them, then up they would go, destroying wagon and team, and leaving a huge crater which would render both roads useless for traffic until repaired. Trees on the side of the road were sawn half-way through and left standing, waiting for a wind to blow them over. This annoyed our people considerably, as trees were continually coming down and holding up the traffic until the road could be cleared. But I think the thing that angered us most was the damage down amongst the orchards. Every fruit tree was cut down and absolutely ruined. This was simple wanton destruction, and without reason.

In our village of Haplincourt, the only cover available was afforded by two cellars dug into a bank. These had been inspected by battalion headquarters and refused on account of the danger of mines. They preferred to build their own shelter from material salvaged from the ruins.

The troops had done likewise. The cellars were unoccupied, and looked tempting. Together with another company commander, I inspected them with a view to occupation. The floors and walls were bricked, with a large fireplace on one side. They were about twenty feet long and about seven feet wide, with a good door at each entrance.

There were niches in the walls where bricks had been removed, evidently with the object of placing bombs in them, but there was no sign of any explosives. The only thing we were suspicious of was a hole in the wall opposite the fireplace and extending under the floor. We had a good look at this, but could see nothing, though we could neither see nor feel the full extent of the hole.

We decided to take the risk and occupy it. The weather was cold, and there was six inches of snow on the ground. It would at least be dry and warm in the cellar. There was plenty of timber to burn amongst the ruins of the village. We left it to our company officers to please themselves. They all decided to join us. There was just room for us all to get in when our valises were laid out and the door was shut. The signallers of both companies occupied the cellar next door at their own risk.

After we had been there four or five days an engineer officer, with a couple of men, came to look over the cellars to certify them fit or otherwise for occupation. Though they found nothing in our cellar, they were a bit worried about the hole in the wall, and advised us to move. They then inspected the signallers' cellar, where they succeeded in locating three bombs, which they brought up and took away after extracting the detonators. They renewed their warning to us before leaving. We considered the situation, and decided it was a very comfortable place. Everybody agreed that we could not build a shelter that would be half as comfortable. And anyway, a shell might hit it, and we might as well go up one way as another. We stayed. That night we all solemnly shook hands and bade each other farewell before turning in. We repeated the formula each night until, at the end of a fortnight, we were relieved. Nothing happened, but I think we were all glad to get away. It is not a comforting sensation to feel you might be sleeping on a mine.

Our next billet after leaving Haplincourt was in the Beaulencourt Sugar Factory. We were interested to see the inside of this building. For months, we had gazed at it from the old front line and wondered if we would ever get near it. It was one of the outstanding landmarks, about three miles to the right of Bapaume, where we could see the factory buildings and tall chimney on the skyline.

The factory was a three-storeyed brick building, which, though more or less damaged, provided good accommodation for the whole battalion, while the officers were accommodated in the manager's residence. We were still in a reserve position, standing by, ready for emergencies, and were employed in the daytime digging and wiring a line of defence to be held in the event of a further German advance. It did not seem likely to us that it would ever be used, as the German movements for the past year or so had been mostly retirements. It nevertheless proved a good precaution. During the great German advance of March 1918 a year later, the British Army occupied this line and held up the advance for two days.

There were quite a number of German soldiers caught within our lines and wearing our uniform during this time. It was a fairly simple matter for them to sneak in at night through our outposts, collect what information they could during the day, and get back to their own lines the next night. It was a very risky procedure for the individual, and they were very brave men to attempt it, for of course if caught wearing our uniform they were treated as spies, and they knew the penalty. It meant a firing party. But, though a number were caught, there must have been a far greater number who were not. It was probably on account of these activities that, while at the sugar factory, we were ordered to supply a guard daily on the billets and brigade headquarters, which was also located there. We did not mind; it was a spell from wiring, each company getting its turn as duty company every four days.

A few days after our arrival at the factory, a batch of reinforcements, 140 strong, arrived from England. Company commanders were sent for to receive their quotas. They were a good-looking lot, and a very welcome addition to the unit. After inspection and checking rolls, I welcomed them to the company, allotted them to platoons, and handed them over to platoon commanders. The next evening, we were due for guard duty. The company sergeant major appeared with his duty roster, preparatory to warning the men for duty. I suggested that he had better put the new men on guard and give the old hands a spell. Having just come from a training camp, they should be well up in rifle exercises and guard duties. He could try them out in the morning. The sergeant major agreed. It was the usual procedure for the guard to undergo an hour or so of instruction before going on duty.

Next morning, the sergeant major came and asked me if I would inspect the men he had picked for guard duty. Putting on my cap and belt, I accompanied him downstairs and across the yard to where the guard were fallen in.

'I suppose these fellows are pretty good, Sergeant Major,' I said.

'Well, no, I am afraid they are not, sir,' he replied. 'That's why I wanted you to see them. There is not one in the whole batch who knows how to fix his bayonet, and very few have ever fired a rifle.'

'Good Lord!' I exclaimed. 'They have just come from Salisbury Plain, haven't they?'

'Yes, sir,' he replied. 'But they have done practically no training. They say they were rushed onto a ship in Australia as soon as they got their uniforms, and when they arrived in England they were sent straight across here.'

I was astounded, but it was true. This was the result of the defeat of the Conscription Referendum, and the rotten tactics of our politicians who did not have the guts to pass the Bill on their own responsibility, for fear of offending some of their constituents and so risk the loss of their seat, which of course meant the loss of their pay, the main attraction for some of them. Professional politicians are a curse to any country, but I suppose a country deserves to be cursed for putting up with them.

Recruiting at home was so poor that men were being sent to the front as soon as they enlisted, and the medical standard was so reduced in order to keep up the necessary numbers, that 50 per cent of the men arriving in England were being returned immediately to Australia as being medically unfit.[2]

Here were these men, none of whom knew how to fix a bayonet,

---

2 Some recruits arriving in England were indeed returned immediately to Australia as unfit, but 50 per cent is a highly exaggerated estimate.

let alone how to use it, having joined their battalion in the front line, now in a position where they were liable to be called out at any moment and rushed up to the front to engage in hand-to-hand fighting. And actually, three nights later, this occurred.

I was very annoyed about it, but of course the men were not to blame. I was sorry for them, and realised the rotten position they were in, being sent into the front line without the least idea of how to use their weapons or to defend themselves. It was hopeless, of course, to think of putting them on guard. We had to fall back on the old hands after all — and to make matters worse, officers and N.C.O.s had to do extra duty as instructors to train our reinforcements.

I kept them hard at work for the next few days, for their own sakes, for I knew that it would be little short of murder to send them into action untrained as they were. It was distinctly unfair in two ways, for of course my company strength was augmented by so many, whereas I knew if we had to go into action they would only be a hindrance and a worry to me. We would not have time to wet nurse them during a fight.

At three o'clock in the morning of the third day after their arrival, I was rudely awakened by someone kicking me in the ribs. Sitting up, I enquired what was wrong, not very politely I'm afraid, and saw the adjutant standing over me, grinning.[3]

'Better get up, Dan,' he said. 'There's a job on.'

'What is the job?' I asked. 'Why, it's not daylight yet. What time is it?'

'It's three o'clock, sir. The enemy have broken through at Lagnicourt, and we have got to go up.'

---

3 The 60th Battalion adjutant was Howard Kingsley Love, a 21-year-old electrical engineer from St Kilda. An 8th Battalion reinforcement, he had been wounded at Gallipoli before becoming, like Richards and Calder, one of the veterans transferred in February 1916 to form the experienced core of the 60th. Love left the AIF in January 1918 to become a pilot with the Australian Flying Corps, but was shot down (safely) in April and became a prisoner of war. Soon after his release following the Armistice, he married his English fiancée, and they sailed to Australia in 1919. Love founded Kingsley Radio Pty Ltd, a manufacturer of radios and radio parts. He died in 1948.

'Hell!' I exclaimed, now thoroughly awake. 'Honest?'

'Yes, it's a fact,' he said. 'Wake your officers, and get your company out, will you?'

'Right,' I replied, springing out of bed. In a few minutes, I had roused my officers, and we were all hurriedly dressing. Dashing across to the factory, we found the troops were already roused, and were busy dressing and packing their kits.

We completed our own as quickly as possible, and it was not long before the battalion was ready to move.

We could not, of course, get any detailed information of what had occurred, except that the enemy had launched a strong attack in the vicinity of Lagnicourt, had driven our infantry back, penetrated as far as our artillery lines, and had captured a number of our guns.[4] We were required to help push them back again. It sounded as if it might be a sticky job.

I instructed platoon commanders to distribute the new men through their platoons and tell the old hands to look after them, intending to ask permission to drop them out if we got into severe fighting.

In the early morning, the battalion moved out along the road to Bapaume. Nearing Bapaume, we passed the 8th Battalion, also on their way up. There was a running fire of greetings right along both columns between old friends of the two units, and my old company gave me a cheer as I went by. I felt very homesick as I passed them.

Reaching Bapaume, we were met by a staff officer who informed us that the situation was now in hand, and instructed us to occupy the quarters vacated by the 8th Battalion, just outside Bapaume. We were to hold ourselves in readiness to move in the event of further developments. Proceeding through the town, we moved into a camp composed of bell tents situated in a field on the outskirts of the town.

What had happened was that the Germans, taking advantage of a thick fog, had launched a very strong attack and succeeded in penetrating our outpost line before our troops realised what was

---

4 The Germans attacked near Lagnicourt, and broke through initially, on 15 April 1917.

happening. Though they put up a stubborn resistance, they found themselves surrounded and their position hopeless. The enemy pushed on so quickly that they got right back to our artillery lines before the gunners got the alarm. The gunners just had time to jump up and run to avoid capture, many of them not even having time to grab their trousers. They fled, clad only in their shirts. The situation for the moment for our people looked rather bad, but the 6th Australian Brigade, under Brigadier General 'Bob' Smith, who were at the nearest point in support, were quickly on the move and coming up at the double, and they succeeded in pushing the Huns back again and recapturing the artillery. As soon as they got them clear of the guns, the gunners returned and found, to their delight and amazement, that the guns, except one, had not been damaged. The enemy had missed a great opportunity. Instead of putting our guns out of action, their troops had gone looting. Other troops came into action in support of the 6th Brigade as quickly as they could reach the scene, and it was not long before the Huns were on the run for home. And then they copped it, getting back through their own wire. The Hindenburg Line was protected by tremendously strong barbed wire entanglements, row after row of it, each row about fifteen to twenty feet wide, and absolutely impenetrable, except where narrow openings had been left for that purpose and masked. As the troops converged to get through these openings in full view of our artillery, they were caught in a terrible hail of shrapnel, and 3,000 of them were killed in their own wire.

We remained in Bapaume for two days, and then, as the enemy showed no further inclination to attack, we were ordered back to Beaulencourt. Early in the morning, Captain Cooke of the 8th Battalion arrived on horseback to take over the camp as Billeting Officer for his unit. From my company lines, I saw him talking to the C.O. and one or two others outside headquarters tent. As I approached, I saw his horse trying to reach a bucket of water standing outside the tent. Cooke, who was dismounted, jerked the reins, and the horse threw his head up. But he was evidently very thirsty. He tried again, and again his head was jerked away. This happened four times. On the last occasion, the horse's bit caught in the handle of the bucket. The bucket flew into the air, turned upside down at the top of its flight, and came neatly to rest on Cooke's head, fitting almost to his shoulders, and drenching him from head to foot with the full contents of the bucket. It was the funniest thing I had seen for a long time, and of course it evoked roars of laughter from all who saw it. The only person who did not appreciate the joke was Captain Cooke. He could perceive no subtle humour in the remark by someone that it was a cold morning for a shower. But the old horse looked as pleased as Punch. He had a look in his eye which seemed to say, 'That'll learn you to jerk my reins.'

Soon after our return to the sugar factory, I learnt that my brother was at Contalmaison, a village away across the old Somme Battlefields, a few miles from Pozières. Getting leave for the day, I took my horse and rode across the battlefield to find him. He had been in France now for quite a time but we had never met. It was strange riding back over the places I had known so well, to find them all deserted and desolate now. I came across the body of a German soldier lying in a shell hole in what had once been No Man's Land. Poor devil. He looked as if he might have been young and was probably a decent chap. I could not help wondering why it should all be, why he should be lying there, not even buried, one of thousands — hundreds of thousands — cut off in their youth to satisfy the ambition of a few self-seeking political hypocrites. But a soldier cannot afford to harbour those thoughts. I saluted him and passed on.

At this stage again, I wonder when people will wake up. After all the lessons of the last war, from which the Nations have not yet recovered, the situation in the world today is worse than it was in 1914, and those self-same politicians, perhaps different individuals in some cases, but just as stupid if not more so, are heading us straight into another world war, which promises to be ten times more fearful than the last one, and which I can see no possibility of evading within the next two years.

On arrival at Contalmaison, I was disappointed to find that my brother's unit had moved the day before and he was now at Vaux, just beyond Bapaume, and within easy distance of our own billet. I gladly accepted an invitation to lunch, then started on the ride back. Having the afternoon before me, I decided to return by a different route, and made for the Albert–Bapaume Road, intending to take a quiet look at the Pozières village, the windmill, and Mouquet Farm on the way back.

There was very little traffic on the road, and I rode quietly along until, recognising certain landmarks, I knew I must be getting close to Pozières. Further on, I became puzzled at seeing no sign of the village. Stopping to get my bearings, I felt convinced that I should be close to it. However, I knew I must come to it if I stuck to the road, so I rode on. A few hundred yards further, I came across a party of men of a labour battalion working on the road. Stopping to enquire the whereabouts of the village, a man replied, as he straightened up and leant on his shovel, 'Pozières, sir? This is it. You are right in the centre of the village.'

'Not much sign of a village here,' I said, thinking he was joking.

'No, sir,' he replied. 'They made a pretty good job of it. But this is it alright,' and, pointing to the side of the road opposite where we were standing, he continued, 'The church was there.'

There was absolutely nothing to indicate to a passer-by that a village had ever existed there. But it was so. And the material they were using on the road was composed of fragments of bricks which once had formed the walls of the church.

Riding on, I came to the old windmill, but the ground had been so fearfully torn up by shellfire that many of the old trenches were almost obliterated and were difficult to recognise. Had I the time, I could no doubt have located the old places alright, but I still had a long way to go. I rode on, past Mouquet Farm, until I came to the famous 'Butte de Warlencourt'. Although we had never occupied this sector, I was interested in the 'Butte' as a famous German strongpoint, and also because it was here that my brother got his first big fright in the war. He was in the 2nd Division. He had tried hard to enlist, and come with me in 1914, but was declared medically unfit on account of an injury to his knee, sustained playing football. After several unsuccessful attempts to pass the doctor, he at last underwent an operation at his own expense, and eventually succeeded in being passed fit, and joined his unit in France, just in time to accompany them on a tour of duty in front of the 'Butte de Warlencourt'. The 'Butte' was a huge mound held by the Germans, and simply bristling with machine guns and snipers, and was, at that time, one of the nastiest places on the Somme front.

On his first night in the line, my brother took part in an attack on the 'Butte'. The attack failed — it could not do otherwise, and he was one of a very fortunate few who survived. I remember him writing to me afterwards, telling me of his experience, and the fright he got, and asking me if I could explain, with my longer experience, where all this 'glamour' was that people talked about in connection with war. I could not help laughing. I knew his feelings exactly. I had experienced them myself, but I could not supply the answer to his question.

Neither could I understand, nor can I yet, why the British Army in France persisted in the long out-of-date tactics of making frontal attacks on impregnable positions. They served no purpose, were a useless sacrifice of valuable lives, and tended more than anything else to destroy the morale of the troops.

An inspection of the 'Butte' did not help towards an understanding. I could only think that the person who ordered the attack was sadly lacking in imagination.

I rode on, and reached the sugar factory in time for the evening meal. Reporting my return and the result of my trip, my C.O. was good enough to suggest that I take leave next afternoon and find my brother, for which I was duly grateful.

I found him, in more or less comfortable quarters, in the ruins of the stables of a chateau in Vaux.

It was great to meet him. We had a long talk, swapped the latest news from home, and enjoyed a laugh over some of our experiences. He was also able to give me news of our elder brother, who was in Palestine with the Light Horse, and of whom I had not heard for some time. I was relieved to know that he was still alright, and could not help feeling that we were remarkably lucky. The war had been going on for two and a half years, and the three of us, two in infantry and one in a light horse regiment, were still alive and with our units.[5]

That afternoon, I saw the remnants of the 4th Brigade returning from their attack on the Hindenburg Line, after carrying out one of those shows which always appeared to the ordinary soldier to be so useless and unreasonable, doomed to failure from the outset. They had been ordered to carry out an attack on Bullecourt village with the object of 'testing the strength' of the Hindenburg Line. The very reputation of the Line appeared to us to be sufficient to know that one brigade would not break it. However, they tried, with the result that the brigade was practically decimated. They suffered frightful casualties, and a very large number were taken prisoner.[6]

We watched them go by in silence, and every man's heart went out to them in sympathy. They trudged past with their heads down, stunned by their appalling losses, grieving for their mates who had been so needlessly sacrificed. I had seen units come out of a fight before with pretty thin ranks, but still retaining a glow of pride in a job well done, but I had never seen anything like this before. Companies were represented by perhaps an officer (and perhaps not) and fifteen to twenty men, all feeling that the job they had done was not only hopeless from the start, but absolutely useless, and their mates had gone for nothing.

---

5 Sydney William Barrie, a 28-year-old bank clerk, enlisted in May 1916, and joined the 23rd Battalion at the Western Front in December. He later transferred to the AIF Provost Corps. The eldest brother, Alexander McIntosh Barrie, was a 36-year-old clerk when he enlisted in August 1915. His service in the 4th Light Horse was restricted by sickness, and he returned to Australia in 1917. All three brothers survived the war, although Alex's death in 1931 was attributed to his wartime illness. The Barrie brothers had two older sisters; another sister had died in infancy.
6 The attack on the Hindenburg Line near Bullecourt on 11 April 1917 was a catastrophe for the AIF. It involved the 4th and 12th Brigades. Tanks instead of artillery were supposed to pave the way for the attackers, but the tanks failed and the AIF infantry had to take on the mighty Hindenburg Line unaided. They did extremely well in the circumstances, but the casualties were devastating.

I rode back in the late afternoon, after my brother had promised to come and see me within a couple of days. He came two days later, and we had another good afternoon together.

The next day, we left the sugar factory, and moved back to Mametz for a long-promised three months' spell. Everybody was sceptical. We had heard of these spells before, and the mere mention of it now was treated as a joke. We were assured that this time it was true.

Chapter Nineteen

The camp at Mametz was a good one, composed of Nissen huts, and big enough to accommodate the whole brigade. Messes were re-established and old acquaintances renewed. I knew quite a lot of fellows in the other battalions, but many of them I had not even seen since joining the brigade.

It seemed to be an assured fact that we were to have a long spell. We embarked on a moderate syllabus of training to keep the troops fit, but leaving plenty of time for recreation. There was generally a game of football on the parade ground in the afternoon, in which the brigadier very often joined. He had been a good player in his college days and after, and could not resist the lure of the game. He was a big man and heavy, but very active, and it was amusing to watch the play when he was on the ball. As soon as he heard it going, out he would come from brigade headquarters in his shirt sleeves, and barge straight in. Then the fun would start. Fellows who had been doing very well up to then no longer had it their own way, and were sent sprawling all over the field. Some, who did not know him so well, were a bit dubious about returning the knocks, and kept out of his way, not knowing what might happen to them if they brought the brigadier down. But they need not have worried. Pompey was not like that; he forgot about military ranks when he was playing football, and it was all the same to him whether he was up against a major or a private. Others determined to get even with the 'old man', and the harder they tried the better he enjoyed it. But it was no good.

Those who cannoned into him just cannoned off again, to the added amusement of the onlookers. Everybody enjoyed those games, and none more than Pompey.[1]

On our first Saturday there, our Padre, Captain The Rev. Father Gilbert, asked permission to hold a communion service on Sunday morning, and for leave to visit Meaulte that day to buy some wine for the purpose.[2] He was of course readily granted permission, and at about 9.00 a.m. started for Meaulte. Meaulte was about seventeen kilometres distant (equal to about twelve miles), and there was a big army canteen there. At about 4.30 p.m., I was sitting in the mess writing a letter, the room being otherwise empty, when in strode the Padre. I greeted him with, 'Hello, Padre. You're back.'

'Yes.'

'Did you get your wine?'

'I did,' he replied, as he pulled two bottles out of his pockets and placed them on the table.

I continued my writing, but as he put the second bottle down it struck me that there was something peculiar about it. I looked hard at it against the light of the window, then rose and made a closer inspection. Both bottles were empty.

'But, Padre,' I said, 'there is something wrong. Both these bottles are empty. I thought you said you brought the wine.'

'Yes, my son,' he replied, 'so I did, and there are the bottles to prove it.' Then, with a twinkle in his eye, he continued, 'But the boys will need a stomach pump to get it now.'

I roared. He had drunk every drop on the way home.

Then he told me the story. It was a very warm day, and he had started off on foot, fully confident of getting a lift on a busy road.

---

1 Pompey Elliott had played football for Ormond College during his law course at Melbourne University. His brother George was a well-known footballer who captained University's VFL team and represented Victoria. George Elliott and Keith Doig had been medical students together, as well as football teammates. Captain George Elliott MC became the 56th Battalion's doctor, and was killed in September 1917.
2 James Patrick Gilbert was a 40-year-old Catholic priest from Randwick. He had left Sydney in July 1915, and joined the 60th Battalion nine months later.

But on the way down, the traffic was all going the opposite way, and he did not meet with a single vehicle of any description going in his direction. He arrived at Meaulte having walked the whole distance, hot, tired, and thirsty. He had a long, cool drink, ordered his wine, and had lunch. Then, after a short rest, he started back, confident of getting a lift on the return journey. To his astonishment and confusion, he found the traffic again against him. Vehicles which had gone up loaded in the morning were now returning empty. He walked on and on, hot and dusty, searching amongst the ruins of every village he passed for a water tap, but failing to find one. At last, his thirst got the better of him. He smiled at the ludicrous situation of himself dying of thirst with two bottles of wine in his pocket. He could not go further without a drink, and decided that one little nip would not matter. He had it, and proceeded on his way refreshed. But his thirst got the better of him again, and he was persuaded to have another nip. He was sure he would be alright now, and stepped manfully out on the road again. But he could not quench that thirst. The wine seemed to increase it, rather than quench it, and, before he realised it, one bottle was gone, and he was still far from home. However, he still had one bottle, and he could manage his service on that. He gritted his teeth and continued his journey. His thirst got worse and worse, his mouth was parched, his tongue dry, and his eyes and nose full of dust, but he refused to open the other bottle, until finally he was compelled to rest from sheer exhaustion. He could go no further, and was forced to open the second bottle to revive himself. After a rest, he continued on his way, but the second bottle went the way of the first before he reached his destination.

Dear old Padre. He had walked twenty-four miles and brought home two empty bottles. The story did not take long to get around the battalion, and the troops appreciated fully a good joke against the Padre.

Next morning, though he had to dispense with communion, he had the biggest attendance at his early service that he had seen for a long time. Men of all denominations attended to show their appreciation of a good sport. The old Padre was well liked by all ranks, and all the time he was with us he never failed on his job. He was not a young man, but during the whole of the winter on the Somme he had accompanied the battalion on every tour of front-line duty, establishing himself with the R.M.O. at the first-aid post, where he assisted in caring for the wounded and giving comfort to the dying, and every night at midnight had a kerosene tin full of hot cocoa for each company in the line. This was a wonderful comfort to the troops, and appreciated all the more because the cocoa was not on issue, but was provided by the Padre himself. Where he got it, no-one knew, but it always came.[3]

He could also be depended on at all times to have a bottle of whisky in his possession, which he kept, not for his own comfort, but for the comfort of anyone who needed it.

His was a brand of Christianity which men understood and appreciated, and though I was not a member of his flock I cannot refrain from paying this tribute to him and others of his Church whom I met in the fighting units, all of whom were of the same type. They were at the service of all, at any time and under any circumstances, irrespective of Church or Creed.

I regret I cannot speak so highly of Padres of other denominations. Although there were undoubtedly some good men amongst them (Padre Booth of the 8th Battalion was one of them),[4] there were others who were not so good, and some who brought the Cloth into disrepute.

I remember one who was with my battalion for six months, and who during that time never once went near the line with his unit. As soon as we approached a reserve position where there was any possibility of a long-range shell reaching us, the Padre approached the C.O. with the suggestion that he was afraid he couldn't be of

---

3 Captain Gilbert was awarded the Military Cross 'for distinguished service in the Field'. He returned to Australia in 1919.
4 J.J. Booth, a Yorkshire-born immigrant who arrived in Melbourne in 1910, was a widely admired AIF chaplain at the Western Front. He became a respected Anglican archbishop, and served as senior chaplain at AIF Headquarters in World War II.

much use to the battalion right now, and if the colonel didn't mind he would go to the nearest C.C.S. (Casualty Clearing Station), where he might be of use ministering to the sick and burying the dead. He would then join us when we came out of the line again. The colonel didn't mind. He was glad to get rid of him. But we all knew that it was not out of consideration for the patients that he went to the C.C.S., but because he knew he was reasonably safe there under the Red Cross. The only thing that Padre was useful for was finding billets when we were on the move. I was on battalion headquarters at the time, and arriving at a village where we were to spend the night at 4.30 p.m. after a long, hot march, the C.O. called for his batman, who was attending to the baggage.

'Sandy,' he said, 'never mind the baggage now. Get a fire going and get us a cup of tea. Afterwards, you can find out where the Padre is located. He will have the best billet in the village. Put my kit there, and tell him he has made a mistake. And you can act on that in future, Sandy. It will save you a lot of trouble — we will get a cup of tea, and I will get the best billet in the village.'

Sandy took this advice, and it worked splendidly. Everybody was satisfied by the Padre.

During the six months that Padre was with us, he only held one service, and that one he was ordered to hold by the C.O., who accompanied the request with some very trite remarks on the Padre's neglect of duty. We were a long way from the line, and it was a quiet, sunny Sunday morning. In the middle of the service, a very long-range shell landed and burst about half a mile away. The troops did not bother to turn their heads to look, but the Padre did not wait. He hurriedly concluded his service, grabbed up his books, and ran for his life. The battalion laughed; officers called their companies to attention, and we moved back to quarters. In the winter, when sheep-skin jackets were issued to the troops as protection against the cold, the Padre was the first man in the battalion to draw one. As the issue was short, officers and many N.C.O.s refrained from drawing them, so that the troops should not go short. The Padre stuck to his, and in doing so gained no respect from the troops.

Nor did one whom I afterwards came across in Wandsworth Hospital, London. He was a very pompous Scotch Presbyterian. He entered the ward one day, and looked behind the door where a list of patients was supposed to be kept. It was not there. He knocked on the floor with his stick. The sister in charge appeared. She did not look overjoyed to see him, but bade him a courteous 'Good afternoon'.

'Good afternoon, Sister,' he replied in a pompous tone of voice. 'I was looking for your list of patients. It doesn't seem to be there.'

The sister explained that it was out of date, and she had been too busy to renew it, but she could tell him about the patients as they visited each one.

'Would you come round with me?'

'I won't bother to go round,' he replied. 'Just point out any Presbyterians.'

'There is one there,' she said, pointing to a bed next to mine. 'He is a Canadian. There is one in the next bed,' pointing to me. 'He is an Australian.' And pointing to the bed opposite, 'There is another one there, he is a South African.'

'I see,' said the pompous old fool. 'Have you no Englishmen or Scotchmen?'

'No,' replied the sister, 'Those three are the only ones in.'

'Thank you, Sister,' he said. 'I don't want to see any Colonials. Most of them don't know who their grandfathers were, you know. Good afternoon. See you have your list up when I come again, won't you?' and he stalked out.

Our sister gasped and went red. She would dearly love to have slapped his face, but he had gone. She just said 'Oh!' and stamped her foot. But what a wealth of expression.

I laughed and said, 'What's the matter, Sister?'

'Did you hear what the old bastard said?' she asked.

'Yes,' I replied, 'but don't worry about him. I don't think his ministrations would help one far along the road to Heaven.'

'I don't think they would either,' she agreed. 'But the insult!!'

'Never mind,' I said smiling, 'I happen to know all about my grandfather. He might be interested next time he calls.'

'I hope he never comes here again,' she said, and we all agreed.

The South African was a member of one of the best known and titled South African families, and I could trace my own pedigree probably as far, if not further, than the old fool himself, into a well-known and historic house. But who cares about that. It is not my conception of Heaven that the Golden Gates are opened only to Scotch Presbyterians with a pedigree in their pocket. The thing that hurt me most was that he would be adjudged a product of Scotland. Still, perhaps if one searched far enough, it might even be possible to find a bad Scotchman. The result of a mixed marriage probably.

We celebrated the second anniversary of the landing on Gallipoli at Mametz. A holiday was granted to the troops, and a sports meeting arranged, which General Birdwood promised to attend. One prize was allotted for the best kept cooker in the brigade, to be judged in the lines at 11.00 a.m.

I worked my cooks up to a pitch of enthusiasm for this competition. The cookers were in good order, and we chose one for our entry, relieved it of duty for a day before, and all hands set to work polishing. They made a good job of it, and to show my appreciation of their efforts I remained in camp for the judge's inspection and to hear the result. The cooks appeared quite bucked at the interest I took in their work. At 11.00 a.m., everything was ready, and I congratulated them on their job and hoped they would win. There was no sign of the judges. At 11.45 a.m., we were still waiting when a runner approached, intimating that I was wanted in the Sergeants' Mess.

'What for?' I asked.

'Don't know, sir,' he said. 'There appears to be some trouble.'

'Well, you had better get the orderly officer,' I suggested.

'They told me to ask you to come, if you wouldn't mind, sir,' he replied. 'They said you would be able to handle it better.'

'Alright,' I said, and off I went, wondering what the trouble was. As I entered, I noticed a group of five or six sergeants talking together, but everything seemed quiet and orderly.

Bidding the sergeant in charge 'Good morning', I enquired the source of the trouble.

'Well, sir,' he said, 'there is no trouble exactly — yet. But as it is Anzac Day, some of the old boys want you to have a drink with them, for old times' sake.'

Then the little group came forward, grinning, and disclosed themselves. They were all original members of the 8th Battalion, and had all taken part in the Landing. They apologised for the ruse they had employed to lure me in.

'That's alright, you devils,' I said. 'It will cost you something to get me out now.'

They laughed at that, and I enjoyed an hour's good yarn with them over old times.

The judges did not appear until after lunch, but we won the cooker competition. The sports were a great success. Everybody had a great day, and at the finish of the program the brigade marched past General Birdwood. In the evening, everybody visited everybody else, there were representatives of every battalion in each mess, and the brigadier visited them all. It was midnight before we closed down and retired, tired but happy.

I could not help being struck with the wonderful spirit of the 15th Brigade. They were very strong in 'esprit de corps'. Nobody spoke of belonging to any particular unit in the brigade. It was always 'the 15th Brigade'. It was typical of Pompey. He made it, and was definitely the Father of the Brigade, and they loved him.

Chapter Twenty

We had been in Mametz for three weeks. People were beginning to believe that the promised spell was an assured fact. Then, one afternoon, all officers were ordered to report to battalion headquarters. When the gathering was complete, the C.O. broke the news that we were ordered to return to the line, and would move out early next morning. He qualified this by stating that we were only required temporarily, to hold the line for a few days until an English division, which was on its way, arrived and took over. Our 2nd Division was holding the line, but had suffered very heavy casualties, and had to be withdrawn. The 1st Division, due for a spell, had been sent in again to relieve the 2nd, and we were now to relieve the 1st.

When we halted outside the village of Vaux for a rest, my brother came out to see me again. We talked for ten minutes or so, and I promised to look him up again, if possible, on our way back after our relief. He was pleased to hear that we were not going into action, and promised to look out for us coming back. We said farewell as the battalion started to move, and I took my place in the column. The next time I saw him was in Australia, two and a half years later.

The 57th and 58th took over the front line, with the 59th in close support at the railway embankment a few hundred yards in rear, and the 60th in brigade reserve at Noreuil village.

We were again assured that we would not be required for front-line duty, and the C.O. was given permission to proceed on leave to England. He left the next day. The second-in-command also left for

Amiens to attend a court-martial, and it certainly looked as if we had nothing to worry about.

We were accommodated in small dug-outs, dug in the sides of a sunken road just outside Noreuil village and running at right angles to the front line. Just below us, the road crossed a small valley, which was used as a field artillery position. Our quarters were not altogether comfortable, as the German guns could fire straight down the road, and everybody had to scuttle for cover when they opened. Even then, it would not have taken a large shell to blow in any of our dug-outs, and on account of the proximity of the artillery we were treated to rather more than our usual share of shelling. Fortunately, they treated us mostly to shrapnel, which did not worry us to any extent once we were under cover.

On our second or third night there, I was awakened some time after midnight by voices shouting my name. Other voices took up the cry, until there was a regular clamour. Jumping out of bed, I stepped outside and enquired what it was all about. It was a fine moonlight night, and very quiet. Fifty yards away, a crowd of men were crossing the road, and some were standing on the opposite bank, calling. As I approached them, I shouted, 'What the devil's up? Who wants me?'

'That you, Dan?' a familiar voice enquired.

'Yes,' I replied. 'Who are you?'

It was my old pal, Captain Joe Catron, and my old company of the 8th Battalion. They had just been relieved from the front line, and were on their way down for a spell. Hearing that the 60th were here, they had determined not to go past without seeing me. It was great to see them all again. All the old hands gathered round, with a cheery word of greeting and a handshake. It was well worth getting out of bed for, but too soon over. In a few minutes they had to go off at the double to catch up and take their place in the column. I remained on the bank until the tail of the column had passed, and saw several more that I knew as they went by. Then I watched them out of sight.

It was a great battalion, and I was proud to be associated with it. As the tail of the column disappeared in the moonlight, I slowly turned and went back to bed. Although I liked the 60th, and was quite happy there, I could not help feeling sad at having left the 8th. I had a great affection for my old company, and I knew they had not forgotten me.

A couple of days later, I received a message requesting me to report to battalion headquarters. I duly presented myself, and was informed by the adjutant that I was required to report to brigade headquarters at 3.00 p.m. that day, and to take one other officer with me.[1]

'For what reason?' I enquired.

'I don't know,' the adjutant replied. 'I have no particulars, except that you are to go, and one other officer. Apparently you can take who you like. Who do you want?'

I nominated Lieut. O'Connor.[2] At brigade headquarters, we found quite a crowd assembled, representative of every unit in the brigade, all wondering what was in the wind. We were not kept wondering for long. The brigadier appeared, and once we were reported 'all present', he quickly got down to business. It had been decided, after all, to give us a job to do. The sector held by the 57th and 58th Battalions was actually in the Hindenburg Line, a small portion of which had been captured and held by the 2nd Division a short time previously.[3] At each end of this sector, a communication trench had been dug, part of which was held as a front line for protection of the flanks, with a bomb block at each end of the main trench between us and the enemy. It was about as nasty a position as one could imagine. The Germans naturally resented us sitting in their much vaunted Hindenburg Line, and were very spiteful about it. It was now decided to extend our holding from the left of our sector held by the 58th to, and including,

---

1 Hugh Wrigley had recently resumed as adjutant. A 25-year-old clerk who had served at Gallipoli, he became an officer after the evacuation. He had been the 60th's adjutant in mid-1916, but was severely wounded at Fromelles, where his gallantry earned him the MC. Wrigley held various senior positions during World War II, and distinguished himself as a brigadier at the battle of El Alamein.
2 Irish-born Daniel O'Connor was a 28-year-old shipping clerk of Albert Park.
3 Two AIF brigades had launched a renewed assault against the Hindenburg Line near Bullecourt on 3 May 1917.

Bullencourt village. Some Scottish troops were to co-operate on our left and to attack the village; the supporting companies of the 58th were to attack the sector adjoining the bomb block itself.

My job was to take in 100 men to assist the garrison in holding the front line against possible counter attack, and help in the attack on the bomb block. The plan was very carefully explained, and detailed instructions given.

I was not very enamoured of the scheme, and looking around the other faces it was not hard to see that the others felt the same. It sounded almost like a forlorn hope to me. Of course, no-one said a word. Everybody listened attentively and took notes on the instructions applying to their own particular job.

When it was all over, the brigadier asked if all was clear, a few questions were asked, and we were dismissed. The conference broke up in silence, and even outside nobody had very much to say.

Taking O'Connor with me, I went straight off to the front line for a reconnaissance of the position. My instructions were to have my party in the line by midnight the next night. Zero hour was 3.40 a.m. the following day.[4] We had barely reached the front line when O'Connor was hit in the chest by a sniper's bullet, and fell, badly wounded. I thought at first it was the end of him; both his lungs were injured, and I never expected to see him again.[5] The 58th M.O. attended him, and sent him down, but I am glad to say he recovered, and I met him some months afterwards in London, looking as fit as ever. I completed my reconnaissance and returned to Noreuil alone. Everybody was surprised and sympathetic when I reported the result of my visit to brigade headquarters and the loss of Lieut. O'Connor. I nominated Lieut. Leslie to take the place of O'Connor, and was given a free hand with my other arrangements.[6]

---

4 That is, 12 May 1917.
5 O'Connor was admitted to hospital with wounds in his back, both arms, left shoulder, and right leg.
6 Charles Leslie was a 31-year-old salesman from St Kilda. Married, short in stature, with fair hair and hazel eyes, he had joined the 60th in November 1916.

When I returned to my quarters, I sent for my company officers and sergeant major, and told them the news. Turning to Lieut. Leslie, I said, 'And I have asked for you, Leslie, to take the place of O'Connor. Are you game?'

'Yes, sir,' he said. 'Fall the company in now and we will tell off the men.'

In a few minutes, the company had fallen in, and I explained to them as much as was necessary of the job in hand. I did not attempt to gloss the show over, but made it quite clear to them that in my opinion it was going to be a man-sized fight and I would prefer to take volunteers rather than detail them.

'I want one hundred men,' I said. 'Who'll go?'

The whole company stepped forward.

'Well,' I said, laughing, 'you are a bloodthirsty crew. I wouldn't have thought it of you. But I can only take a hundred. So the question is "Who'll stay home?"'

They grinned and stood still.

I had to detail them after all. Or rather, it was a case of elimination rather than detail for duty. I tried to do it as fairly as possible, taking an equal number from each platoon and eliminating those who were least fit, or, through length of service, were most deserving of a spell. Some of them were quite hurt at being left behind, and voiced their protests. They were great fellows, and I felt proud to command them. Before dismissing them, I told them so.

The next evening as dusk was approaching, I fell the party in and checked them over. Finding them all present and correct, I reported to the adjutant that I was moving off, and handed him a copy of the roll. I decided to get an early start so that we could take our time going in.

The adjutant returned with me to see us off and wish the party luck. The remainder of my company were there talking to their mates who were going, and the rest of the battalion were gathered round to see us off. I wondered what our home-coming would be.

We reached the railway embankment with plenty of time to spare. I gave the party a spell here, and permission to smoke, warning them that, from here on, there would be no smoking and no talking, impressing on them the necessity for strict silence.

The line seemed comparatively quiet, and I did not anticipate any trouble going in. Nevertheless, precautions were necessary, and, as it turned out, they proved more necessary than even I realised. We moved from the embankment in single file, and soon reached the communications trench. I took the head of the column and led the way in. About half way up the trench, there was a hole in the parapet where a shell had hit it, and a heap of debris on the floor of the trench. Climbing over the debris, I just got safely round a traverse with the first half dozen men following, when over came a hail of whizbangs, straight into the breach, followed by a cry of someone hit. Running back to the corner, I shouted to the column to halt, and those in the traverse to run round the corner. The traverse was soon clear, and we hugged the parapet until the firing was over, comparatively safe.

It lasted about ten minutes, and though we suffered no casualties after clearing the traverse, those first few rounds cost us six, of whom one, Private Challis, was killed, and all of them crossing the breach or in the traverse.[7] It was rotten luck. We had obviously been seen crossing the breach. In fact, when I reported the occurrence at 58th Battalion Headquarters later on, the C.O. told me that several parties had been caught there.[8] The Germans evidently had a spotter in No Man's Land who signalled the guns when he saw a party crossing it. He said I should have been warned about it. I thought so too, but I wasn't. However, I suspected something of the sort, and to avoid a repetition I posted the C.S.M. at the breach to warn the remainder of the party not to expose themselves passing that point, and to hurry round the traverse. We got them safely past without

---

7 The famous Carlton footballer George Challis had been in the 15th Brigade, but this was a 33-year-old railway worker, Francis Henry Challis of Sandringham.
8 The 58th Battalion commander was Lieutenant-Colonel Charles Denehy, a 37-year-old schoolteacher who had served in the pre-war militia and, as a 7th Battalion lieutenant, had been wounded at the Gallipoli landing.

further trouble, and moved on. I reported my arrival and casualties at battalion headquarters, which was only fifty yards behind the front line, and then moved into the line.

Captain Dawson was in charge of the sector.[9] I took over certain posts from him, posting my men in place of his, while he withdrew his men for the attack on the bomb block. The remainder of my party was kept in readiness to assist in the attack. My party was in position a few minutes before midnight. Then came the anxious wait of three and a half hours. That is the worst part of a fight, waiting for it to start. The night was comparatively quiet and time passed slowly.

Leslie and I took turns at trench duty until three o'clock. At three o'clock, Leslie took charge in the trench until the fight was over, leaving me free to go where I was most needed. If my men had to go to the bomb block, I wanted to go with them, or at least I thought I ought to, which amounts to the same thing.

At 3.15 a.m., I ordered 'stand to', and took a final look around the trench. Everything was in order, and everybody was clear as to what was expected of them. At 3.30 a.m., I went to the bomb block. Captain Dawson was there and one of his officers, with the bombing party all ready, waiting for zero.[10]

We compared watches. Ten minutes to go. Everybody was in a state of nervous tension, though outwardly calm. The night was perfectly still, and all was quiet on the front. But we could sense that the Germans were nervous. Their flares were going up, and we could feel that they were suspicious. We knew that our fellows were creeping out into No Man's Land and taking their places on the tape line, if not already there, and we hoped the flares would not betray

---

9 Forbes Dawson of the 58th, a 27-year-old engineer from St Kilda, was the front-line supervisor of the operation. Severely wounded in the last weeks of the war, Captain Dawson DSO, MC had his left leg amputated above the knee.

10 This officer was presumably Lieutenant R.V. 'Mickey' Moon, a 24-year-old bank clerk who had enlisted in the Light Horse as a trumpeter. His platoon had the daunting task of attacking the concreted pill-box bastion of machine-guns located directly ahead. 'You've got the tough one, Mickey', Denehy had observed apologetically when assigning operation roles to his company commanders in the 58th.

them before they were ready.

Another glance at my wrist watch showed five minutes to go. It was still dark, with just the first streaks of dawn appearing in the East. Four minutes. Three minutes. The flares were getting thicker. The bombers were ready to spring over the top. Two minutes. More flares. A minute and a half. The officer whispered to his party 'All ready?' Then up from the Hun line went sizzling a curling yellow rocket. The German S.O.S. We had been discovered. But it did not matter now, it was too late. The rocket had hardly burnt itself out when over our heads came screaming a salvo of German shells and then a loud crash in No Man's Land. All hell broke loose. The first salvo was followed by a hail of shells from both sides, rifles and machine guns roared, the bombers jumped to their job, and bombs flew and added their quota to the din.[11] The fight was on. The tension was broken.

I remained at the bomb block with Captain Dawson, anxiously watching the progress of the fight. It seemed to be going against us. Unfortunately, we had failed to produce that first surprise, which is such a large factor in success. The enemy had discovered us just in time, and they were ready. Their trench was packed with men. The attackers in No Man's Land could make no progress. Our bombers were driven back again and again, but undaunted they grabbed a fresh supply of bombs and tried afresh. The dust was so thick by now that we could not see what was going on in No Man's Land and the din so terrific that we had to shout to be heard. It was broad daylight, and we still made no progress. The enemy were holding their own.[12]

Captain Dawson suggested that I have a look at the front line and see what was happening there. I went the length of the sector. The shelling was terrific, and though the observers were all up in their

---

11 The German bombardment was unusually heavy. Pompey Elliott considered it the worst he had ever been under.
12 Moon and other attackers were soon hit as they encountered fierce resistance from the pill-box. However, he kept rallying his men despite a severe facial wound. Inspired by his leadership, they persevered and eventually prevailed after a ferocious fight. But there was more to do — this pill-box was the first of the operation's objectives.

places and there was no sign of any movement in front, the situation was not so good.

The troops were all at their posts, most of them hugging the parapet and endeavouring to make themselves look as small as possible, which was the only thing they could do. But there were a good many new men amongst my party, most of whom were experiencing their first taste of shell fire, and it was about as bad a dose as I had experienced. Many of these fellows were cowering in the bottom of the trench looking absolutely terrified. I did not blame them. In fact, if the truth were known, I was experiencing something of their feelings myself (and so, I dare say, were most others), but I could not let anybody know about it. I don't think there is anything more nerve-wracking than just to sit in a trench and be shelled, and unable to reply. But they had to be shaken out of that attitude, and little as I felt like it, I had to produce a joke and a laugh, and endeavour to give them the impression that this was nothing and I was thoroughly enjoying it. The result was astonishing. They were on their feet in no time, some of them looking a bit sheepish, for which I was sorry. I stayed and talked with them a few minutes, and then on to the next post, trying to look as if I was having fun, when in fact I was as scared as the rest of them. At the next post, I had to repeat the process, with the same quick result. They were wonderful fellows, and I could not help admiring them. The situation was bad enough to scare the wits out of the oldest soldiers, but all through the fight afterwards I never saw any sign of them faltering again. They stood up to it with the best of them.

Returning to the bomb block, I found the situation not improved. In fact, if anything, it was worse. The fight had been going on for an hour or more, our casualties were mounting and we still had made no progress.[13] Captain Dawson was still there, conducting the bomb

---

13 B Company of the 58th — under Captain Norman Pelton, a 35-year-old schoolteacher — had the task of seizing a sizeable stretch of German-held trench beyond the pill-box that Moon and his men were to capture. This trench formed part of the Hindenburg Line. The 58th Battalion also had to take control of numerous adjacent dug-outs and a tactically vital intersection.

fight. I assured him that things were alright in the line.

'How's the fight going?' I asked.

'No good,' he replied. 'We can't shift them at all. I am afraid we will have to send some of your fellows in. I have lost a good many men.'

'How many do you want?' I asked.

'Can you give me a dozen?' he queried.

'Yes,' I said. 'I'll get them.'

Returning to where my fellows were waiting, I asked for a dozen men. They all got up. Taking the first twelve, we hurried back to the bomb block and into the fight. But it was not good. Try as they would, our men could not get a footing. The Huns were too strong for us, and again we were driven back. Another half hour went by, and we were still no further advanced. The shelling seemed worse than ever. Captain Dawson asked for another ten men.

I was on my way to get them when a shell burst right in front of my face. I saw a red flash and felt a most violent concussion. I remember thinking 'My head is blown off'. Then everything went black, and I fell. I do not know how long I lay there unconscious, but I remember when I came to, my first thought was 'Where's my head?' and I was feeling round the floor of the trench to find it. Then, with returning consciousness, my hands went gingerly to my neck, and then higher, and I found to my surprise that my head was still on — and, more surprisingly, undamaged. Then I sat up and said to myself, 'My God, I'm still alive!' And I was, but oh what a headache! Then I remembered I had a job to do. I picked myself up and went on with it. I was a bit groggy at first, but soon pulled myself together, got the other ten men, and went back to the block.

Dawson again asked me to have a look at the front line. I found the situation as satisfactory as one could expect. The men were at their posts, and there was no movement in front. But they were suffering heavily from shell fire.

I went on to the 57th sector to get in touch with them and see how they were shaping. Lieut. Pelton was in charge. He had just gone to company headquarters. His headquarters was in the front trench.

Stopping at the entrance to his dug-out, I saw a group of people at the foot of the staircase.

'Is Mr Pelton there?' I asked

'Mr Pelton's dead, sir,' someone replied.

'Good Heavens!' I said. 'When did that happen? They told me he was in the line a few minutes ago.'

'So he was, sir,' the voice replied. 'He was shot coming in a few minutes ago. Just where you are standing, sir. You had better hop it.'

I hopped it.

On my way back, Corporal Bevan, one of my Lewis gunners,[14] stopped me with a suggestion that he take a gun into No Man's Land, which would bring him in rear of the enemy line beyond the bomb block, and by enfilade fire from the rear he reckoned he could do sufficient damage to turn the scale. It was a wonderful suggestion. I got up on the parapet with him to have a look. It was a sound tactical move alright, but a glimpse over the parapet was sufficient to convince me that the chances of success were about 1,000 to one against. Once out there, he would be under fire from both sides, and it looked as if a rat could not live in it. I shook my head. He pleaded to be allowed to go. I pointed out the risk and the almost impossibility of pulling it off. It was a V.C. job if successful, but a white wooden cross was more probable. Also, he had to have a mate, and I could not order a man to go into that. He was game to go alone, but I could not allow him to do so. I ordered him to stick to his post until I saw how things were going at the bomb block.

His suggestion was an excellent one if it could be pulled off, and I was very intrigued by it. But the chances were very slender. I determined that if we failed otherwise I would let him have a try, and would go with him myself as his Number 2.

Collecting another party of bombers, I reached the bomb block again to find the situation unaltered, except that our casualties had been so heavy that we could not afford to send in many more men, and would be hard put to it to withstand a counter attack. I asked

---

14 This was, it seems, Corporal William Beavon, a 24-year-old English-born metalworker.

Dawson what he thought of it now. He admitted he was afraid we were done, but the troops were still fighting in No Man's Land, so we decided to make one more big effort with every available man. I did not mention Bevan's scheme yet. Time enough for that if this effort failed.

They went over, and fought like demons. The Huns had suffered as much as we had, but still held their own until, though still fighting, we were convinced that we would have to give it up and admit defeat. Then suddenly, to the great astonishment of all, the Huns suddenly chucked it in, and the whole line climbed onto the parapet with their hands up. We had won![15]

Our fellows were into the German line immediately, and shelling ceased. The prisoners were hurried down — 177 of them came through our trench — and all hands got busy preparing to meet a counter attack.[16]

We had not long to wait. We had just cleared the prisoners when one of my gunners (Corporal Bevan) shouted, 'Here they come, sir!' Jumping up onto the parapet, he pointed to a column of infantry moving along a road towards the line. It was a beautiful target, and I gave the word to fire. Bevan's gun and a Vickers gun alongside opened simultaneously and got right onto them. It was funny to see them scuttling right and left like rabbits. They swept right along the column, and finally the whole column broke and ran, and that was the end of it. The attack never developed. The guns ceased fire, and I sent for my C.S.M., and we proceeded to make up our casualty list

---

15 Moon's splendid leadership had been decisive. Though wounded, he led his men from the pill-box they had captured to the fight for the second objective, where Pelton's company had been unable to overcome the German reinforcements emerging from their extensive dug-out system. Moon positioned a Lewis gun so it could partly enfilade the Germans along the trench. When they fell back, Moon pursued them (initially alone), which prompted them to seek sanctuary inside their dug-out entrances. They had intended this refuge to be temporary, but Moon and his alert comrades detected a fleeting opportunity and pounced, rushing to the dug-out entrances and firing inside, thereby trapping their adversaries.

16 Moon and about 15 of his comrades had captured most of these prisoners.

and to prepare a report.

We were sitting in a traverse just below the Vickers gun, which was still on the parapet ready for action, when the enemy, evidently annoyed with this gun for having 'biffed' their counter attack, fired one last spiteful shell. It was a beautiful shot. It landed right on the parapet and under the gun, and blew it off the parapet, and with sheer rotten luck, three pieces of shell case hit me, one on my right hand as I was writing, and two in my left leg. I am afraid I swore. The fight was over, and I was congratulating myself at having got through safely, and then to be shot sitting! It was not sporting. I was very annoyed about it.

Sending for Lieut. Leslie, I instructed him to take charge and complete my report while someone assisted me to the first-aid post, which was only fifty yards away.

I was more badly injured than I had thought, and, to my great regret, I never saw my company again. I had fought my last fight.

The whole brigade was relieved at midnight that night, and the long-promised spell materialised at last. They did not go into action again for four months, while I spent the whole of that time in bed.

Poor Leslie was killed later in the day, and at midnight my company sergeant major led out the remnants of my party, totalling thirty men. Our casualties were 70 per cent, but it was a great fight.[17]

---

17 Also among the casualties was Corporal Beavon, whose wounds included a fractured jaw. Promoted to sergeant and awarded the MSM in 1918, he suffered another head wound, but survived the war.

Chapter Twenty-One

The first-aid post was crowded with stretcher cases waiting to be evacuated. After having my wounds attended to, I was laid down amongst them, but the bearers had a long carry, and it was slow work getting them away. I decided that I was fit enough to walk. Leaving a message for the doctor, I started off, and found I could manage fairly well, supporting myself with my left arm against the trench wall and hopping on my good leg. With frequent rest stops, I managed to get about 500 yards, nearly to the end of the communication trench, but my leg was getting very painful, and progress more difficult, and finally I collapsed in a heap and lay there unable to move. I was eventually picked up by a stretcher party and carried to the collecting point near Noreuil, where I was laid with a crowd of others to wait for the ambulance. On the way down, a party of our officers waylaid my stretcher party. I had been reported a casualty by telephone, and they had come to find me and express their regret and hopes for my recovery. It bucked me up a lot to see them. We talked for a few minutes, and then pushed on.

I have only a hazy recollection of my journey to the C.C.S. I had a good deal of pain, and seemed to be only semi-conscious. A horse ambulance picked us up first, and I went in the first load. I remember I protested that there were others before me, but they put me on just the same, and I felt too bad to argue. I have no idea where we changed from the horse ambulance, but vaguely remember doctors doing something, and then another journey in a Ford motor ambulance. The next thing I remember clearly is waking up the next day in a hospital marquee at the C.C.S. at Achiet-le-Grand, after an operation of which I have no recollection.

In the next bed to me was an old pal, Lieut. R.A. Moon of the 58th. I had seen him coming out of the line after the fight. He had sustained four wounds, but carried on. The fourth one fractured his jaw, and he was in a bad way, but still game. He recovered, and was awarded the Victoria Cross.[1]

Next morning, I was put on a hospital train bound for the base at Camiers. There were two tiers of bunks in the train, but my stretcher was laid on the floor. I remember protesting to the C.O. about it, but he laughed and told me not to worry.

'You see,' he said, 'there are so many bad cases on the train that I thought you wouldn't mind the floor, as you are not so bad.'

I assured him I did not mind, but as the journey progressed I began to wonder what the idea really was, for at intervals of about a quarter of an hour throughout the whole journey, either the doctor or a nurse knelt down beside me and inspected my wound. I discovered afterwards that the real reason for my being on the floor was the fear that they might have to operate again on the journey. One of the main arteries of my leg had been severed, and though this was tied at the C.C.S. another large vein had also been cut, and missed — and I had been bleeding from this all the time. On arrival at Camiers, my stretcher was grabbed almost before the train had stopped. I was pushed into an ambulance, and without waiting to fill up it went off at top speed for the hospital. On arrival there, I was carried straight through to the operating theatre, through rows of stretchers waiting their turn, and was operated on at once. For ten days, I was too ill to be moved, and was then evacuated to England and sent to the Third London General Hospital at Wandsworth.

I will never forget the commotion I caused on the evening of my arrival. After being put to bed, I felt something crawling on my back. I suspected a louse. A medical orderly had thrown a blanket over me

---

1 Moon was the only soldier in the 15th Brigade to be awarded the VC.

at Calais, and I still had it on arrival at the hospital.

Being helpless myself, I sought the aid of the sister in charge to run him down. She did so, and exterminated him. It was the first louse I had found on me, being one of those fortunate beings who for some reason was usually free of them. But to think I should find him here, of all places. The dear sister was horrified. A louse in her ward! Where had I got it? Where had I come from? I had committed an unforgiveable sin in bringing a thing like that in with me. Such a thing had never been known before. I told her about the blanket. She rushed to the phone and rang up the secretary, then rounded up all the orderlies within sight, and in a few moments the whole hospital staff was on the track of that blanket. It was finally discovered and burnt, and the excitement subsided. That poor little louse; little he knew of the commotion he caused. The patients thought it was a great joke, and roared with laughter. But poor Sister was filled with indignation.

What a chance for a humorous artist to sketch that scene, along the lines of that famous picture 'The Guardsman Who Dropped It', to be entitled 'The Man Who Brought the Louse to Hospital'.

Next morning, in accordance with the usual routine, I was prepared for inspection by the medical officer. At about 10.00 a.m., Sir Francis Pearse-Gould came and looked me over. Sir Francis was rather an austere person, and very dignified. He was Honorary Surgeon to the King, mid-Victorian in appearance and manner, with side whiskers, and a very soft heart when one got to know him, and a gentleman for whom I have the greatest respect and to whom I owe a very deep debt of gratitude. Sister Beecham attended him on his inspection. It did not take long. After a glance at the wound, he asked for my chart, put a few questions to the sister, then they both turned aside and held a whispered consultation. I could not hear what they were saying, but I overheard the word 'amputation'. My heart fell, but I decided at once to fight them on that point, and was fully determined I would not submit to that except as a very last resort.

Presently, Sir Francis turned to me and said, 'Well, old chap, I will operate at ten o'clock tomorrow.'

'Very well, sir,' I replied, 'but I have had two operations already. Might I enquire the nature of this one?'

He looked at me a moment before replying.

'Well, you know, your leg is rather bad. I'm afraid it will be necessary to amputate.'

My worst fears were realised — but I was still determined it would not be, if I could help it.

'Surely it is not as bad as that, sir,' I replied, 'and anyway, am I not right in thinking that the patient has the right to decide in such a case?'

'Quite,' he replied, 'but I would not suggest it unless I considered it necessary.'

'I quite believe that, sir, but I am very anxious to avoid it, if at all possible.'

'Well, old chap,' he said, 'it is not merely a case of saving your leg, but of saving your life. Have you seen the wound?'

I admitted that I had not.

'Sit up and have a look at it,' he said.

The sister raised me up, and I certainly got a shock when I saw it. It was black. She lowered me on to the pillow again, and for a minute no-one spoke. Then in a kindly voice Sir Francis asked, 'Well, now what do you think?'

I shook my head and replied, 'I'd hate to lose it.'

'But if it is a case of saving your life,' he said, 'surely a limb doesn't matter. Why are you so anxious to retain it?'

'Well, sir, if I have got to die, I think I would sooner die with two legs, for how could I climb the Golden Stairs with only one?'

Dear old Sir Francis laughed. He put his hand on my shoulder and said, 'Well, I will tell you what I will do. Though I can't hold out much hope of saving your leg, I will attend to it myself, and will do everything in my power to save it, if you will leave the final decision to me. And I give you my word, I won't amputate unless it is absolutely necessary.'

'Thank you, sir,' I replied. 'I will leave my fate in your hands.'

I have never ceased to be grateful to him for what he did. Although he must have been a busy man, he would not allow anyone else to touch me, and took sole charge of me himself, changing my dressings daily and arranging special treatment until, at the end of six weeks, he pronounced me out of danger, and handed me over to the care of Sister Beecham. Then the sister did the same thing for a further six weeks, until she considered I was far enough recovered to hand me over to the nurses.

Sister Beecham was wonderful, and I soon began to realise how lucky I was to be in her charge. I have often wondered since whether the fellows who spent any time in hospital during the war fully appreciated how much the soldiers owe to the nurses. During the time I was in Wandsworth, there was an Australian officer in the medical ward dying of pneumonia, and Sister Beecham, working under the direction of the medical officer, had been with him every spare moment of the day and night, on duty and off, trying to bring him back to life. It was a losing fight, and it seemed as if nothing could save him. One night, it looked as if the end had come, and she sent for the doctor at midnight. At 2.00 a.m., the doctor gave up all hope, and said, 'Well, Sister, it is no use me staying any longer. He is beyond all medical aid. There is nothing further I can do.'

But there was still a spark of life, and the sister was loath to give up hope while that remained.

'Doctor,' she said, 'would you mind if I have a try?'

'No, Sister,' said the doctor. 'Personally I can't think of anything that can possibly save him, but if you can, try by all means. You can do what you like. I can do no more.'

The sister immediately had his bed removed to an open verandah at the end of L Ward, had a bed erected for herself, and for six weeks she never left the hospital. She devoted every moment of her time off duty and all the time she could spare while on duty to the task of dragging him back to life. And she succeeded. I will never forget the day when her patient was strong enough to get up for the first time, and she proudly brought him in to the ward, supporting him as he walked. The other patients sat up in bed and cheered her. And poor Sister blushed and looked quite embarrassed. She was tremendously proud of the job she had done, but she did not expect any demonstration about it. To her, it was her job, and that was all there was to it.

But how her patients loved her! And she had the reputation of being the strictest sister in the hospital, so that the nurses used to try to avoid duty in her wards.

There was no nonsense in L Ward. Perhaps the patients admired her for that, too, but with all her strictness, no trouble was too great for a patient, and no-one was quicker to appreciate a good joke. It was a happy ward, and although I spent many weeks of pain there I have only pleasurable recollections of the four months I spent in it as a patient.

There was a good deal of humour in a hospital ward, and I think one of the best jokes was perpetrated by two Welsh officers in M (the medical ward) on the occasion of a Welsh Festival Day. These two dressed themselves up to represent Sir Francis and the matron, and carried out an inspection of the wards.

The matron was a very fine woman, rather stout, with golden hair, and always immaculately starched. One of these lads, having borrowed a nurse's costume, teased out a piece of rope to represent her hair, and with a pillow as his bosom made a remarkably good impersonation.

His companion was equally good as Sir Francis, with side whiskers complete, and even to his dress. It was very well done and well acted. We heard shrieks of laughter coming from M Ward, and wondered what the joke was.

Then the door of L Ward opened, and in they came, and proceeded to make an inspection of our ward. They acted their parts well. Sister Beecham was out of the ward, and the mirth was unrestrained. They had got as far as my bed, the third from the door, when the door opened again and in walked the real matron and Sir Francis. They stopped dead. The matron gasped and went red in the face. Sir Francis, looking furious, exclaimed,

'What's this! What's this!' then turned on his heel and hurried out, followed by the matron. It was a wonderful climax to a good joke, fully appreciated by all except the masqueraders, and even they saw the humour of it when they had recovered from the shock. But the inspection ceased, and they hurried back to their ward to prepare themselves for the interview which seemed indicated.

Realising that I was likely to be unfit for service in infantry for a long time, and not wishing to return to Australia until the war was over, I applied for transfer to the Australian Flying Corps. Two officers of my battalion had already transferred and were stationed at Market Drayton, one in command of the flying-training school. He promised to push my application through. For some time, I heard nothing of it, but was not worrying as I was not yet out of bed. Then came the time when I was allowed to get up for two hours a day, and shortly afterwards I was instructed to appear before a medical board in London. I was declared 'unfit for further service, and to be returned to Australia'. I protested against the decision. Sir Charles Ryan was president of the board. He was very sympathetic, and explained that his instructions were definite in regard to people who would be unfit for some time — but after a deal of argument, he modified his decision to 'eight months leave to Australia', and in the meantime I was to go to a convalescent home.

Next day, I left Wandsworth for Cobham Hall, the home of Lord Darnley, in Kent. Lady Darnley was a Victorian, and they had given up part of their home as a convalescent home for Australian officers. It was a magnificent old place, and I wish I could have seen more of it. I still had an open wound which required dressing twice daily, and was only allowed out of bed for two hours per day. I was confident of being allowed to remain there for some time.

To my surprise, on the fifth day after my arrival, in company with another officer, I was ordered to report at Horseferry Road (our administrative headquarters in London) by the first available train. On arrival there, late in the afternoon, I was informed that I had been appointed adjutant of a hospital carrier sailing for Australia from Royal Albert Docks in two days' time. My companion was appointed to another ship of the same convoy, and we were allowed forty-eight hours leave before sailing. I protested that my appointment must have been made in error as I was not fit for duty. The clerks replied that they were afraid I would have to go. There had been some trouble on one or two transports recently, and I had been chosen on account of my length of service and experience. Being an original officer of the A.I.F., it was considered that I would be capable of handling any little troubles that might arise on the voyage. Very nice. I accepted the compliment, but determined I would not accept the job, if I could avoid it.

I went straight to the Flying Corps office to enquire about my transfer. I was lucky enough to find Captain D'Arcy there in charge. D'Arcy had been in my platoon in 1914, and I knew I could count on him to do what was possible.[2] My transfer was approved, but had been held up until I was fit enough to join. I explained the situation to him, and he promised to get it moving at once. Next day, I saw everybody it was possible to see, but to no avail. They all had the same answer. I had been chosen for the job, and as the ship was sailing the next day it was too late to find anyone to take my place. D'Arcy had done everything possible, but my papers, though on the way, had not arrived. They arrived the next afternoon, but too late for anything to be done. Everybody was sympathetic, but could do nothing for me. The ship was due to sail within a few hours, and I was regretfully forced to join her.

Late in the afternoon, in a disconsolate frame of mind, I boarded a train for the docks, and reported myself aboard the *Port Lyttelton*. There were only two medical officers and one other who had been appointed quartermaster on board. The troops were to be picked up at Plymouth. We sailed next morning, and, to my great disgust, had to wait a week at Plymouth for the troops to arrive. The O.C.-Troops arrived a few days beforehand, but remained ashore. In

---

2 John Pryde D'Arcy was born and lived much of his life in South Africa. A 24-year-old farmer when he enlisted in August 1914, he was wounded twice at Gallipoli. He joined the Australian Flying Corps in July 1917, and became a lieutenant in October, the month when Barrie asked him to expedite his transfer. D'Arcy was court-martialled in 1918 and dismissed from the AIF, having been found guilty of forging a railway warrant.

company with the medical officers, I went ashore to meet him, and as there was nothing to keep us on board we also stayed and did our best to enjoy our last few days in England. My interview with the O.C.–Troops did not improve the prospects for the voyage. He was practically an invalid, had seen no service, having recently arrived from Australia on transport duty, and after a short leave in England was now returning home.[3] He was good enough to warn me that I would have to run the ship, as he expected to be confined to his cabin for most of the voyage, and in fact he was. I was not looking forward to the trip.

A hospital carrier, as the *Port Lyttelton* was designated, differed from a hospital ship in that she carried troops who had recovered from wounds or sickness, and required little or no medical attention, but were unfit for further service — and in addition, she carried any who were being sent home for 'other reasons'.

And therein lay the catch. Included in the draft were about twenty men with more or less bad records. There were only four officers in addition to the staff, one of whom was being sent home to complete his medical course at the university. He was alright, except that he was young and of little experience, and I doubted his ability to handle a troublesome situation.[4] One of the others was being returned on account of age, he being over the retiring age for the rank he held before obtaining his commission in Australia, and had seen no

---

[3] The OC–Troops was Major J.H. O'Halloran, a 38-year-old businessman from Singleton (New South Wales). Though now restricted to transport duty, he had in fact served at Gallipoli with the 20th Battalion, and had endured a nervous breakdown as a result. According to medical reports, O'Halloran had always been an anxious type, but had never had a complete breakdown until his harrowing two months at Gallipoli. He had three daughters, and had recently become a widower.

[4] This was Cyril Tonkin, who had more experience than Barrie realised. A married 28-year-old chemist, Tonkin had enlisted in the first fortnight of the war, and served at Gallipoli. Having risen through the ranks, he became a lieutenant in March 1916. Hernia trouble caused his evacuation from Gallipoli, and in France his right leg was fractured. Tonkin graduated in medicine in 1921, and became an admired pharmacist-doctor. He was awarded the OBE, and a major university scholarship perpetuates his memory.

service. Another, although not actually under arrest, was under definite instructions for discharge on arrival in Australia to avoid court-martial in England; and the fourth was already in plain clothes, having been court-martialled and cashiered in England. It appeared that I could not expect much support from the officers, and, with an invalid C.O., it looked as though the voyage was not going to be a very happy one for me.

I chose an orderly-room staff, and appointed N.C.O.s to certain definite jobs, organised the troops into companies, and allotted officers and N.C.O.s to duty. That being done, I could only hope for the best and keep my eyes open.

It was not long before the bad element showed their hand.[5] After a few days at sea, little troubles began to occur, and always the same crew seemed to be at the bottom of it. I held a conference with the orderly-room staff and senior N.C.O.s to devise the best method of dealing with the troubles and locating the ringleaders. My orderly-room sergeant confided to me that he knew the ringleader and had been expecting trouble from him. The sergeant was a member of the C.I.D. in Sydney in civil life, and this other man was a well-known criminal. The sergeant had been sent on one occasion from Sydney to Melbourne to arrest him and take him back under escort. He then produced his papers. The man had evaded embarkation thirteen times in Australia, and was finally put on a troopship under guard. He had done the same thing in England several times, and was placed under guard there to ensure his embarkation to France. He had escaped from the guardroom, and was known to have intentionally contracted a filthy disease to avoid active service, and was now suffering from a valvular disease of the heart in consequence. It was interesting information. I decided to take no action at present, but to let him have his head, and he would probably become bold enough to do something with which we could charge him and keep him out of mischief for the rest of the voyage.

The ship's captain was becoming perturbed and requested my

---

5 The *Port Lyttelton* departed on 20 October 1917.

presence at an interview in his cabin. He had never carried Australian troops before, and was under the erroneous impression that they were wild men, entirely lacking in discipline, and he feared for the safety of his ship. He insisted that some system of training be carried out, and discipline tightened up in case they got out of hand. To some extent, I agreed with him, but showed him my instructions for the voyage, which specifically forbade any work of any kind being done, to allow the troops to rest as much as possible. After all, the responsibility rested with the O.C.-Troops, and he refused to bend a regulation. This was another example of political stupidity and interference. To send a ship to sea on a voyage of six to seven weeks with over 800 comparatively fit men, with instructions that they were to do no work of any description was simply inviting trouble, and in several cases the officers in charge were made the scapegoats on arrival in Australia.

This was especially the case if there happened to be a soldier M.P. on board. These people were the bane of a soldier's life. In most cases, they enlisted with a flourish of publicity, used their political influence to secure a safe job, and returned home without having fired a shot or risked their precious lives. They would then be hailed as heroes by an unsuspecting public, and so secure the safety of their seats.

In one notable case, one such person was the instigator of all the troubles aboard a particularly bad ship. On arrival home, he made a report to Parliament on the happenings on the voyage, and demanded the punishment of certain officers concerned. Parliament ordered an enquiry, which was given great publicity, with the result that a well-known and very capable senior officer — who had served with honour and distinction from 1914 until nearly the end of the war, when he was invalided home in consequence of wounds received in action — was made the scapegoat and punished in order to enhance the political aspirations of this hypocritical waster, who himself should have been punished for evasion of service. The crime of which this officer was actually guilty was that of taking certain necessary steps to avoid a mutiny on the ship, which had been instigated and fermented by the wastrel who laid the charge. Unfortunately, it was only those behind the scenes who knew the true story and the true character of those who gave witness against him, but his character was too well known for his friends to lose faith in him. They admired him for his handling of a very nasty situation which had been forced upon him.

My interview with the captain ended stormily. As I was adjutant of the ship, he held me responsible for the conduct of the troops. I admitted the responsibility, and endeavoured to point out to him how my hands were tied. He was not interested in military regulations, but he knew what I ought to do. He became very angry, and as I did not wish to get heated myself and say things I did not want to say, I left him with the assurance that if he looked after his job, I would manage mine. I am afraid this left him very wrathful, and for three days we were not on speaking terms.

I was not unduly worried. I knew that at least 95 per cent of the men on board were good soldiers and, if handled rightly, I was confident of their support. I had handled and fought with them for three years, and I knew how utterly dependable they were, if well led. Although the draft was composed of individuals of almost every unit in the A.I.F., and entire strangers to me, provided I did not funk my job, I knew they would support me to the limit. And I had made up my mind what to do.

On the third day after my quarrel with the captain, it happened. I was sitting on the boat deck reading on a beautiful sunny afternoon, when suddenly the captain came running down from the bridge in a state of excitement and almost alarm.

'There you are,' he cried. 'I knew it would happen. A damned mutiny! Go and look at the deck.'

I went and looked, the captain abusing me all the while. It certainly looked nasty. The whole of the troops were congregated on the forecastle deck in a seething mass, with a fight proceeding in the centre.

'What happened, sir?' I asked the captain.

'I don't know how it started,' he replied, then, pointing at the known ringleader, whom I shall just call 'Dodge', he said, 'but I saw that fellow hit one of your military policemen from behind and knock him over amongst the winches.'

'Good!' I said. 'That is the fellow I want,' and I made for the companionway.

'Where are you going?' asked the captain.

'I am going to settle the argument,' I replied.

'You can't go down there,' he said, making a grab at my arm to stop me.

I evaded him, and slid to the deck below.

'Can't I?' I replied laughing. 'You watch me.'

'If you go out there, they will throw you overboard,' he shouted, 'and I won't stop the ship for you, we are still in the danger zone.' He said this in all seriousness, and really thought I was taking my life in my hands.

'I will be alright, Captain,' I said. 'Don't worry about me,' and I made for the orderly room.

I sent two runners out hot-foot with instructions to request all officers to report to me there at once. They returned in a few minutes, and reported having failed to find any officers. I was not surprised.

My orderly-room staff were present with the Sergeant in Charge of Police and two or three of his men, all of whom were good soldiers and appointed by me for the voyage.

No-one knew the cause of the riot.

'Alright,' I said, 'on the captain's evidence I am going to arrest Dodge. I want an N.C.O. and a file of men to come with me. Who will go?'

Their faces lit up at once.

'By Jove! If you get him, you will stop the trouble, sir,' they all agreed.

They all volunteered to go with me. I took the Sergeant of Police and two of his men, whom I had known in the 2nd Brigade and whom I had specially chosen for the job. My orderly-room sergeant also insisted on coming, and I let him. I was not sure of the temper of the troops as I sallied forth from the orderly room at the head of my little procession, and I instructed my men to keep close to me.

I found little difficulty in forcing a passage through the crowd, and in fact the troops themselves took up the cry, 'Make way for the adjutant.' As I had thought, the great majority were merely onlookers, but nevertheless I also knew that this was the crisis that would decide who was going to run the ship — and I determined it was going to be me. The crowd parted and a lane was made, through which we moved right into the centre of the disturbance. The fight ceased. Private Clohesy, the man who had been hit, was there.[6] I asked him what the trouble was. He confirmed the captain's story. Turning to Dodge, I asked, 'Private Dodge, did you hit Private Clohesy?'

'No, sir,' he replied.

'Private Clohesy, is this the man who hit you?'

'Yes, sir,' replied Clohesy.

'Very well,' I said. 'The ship's captain confirms that, Dodge. You are under arrest. I advise you to come quietly. Fall in the escort.'

The escort fell in, one on each side of him, with two sergeants in rear.

'Don't I get a say, sir?' Dodge asked in a truculent tone.

'Yes,' I replied. 'At ten o'clock tomorrow morning you can say all you like before the C.O. In the meantime, prisoner and escort — quick march!'

There was a dead silence amongst the troops. I was still uncertain as to what would happen, but again they parted to let us through. Just under the bridge, I stood aside at a companionway while the prisoner and escort descended. As they disappeared, the whole of the troops (with the possible exception of a dozen or so of Dodge's pals) took off their hats and cheered. Then I knew I had won. The ship was mine.

Detention cells were forbidden on the ship, but I knew there would be no peace on board as long as Dodge remained at large. I had decided to take the risk and make my own arrangements. He was escorted below to the quartermaster's store below the men's deck. The

---

6 This was probably John Clohesy, a tall, solidly built, 43-year-old labourer from Bolwarrah (near Ballarat), whose knee had been operated on after he was kicked by a horse before the war. He enlisted in the 8th Battalion in 1916, but his knee was unable to cope with arduous AIF marches in France.

Q.M. had three compartments inside his main store, each with doors and padlocks.[7] I found him there, quite unaware of the happenings on deck. When I explained the situation to him and requested the use of one of his compartments, he willingly acquiesced, and immediately set to work with his staff to clean out his stores. In a few minutes, Dodge was safely locked in the room under guard, and I returned to the orderly room. The situation on deck was quiet, and the troops had mostly dispersed. Several N.C.O.s were present.

Enquiring if there was any further trouble, they all replied, 'No, sir, the troops were glad to see Dodge go. If you can only keep him out of the way, that will be the end of it. The rest are all "rats" and won't be game to do anything without the ringleader.'

So I thought, and so it proved. But I knew it would be very difficult to keep him locked up. He would have to be formally charged and dealt with by the O.C.–Troops, and I also knew that I would have a tremendous job to persuade him to break a regulation by ordering detention.

I was just leaving the orderly room for his cabin to make my report when the ship's quartermaster appeared with a message that the captain would like to see me in his room.

This surprised me, as the captain had not spoken to me for three days. Wondering what he had to say now, I went immediately to get it over with. Knocking at his door, he bade me 'come in'. As I entered, he was opening a bottle of whisky, which further surprised me.

'You wanted to see me, sir,' I asked.

'Yes,' he replied, pushing a glass towards me. 'Will you have a drink?'

'Thanks very much,' I said, and poured one out. As he was helping himself, he said, 'You know, Barrie, I said some very rude things to you the other day.'

'Yes,' I replied, grinning. 'And I'm afraid I reciprocated to some extent.'

---

7 The quartermaster was Lieutenant R.J. O'Connor, a 26-year-old Oakleigh surveyor, whose service with the 24th Battalion was curtailed by appendicitis and the aftermath of several operations to deal with it.

'Well,' he said, extending his hand, 'I want to take back all I said. Will you shake?'

'Rather,' I said, and we shook hands. He then proceeded to congratulate me on the way I had handled the situation, and he said that he really thought I was taking my life into my own hands when I went out onto the deck. I endeavoured to disabuse his mind of that and to make light of the situation, explaining to him that, with the exception of about twenty bad characters, all those men had been soldiers, and I had sufficient experience to know how to handle them.

'What have you done with Dodge now?' he asked.

I told him what had occurred and of the difficulties I anticipated in being able to keep him where he was. I suggested that he might be able to help me to persuade the O.C.–Troops of the necessity for ordering detention, and also give evidence at Orderly Room next morning. He readily agreed.

'You call me as evidence,' he said. 'I'll see the blighter doesn't go at large, if I have to lock him up myself.'

Splendid. I left the captain's room much happier than I had entered it, not only because of the fact that we were now firm friends, but because I knew that I had his wholehearted support.

My interview with the O.C.–Troops was not so satisfactory. He was obviously afraid to take the risk of ordering detention, though I pointed out as strongly as possible the danger of a repetition of the trouble if Dodge was allowed to go free. I could see I would have to make out a very strong case to get any punishment at all.

Orderly Room was arranged for ten o'clock the following morning. All witnesses were warned, Dodge's record and medical sheet produced, my orderly-room sergeant warned for evidence of previous character, and I reported to the captain the result of my interview with O.C.–Troops.

'Alright,' said the captain. 'Leave it to me. I'll fix it. You demand detention, and I will support you — and what's more, I'll see that he gets it if I have to do it myself.'

At ten o'clock, Orderly Room was held in the Saloon. The weight of the evidence and record of Dodge's previous character was sufficient to impress the O.C.–Troops of the seriousness of the charge, but when at the close of the case I asked that he be committed to a period of detention sufficient to cover the rest of the voyage, the poor old colonel became very worried. He quoted regulations, and pointed out the impossibility of doing it, and even spoke of the grave risk attached to my action of locking him up the previous day.

In reply, I drew attention to the fact that, he being an invalid, practically the sole responsibility of running the ship devolved upon me, and as I was physically unfit (I still had an open wound which required dressing twice a day) I would accept no further responsibility for the conduct of the troops as long as Dodge was allowed to go free.

Then the captain asked permission to speak. This being granted, he said, 'Well, Colonel, I don't know anything about your regulations, but I know that I am responsible for the safety of my ship, and while you are responsible for the conduct of your troops, I am in supreme command at sea. I know this fellow Dodge, I have watched him ever since we sailed, and I consider my ship is not safe while he is free. Therefore, I want to support the adjutant's recommendation, and also to warn you that if you don't order his detention, I will. I will have my own men arrest him for the safety of the ship, and I will put him in irons for the rest of the voyage.'

That settled it. With obvious reluctance, but feeling he was between the devil and the deep blue sea, the poor old colonel was practically forced to award him twenty-eight days detention, and so, except for periods of exercise, Dodge was confined to his little room for the remainder of the voyage.

There was no further trouble, and from then on we were a perfectly happy ship.

I quote this incident as a further illustration of the stupidity of political interference in military affairs, and how politicians, by their vote-catching measures, undermine discipline and render the soldier's task unreasonably hard, and often farcical.

We arrived home on the 15th of December 1917, and strangely enough, before I left the ship, I was offered and accepted the command of the Australian Flying Corps Reinforcement Camp (afterwards known as No. 1 Home Training Depot, A.F.C.) at Point Cooke, Victoria, where I remained until after the Armistice.

So I served with the Flying Corps after all, and had the satisfaction, though still unfit, of performing a useful job until the end.

Nothing more was heard of Dodge. I expect a benevolent government pays him a pension for 'disabilities received as a result of war service'. They generally do to his sort.

Afterword

By Judy Osborne

After the war ... luckily for John Charles Barrie, there *was* an 'after the war'. So many fine young soldiers from the First World War did not have the privilege to live and to tell their story.

After the war, my grandfather ('Captain Barrie' at that stage) realised his long-held desire to 'go on the land'. In 1920, he purchased the 300-acre homestead block of Killingworth Estate at Yea, Victoria, under the Soldier Settlement Scheme.

One day, soon after his arrival at Killingworth, he noticed a fine young woman riding a beautiful horse around the streets of Yea. He followed her for a while, introduced himself, and complimented her on her riding. Her name was Daisy Lang, and his time that day was well spent. On 9 November 1921, he married Daisy in the Presbyterian Church at Cheviot, the site of which had been gifted from her family's property, Kimmel Park.

Charlie and Daisy had a long and loving marriage, but their early married life was tinged with sadness. Daisy gave birth to their first daughter, Margaret, in October 1923. Margaret lived for one week before she died of an unknown illness, possibly pneumonia. In July 1925, Daisy was pregnant with twin boys, Alexander and John, when she miscarried. Finally, in May 1928, she gave birth to a healthy baby girl called Isabel, my mother.

Charlie's writings include the following description of the Soldier Settlement Scheme, written in the early 1930s, and I believe that this passage helps to explain his unwilling departure from Killingworth:

The settlement of ex-soldiers on the land at the termination of the last war was one of the greatest scandals in the history of governments in Australia. It appears that Parliament meant well enough in passing the Acts for that purpose, but the administration of the Acts was left in the hands of civil servants, men who had never been on a farm in their lives, and were totally incompetent to carry out the job. With millions of acres in the country waiting to be settled, which might have been given to the soldiers for nothing or at most a few shillings per acre, and in reasonable sized areas which would assure them of a decent living and the success of the scheme, expensive estates were purchased, in most cases at prices very much above their value, cut up into small areas, loaded with the cost of survey and roads, so that the settler was doomed to failure before he took possession of his block. Hundreds have left their blocks, having lost everything they possessed, and the remainder are hanging on in the vain hope that they will receive some measure of justice one day …

One soldier purchased a homestead block and agreed to pay a certain amount in cash for the homestead buildings. Before taking possession he proffered his cheque to the Department. They refused to accept it, saying they would let him know when they wanted it. In his innocence, thinking government departments were honest, he went on with his job. Three months later, when he had spent so much money on the property that he could not walk off and leave it, he received a sudden, peremptory demand for 1000 pounds more than he had agreed to pay, accompanied by a threat to cancel his lease if the amount was not paid within seven days. As it was not the 'policy' of the Department to make written agreements with soldier settlers, and he therefore had no documentary evidence, protests were unavailing. He had to find the money. This crippled him from the outset, and after paying to the Department over 3000 pounds, probably the greatest amount paid by any soldier in this State, he was eventually ejected from his property in the middle of this period of depression, and left to starve. That was of no great consequence to the Department. The removal of that particular settler meant the covering up of a long string of iniquity. The law would have protected him against such action by a private individual, but against a government department he had no redress. This man fought for three years, from August 1914 in an infantry battalion, was twice wounded, and was moderately well-off before he was foolish enough to become a soldier settler.

I strongly believe that the soldier Grandpa wrote about was himself, and the property he referred to was Killingworth. He did purchase the homestead block of that property, and he had, in fact, fought for three years in an infantry battalion from that very month, August 1914; he was twice wounded, and he had been moderately well-off before the war.

After they left Killingworth in 1932, Charlie and Daisy and young Isabel went to live with Daisy's widowed mother and her brother Archie Lang, Archie's wife, Connie, and their growing family at nearby Kimmel Park. They stayed there for several years, but the farm could not sustain them all. In 1941, Charlie and his family moved to Melbourne. They bought a home in Moonee Ponds, and he took a job at the munitions factory at Maribyrnong.

Writing was, of course, one of his main passions. Horsemanship was another, and one that I inherited from him. In his spare time, he would also build model ships, including a scale model of Captain Cook's *Endeavour*. He was an active Freemason, and he was interested in politics. He was a member of the Service and Citizens' Party, which was founded in 1943 and was later merged with other parties by Robert Menzies to form the Liberal Party of Australia.

Concurrent with his other interests, he remained a military man to the core, and almost always held at least a part-time position with the army. He joined the 20th Light Horse Regiment in 1922. He was promoted to major in 1927 and to lieutenant-colonel in 1936, by which time he was in command of his regiment. He relinquished this command in March 1939 and was placed on the retired list with the honorary rank of colonel.

On the outbreak of the Second World War in September 1939, he immediately volunteered for service with the 2nd AIF, but was rejected on account of age and war disabilities. The bullet from his first wounding on Anzac Day 1915 remained in his chest all his life.

On 18 March 1940, he was called up for duty and appointed to Area Command Headquarters at Seymour, where he was employed on full-time duty until August that year.

He joined the Volunteer Defence Corps (Yea Detachment) on its inception in 1940, and assisted with instruction until he left the district in March 1941 for Melbourne, where he joined the Army Inspection Staff until October 1945.

He lived the rest of his life at Moonee Ponds, until his final weeks, which he spent in the Heidelberg Repatriation Hospital. He passed away on 3 February 1957. He was survived by Daisy and his daughter, Isabel, who by then had married Ken Ruff and produced two boys, Ian and Graham. One year later, she give birth to a daughter — me.

I am honoured to have been the vehicle by which this book has found its way to publication, and I hope that if Grandpa was alive today, he would be smiling.

Index

Note: Page references in italics refer to footnotes on pages indicated.

Adams, Lt Bill, 104, 106, 107, 108, 110
Antill, Brig.-Gen. J.M., *160*, 171, 172, 175–6
  at Gallipoli, *176*
  sidelined, 178–81, *182*
Australia
  depression of 1930s, 274
  militia, 7–9, 12; 5th Australian Infantry Regiment, 7, *11*
  offer of troops to Britain, 10
  Soldier Settlement Scheme, 273–5
  see also Australian Imperial Force
Australian Imperial Force (AIF), 9
  Battalions: 5th, 102, 121, 123, 136, 142, 149, 175, *179*; 6th, *39*, *98*, 111, 121, 123, 126, 142, 175, *179*; 7th, *11*, 22, *39*, 41, *42*, 111, 121, 123, 138, 142; 8th, 11, *12*, *13*, *16*, 22, 39, 98, 100, 103, 110, 111, 116–17, 118, 119–21, 123, 172–4, 204–5, (Gallipoli), 41, *42*, 43–7, (Pozières), 123–46, (Somme area), 175–98, 200–1, 204, 227, 228, 241, 243, (Ypres), 146–171; 11th, *62*; 12th, *62*; 21st, 118; 23rd, *200*; 56th, *235*; 57th, 242, 244, 251–2; 58th, 242, 244, 247, *248*, *250*, *253*; 59th, 242; 60th (Somme area), 203, 204, 204, 206–16, 221–8, 237, 240–54; chaplains, 235, 236–9; medical officers, 178, 179–81, 211, 213, *235*, 237, 245; restructured, *44*, 205
  Brigades: 1st, 97; 2nd, 12, 20–1, 22, 83, 97, 103, 110, 123, 160, 164, 175, 182, 196, 199, 200; 3rd, 26–7, 40, 97, 115, 124, 155; 4th, 119, 232; 6th, 228; 12th, *232*; 15th, 203, 204, 205–6, 220, 221, 234, 241, 244–53
  and conscription 'referendum', 173–4, 225

Corps: ANZAC, 32, 36;
Army Service Corps, 13;
Australian Flying Corps,
226, 261, *262*, 271–2;
Australian Army Medical
Corps, 50, *81*
Divisions (Infantry), 78; 1st,
9, 20, 22, 32, 52, 96, 102,
106, 111, 187–8, 242; 2nd,
97, 170, 171, 230, 242, 244;
4th, 205; 5th, 205, 220; and
mounted officers, 171–2,
228–9, 230; restructured,
205
embarkation 14–18
formation 10–11
Light Horse, *160*, *172*, *176*,
231, *248*
and misbehaving troops,
263–71
recruitment, 12, 225
reinforcements, 41, *83*, 98, 99–
100, *115*, 121, 127–8, 146,
205, 206, 207; untrained,
224–6
relations with British forces, 2,
42, *43*, 52, 107–9
see also Egypt; France;
Gallipoli; Western Front

Baensch, Lt Herbert, 45, *60*
Bairnsfather, Bruce, 198–9
Baker, Sgt Maj. Bill, 111, 112, 113,
138–9
Balfe, Capt. Rupert, *25*
Barrie, Alexander, 231, *232*
Barrie, Daisy (nee Lang), 3, 141,
145, 273, 275
family of, 275
Barrie, Isabel (later Ruff), 273
marriage and children, 276
Barrie, Jessie, 5, *11*

Barrie, John Charles (Charlie)
(civilian life)
background and family, 3–5,
11, 231–2, 240
as bank clerk, 5–8, 12
children, 273; deaths, 273
death, 276
farming, 275; at Yea under
Soldier Settlement Scheme,
273, 275
interests: horse riding, 172,
273, 275; the military, 7,
275; model-ship building,
275; politics, 275; writing,
273–5, (memoirs), 141, 229
joins school cadet corps, 7
lives and works in Melbourne,
275, 276
married life, 3, 141, 145, 273
Barrie, Col. John Charles (Dan)
(military career)
and character, 34; keen to
return to the front, 78–86,
91–4; sense of duty, 34;
sense of humour, 16–17,
21–2, 35, 56, 61, 79, 86–9,
110–11, 114, 126, 154, 162,
165, 186, 235
eagerness to join war effort,
10–11
in Egypt, 19–26; as casualty,
54–7; evacuated, 57–9;
illness, 32–4; pyramids and
other sights, 19, 28–31
embarks, 13–18; for France, 95
in England and Scotland,
93–4; appointed to a
hospital carrier, 261;
convalescing, 59–74, 77,
78–9, 261; declared fit for
service, *81*, 82; hospitalised
from Western Front, 239,

256–61; on leave from front, 199; training courses in machine guns, 76–7, 78; at Weymouth depot, 75, 78–91
in France: at depots in Étaples, Le Havre, 95–111; returns to unit, 113–16; tent climbing, 108; on training course, 219–20
friendships, 48, 60, 83, 87, 89, 118, 124, 140, 149, 195, 199, 256
at Gallipoli: evacuated to Egypt, 53; landing, 40–5; severely wounded, 1, 48–50, 51, 53
joins AIF as an officer (with 8th Battalion), 11–13, 243–4; transfers later to 60th Battalion, 203, 206, 244
joins Australian Flying Corps, 271–2
joins volunteer corps, 7
leadership/authority, 98, 100–2, 105–6, 112; at Western Front, 250
as officer in militia, 7–9, 10, *11*, 102, 155
opinions: on chaplains, 237–8; on commanding officers, 2, 12, 19, 20, 21, 34, 38, 119, 124, 171, 172, 175–6, 178, 181, 187, 190, 241; on English spirit, 66; on politicians in wartime, 23–4, 173, 174, 220, 225, 229, 265–6, 271; on soldiers, 84–5, 96, 99, 105, 110, 111, 132, 133, 136, 158, 159, 177, 193, 207, 209, 246; on troop trains, 218–19
and Pompey Elliott, 2, 11, 78–9, 91, 92, 93, 99, 204–5, 217, 241
postwar; home service during WWII, 276; serves in Light Horse regiment, 275
respected by officers and troops, 91, 98, 110, 137, 138–9, 141, 164, 204, 205, 217, 241, 243, 255
returns to Australia (wounded) as adjutant on hospital carrier, 261–4, 269–71; troubles with troops, 264–8
smoker, 103, 169
training/instructing roles, 1, 16, 79–80, 82–3, 91, 92, 98–9, 105, *170*; on front line, 214, 216, 217, 226
at Western Front (Jul. 1916 – May 1917), 115, 116–24, 146–7, 160–6, 175–83, 197, 233–6, 240–5; evacuation and surgery, 255–6; at front line (Pozières), 125–45, (Somme area), 185–96, 197–8, 200–2, 205–16, 221–9, 246–54, (Ypres), 147–59, 166–71; gassed, 213–14; wounded severely, 1, 254, 255, 256, 258
Barrie, Sydney, 200, 229, 230–1, 232, 242
Beavon ('Bevan'), Cpl William, 252, *254*
Beecham, Sister, 257, 259–60
Belgium and WWI
Broodseinde, *144*, 159
Poperinghe, 164–5, 166, 167
Ypres, 146–7, 149–56
Bennett, Brig.-Gen. Henry, 155, 167

Benjafield, Capt. Vivian, 50, 53, 67
Bird, Capt. Dougan, 37
Bird, Lt.-Col. Fred, *37*
Birdwood, Gen. William, 32, *51*, 76, 240, 241
Blamey, Maj. Thomas, 44–5
Bolton, Lt John, 30
Bolton, Lt-Col. William, *13*, 38, 45, 47
Booth, Rev. J.J., 237
Brand, Brig.-Gen. 'Digger', 119, 121
Britain and WWI
  Australian Depot, Weymouth, 67, 75, *78*; machine-gun school, 76
  British Army, 19, 36, 65, 220; 5th Army, 116; Grenadier Guards, 77–8; King's Liverpool Regiment, 147, 150; 29th (British) Division, 52
  Empire and the dominions, 63
  England, hospitals: Wandsworth (Third London General), 239, 256–60; 3rd (2nd) Western General, 60; volunteers, 60–1
  England, places and sights: Chester, 61–2, 64; London, 67–71, 77, 199; Manchester, 60–1, 67
  Royal Navy, 2, 18, 27, 36, 42–3
  Scotland, 72–4
  see also Egypt; France; Gallipoli campaign; Western Front

Calder, Lt Roy, 208, 211
Campbell, Capt., 50
Canada and WWI, 146

Catani, Carlo, *118*
Catani, Lt Enrico 'Puss', 118
Catron, Pte Bill, *42*
Catron, Lt Joe, 41, 42, 50, 83–4, 121, 195, 243
Caughey, Capt. Ross, 25
Challis, Pte Francis, 247
Challis, Sgt George, *247*
Clohesy, Pte John, 268
Cooke, Capt., 228–9
Coulter, Lt-Col. Graham (C.O. of 8th Battalion), 119–21, 141, 144, 171, 177–8, *179*, 181, 190, 205
Courtney, Lt-Col. Richard, *78*, *82*, *84*
Cowper, Capt. Gerald, *12*, 44
Craig, Col., 67, 68
Crombie, Mr and Mrs, 73

Dabb, Lt Reginald, 145
Daly, C.W.D., *179*
D'Arcy, Capt. John, 262
Dawson, Capt. Forbes, 248, 249, 250–1, 252
Denehy, Lt-Col. Charles, *247 248*
Doig, Maj. Keith, *211*, *235*
Duigan, Lt-Col., 206, 213
Dyson, Will, *176*

Egypt (as AIF base), 17, 18, 32, 54
  Alexandria, 54
  British in, 23, 26, 54, 55
  Cairo, 19, 21, 24–5, 96; behaviour of troops, 25–6, 28
  hospitals, 54; Australian, 33; and casualties, 55, 57; volunteers, 55, 62–3
  Ismailia, 22
  Mena training camp, 19, 21, 24, 32

and Suez Canal, 22–3, 24
Elliott, Capt. George, *235*
Elliott, Gen. Harold ('Pompey'), 2, 11, *34*, *46*
   in England, 78–9, 92, 93
   as footballer, 234–5
   at Gallipoli, 78
   at Western Front, 204–5, 212, 234, 241, 244, *249*
Errey, Lt Len, 158, 159
Evans, Lt, 164
Evans, Lt J.A., 62, 63, 67

Field, Lt-Col. John, 44, *47*
Fisher, Andrew, *13*
Foden, Lt James, 169, 170
Forrester, Pte K.C.A., 129–30
Forsyth, Brig.-Gen. J.K., 124–5, 139, 160
France
   Albert, 115–16, 118, 146, 200, 217
   Amiens, 200
   Australian troops in, 95–107, 146, 200, 217, 233, 234–7, 240–2; eager to return to units, 111–14; entertainment, 234–5, 240–1; profiteering, 100–4; training, 98, 107, 110
   British forces in, 107–8, 114, 116
   Canaples, 121
   damage and destruction in, 114, 160, 221–2, 230, 236
   Étaples, 107
   Mametz, 233, 234, 240
   Pozières village, 230
   Senlis, 114
   see also Western Front

Gallipoli (Weir), 176

Gallipoli campaign
   and anniversary of landing, 240–1
   Australians in: casualties, *13*, *25*, *34*, 39, 43, *44*, 45, *46*, 48–9, 83, *104*, *111*, *134*, *176*, *247*, *263*; digging in, 45; fighting, 83, *263*; illness, *42*, *159*; landing, *25*, 39, 40–4, *46*
   British forces: and landing, 42–3, 52
   casualties, 51–2, 55, 57; evacuations, 53, 54
   digging in, *51*
   evacuation, 78
   French forces at, 36
   landing, 40–2, 52; re-embarkation considered, 50, *51*; and Royal Navy, 42–3
   medical arrangements, *43*, *49*, 50, 53
   preparations, 27, 33, 34, 35–6, 37–9
   topography, 45
   see also Turkey and WWI
Gartside, Lt-Col. Robert, 46–7
Gates, Cpl Stan, 194–5
Germany and WWI, 10, *13*, 68
   defeated, 116
   see also Western Front
Gibson, H.M., 60–1
Gilbert, Capt. Rev. James, 235–7
Goodwin, Lt Frank, 144, 145, 169, 174, 188–9, 190
Grinham, Pte Melville, 162–3

Hamilton, Gen. Sir Ian, 32, *51*
Hardy, Capt. Dudley, 144–5
Harris, Sgt George, 163–4
Hart, Maj. A.G.C., 115

Heane, Brig.-Gen., 182, 188
Heydon, Capt. George, *178*
Hickson, Lt Frank, 158, 159, 162
Hughes, W.M. (Billy), *173*, *174*
Hunt, Pte George, 133, 134–5, 141
Hurry, Capt., 164

India and WWI, 34
   Medical Service, 57
Inger, Cpl John, 135–6, 141

Jackson, Capt. Harold, 69
Jess, Lt-Col. Carl, 138–9, *179*, *182*
Johnson, Lt-Col. J.J., *91*
Joynt, Capt. W.D., 164

Kemal, Lt.-Gen. Mustapha
   (Pasha), 46
Kennett, Pte Les, 134, 135
Kitchener, Lord, 17, 22

Laughter, Pte Charles, 135
Layh, Capt. Bert, *34*
Lemnos, 27, 35–6
Leslie, Lt Charles, 245–6, 248, 254
Lillie, Capt. Cyril 'Ginger', 126–7,
   135, 136
Lodge, Capt. Gus, *120*
Love, Lt Howard, *226*
Luxton, Maj. D.A., 102–3, 111

McCay, Brig.-Gen. James, *20*, *120*
Macdonald, Capt. J., 81
McKenna, Capt. Edward, *25*
Mackenzie, Lt., 61
McWhae, Capt. D.M., *81*
Mason, Capt. Charles, 39, 53–4
Maynard, Sgt, 111
Melbourne, 3, 4
Menzies, Robert, *25*, 275
Midwood, Mr and Mrs, 62–3, 64,
   65, 66–7, 82, 199

Mills, Maj. J.B., *34*, 35
Monash, Brig.-Gen. John, *79*, *138*
Moon, Lt R.V., VC, *248*, *249*, *253*,
   256
Moore, Lt-Col. Newton, *78*
Mostyn, Lt., 58, 59
Mummery, Lt Tas, 176–8

New Zealand and WWI
   ANZAC Corps, 36
   and Egypt, 25
   troops embark, 14

O'Connor, Cpl, 215
O'Connor, Lt Daniel, 244, 245
O'Connor, Lt R.J., *269*
O'Halloran, Maj. J.H., *263*, 265,
   269, 270–1
O'Kelly, Lt Leo, 145–6

Palestine
   Australians in, *160*, 231
Paul, Lt Jack, 39
Pearse-Gould, Sir Francis, 257–9
Pelton, Capt. Norman, *250*, 251–2
Possingham, Capt. Alf, *16*, 46

Red Cross, 66, 238
Richards, Lt Harry, 206, 207, 208,
   209
Rodda, Lt Errol, 127, 136, 145,
   146
Rodda, Fred, *146*
Russian Revolution, 220
Rutherford, Sgt Joe, 138
Ryan, Sir Charles, 261

Sack, Cpl James, 189
Scanlan, Lt Jack, 34
Scott, Lt Daniel, 127, 128, 129,
   131, 153–4, 165–6
Sergeant, Maj. John, 47, *48*

Sheffield, Lord, 61
Slattery, Pte Hugh, 133–4, 135, 137, 141
Smith, Brig.-Gen. 'Bob', 228
South African War, 6, 12, *39*, *48*, *214*
Springthorpe, Lt.-Col. J.W., *33*
Stevenson, Lt-Col. George, *35*
Symons, Capt., 17, 18

Tarrant, Lt., 58, 59
Taylor, Lt Robert, 43–4
Tonkin, Lt Cyril, *263*
Trickey, Maj. Frederick, 214–15, 216, 242
Turkey and WWI
    defending Gallipoli, 27, 36, 41, 48; inflicting casualties, 44, 45–6, 47, 48–9, 51–2
    Suez Canal, 22–3

Ulrich, Lt-Col. T.F., 140

vessels (allied troop- and warships), 95
    H.M.T. *Ascanius*, 17
    H.M.S. *Bacchante*, 48
    H.M.S. *Benalla*, 13, *15*, 17, 18
    Chelmer, 41, 43
    Clan Macgillivray, 36, 37, *39*, 41–3, 51
    Galeka, *39*
    H.M.S. *Hampshire*, 17, 18
    Ibuki, 15
    Ittria, 34, 36
    London, 40
    H.M.A.S. *Melbourne*, 15
    H.M.S. *Minotaur*, 15
    Orvieto, 15
    Prince of Wales, 40
    H.M.S. *Queen*, 38, 40
    Queen Elizabeth, 42, *51*

Ribble, 41
Southern, 18
H.M.A.S. *Sydney*, 15, 16
vessels (German), *13*
    Emden, 15, 16
    submarines, 198
vessels (hospital ships/carriers), 43
    Clan Macgillivray, 43, 49–50, 53
    Gascon, 36
    Letitia, 57, 59, *60*
    Port Lyttelton, 262–72
    River Clyde, 52
    and shipwrecks, 59
Vinnicombe, Lt F.A., 98–9, 104, 106

Wallis, Capt. Robert, *151*
Wertheim, Lt Rupert, 170
Western Front, 23, *34*, *174*
    Australians at, 54, 103, 118–24, 140–1, 142, 147–51, 160–6, 172–85, 196, 204–6; casualties, *45*, 115, 117, 118, 125, 128, 129–30, 131, 133, *134*, 142–4, 145, 146, 158, 159, *163*, *164*, 171, *176*, 190, *195*, 196, *204*, 213, 231, 232, 242, 245, 247, 250, 252, 254, 256; and communications, 175–6, 191; cooks, 161–2, 240; and friendly fire, 151–3, 155, 156, 157, 189; in mud and cold, 182–5, 187, 191, 192–3, 194–5, 196, 197–8, 216–17; trench-digging, 125–36, 139–40
    battles/front line (Australians), 114, 118; Broodseinde, 144, *159*; Fromelles, *146*,

204, *206*; Hindenburg Line, 232, 244–5, 246–53; Menin Road, *163*, *176*; Somme area, 175, 187, 189–96, 197–8, 200–2, 206–17, 221–8, 230, 237, 242, 243; Pozières (first battle), 115, 116–17, *121*, 230, 231; Pozières (second battle), *134*, 142–4, 146, 160; Pozières windmill, 125, 187; Ypres, 146, 149–59, 164, 166–70
British forces at, 114, 116, 117, 147, 150, 224, 242, 244–5; casualties, 117; tactics, 231
Canadian forces at, 146
French forces at, 116
German forces at: (Pozières) 115, 129–33, 136, 137, 142–3, (Somme area), 187, 188–96, 200, 201, 202, 207, 212–13, 226–8, 230, 231, 243, 247, 248, 251, 253–4, (Ypres), 146, 148, 149, 168–9, 171; advance of 1918, 224; casualties, 228, 229, 253; defeat, 253; machine guns, 142–3, 151–2, 156, 168; 'Minenwerfers', 150–1, 153, 156–7, 158; positions, 116, 117, *118*, 166, 187, 188–91, 230, 230, 231; snipers, 130, 131–2, 140, 245
Hindenburg Line, 116, 228, 232, 244–5, 248–53; German retreat to, 219, 220, 221–2, 224
prisoners/prison camps, 146, 186, 196–7, 232, 253
see also France

Wieck, Maj. George, 76, 79
World War I
aircraft in, 212–13
Armistice, 24
begins, 10, *11*
and reluctance to go/return to the front, 84–5, 120, 207–8
Treaty of Versailles, 24
and use of gas, 87, *104*, 107, *134*, *159*, *206*, 213
see also Gallipoli campaign; Western Front
Wrigley, Capt. Hugh, *244*

Yates, Lt Bill, 83, 121, 195
Young, Sgt, 111, 112